Desert Journal

Foreword by Robert C. Stebbins

Illustrations by Gerhard Bakker

Photographs by Raymond B. Cowles and Roy Pence

BERKELEY • LOS ANGELES • LONDON

Desert Journal

Reflections of a Naturalist

by Raymond B. Cowles
in collaboration with Elna S. Bakker

University of California Press

University of California Press
Berkeley and Los Angeles, California
University of California Press, Ltd.
London, England
Copyright © 1977 by
The Regents of the University of California
First Paperback Edition 1978
ISBN: 0-520-03636-0
Library of Congress Catalog Card Number: 74-22959
Printed in the United States of America
Designed by Dave Comstock

1 2 3 4 5 6 7 8 9 0

*To our children
and our children's children,
with apologies for the
state of the world we
bequeath to them.*

Contents

Foreword

R aymond B. Cowles was born at Adams Mission
Station, Natal, South Africa, December 1, 1896.
His boyhood was spent in Africa, at a time when wildlife was
abundant. To help make ends meet, his missionary parents collected and sold scientific specimens of birds to universities and
museums. Young Cowles helped with the family effort. In his
wanderings afield he became enthralled with wild animals.
As a lad, he discovered the nesting of the great Nile monitor
lizard in termite mounds. This observation later led to his
doctoral thesis. When he came to southern California in 1916,
he had already developed a deep appreciation of nature. He
brought with him a wealth of experiences from the African
bush, a fluent speaking knowledge of Zulu, and conserva-

tion concerns that were to strongly influence his later thought and action.

Raymond Cowles, the naturalist, is revealed in the pages of this book. His early experiences with African reptiles set the stage for his pioneer work on reptilian thermoregulation. These studies were so painstaking and revolutionary that an entire scientific discipline in this area of reptilian physiology was created. A tracing of scientific research in reptilian thermoregulation would extend from Raymond Cowles through ever-branching lines to second, third, and fourth generations of students. Even his earliest studies are still cited in current scientific papers.

He brought his naturalist insight to bear on the wild lands of southern California. For forty years he conducted research and instilled his understanding and philosophy of nature into thousands of students in this region of diverse natural wonders. He did so during a time of unprecedented human population growth and technological expansion. He recounts many of these experiences herein. As he does so, the reader will note his deepening distress over the mounting impact of man on the natural scene. As one of his early students I shared many of these experiences and concerns, and we developed a strong friendship. The "Doc," as many of us called him, grew increasingly worried about man's future and the destruction of nature. He was deeply humanistic—a warm and thoughtful person—but he was dismayed by man's collective thoughtless tampering with nature. He saw modern science as an imbalanced approach that failed to adequately address the crucial question of explosive population growth. He was one of the first, if not the first, scientists to see clearly the relationship between the increase in human numbers and the decline in the diversity and integrity of the earth's wild animal and plant life. And he was the first, I believe, to make this connection clear to conservationists (see "The Meaning of Wilderness to Science," Proceedings, 6th Biennial Wilderness Conference, Sierra Club, San Francisco, 1960).

He had made this relationship clear to his students long before the spate of "human population" books, beginning with William Vogt's *Road to Survival* (1948) and reaching a crescendo with the writings and lectures of Stanford University's Paul Erhlich. If the "Doc" had a great disappointment in his life, it was that he never saw full publication of his views on human population. His book on the subject, prepared several decades ago, was apparently too early or too controversial to reach publication. Many of the thoughts expressed therein have found their way into the present volume. Chapter 23 on overpopulation should be read with this in mind.

Raymond Cowles viewed nature holistically. He had a far broader view of science and human affairs than most of his contemporaries. He was people-oriented, but his ethics went beyond man to include the entire biosphere. He enjoyed exposing to the fullest all his senses to nature. On our trips together, he often shared with me the taste, odor, and texture of wild plants—reliving the empirical approach of the aborigine. He lamented the loss of these natural pleasures in a letter to me written a year before his death.

> This is not a farewell note nor a note of grief (although a beautiful scene, sunrise and sunset, the vast deserts and the vaster sea, move me to regret that I cannot forever thrill to the world around me), but I have taken the time to write out these thoughts for the remote possibility that they may be helpful to you as you look forward to retirement. Don't let them become dreary years— travel, keep your sensitivity to beauty, paint, and enjoy music and the music of nature around you. Just last night I was on campus and the students were having dinner and no planes were passing overhead and there were no cars. I just sat and revelled in the sound of wind through the trees and listened to the intervening silence. And above were the eternal stars and the black silhouettes of the mountains. And there was peace.

The "Doc" has now left us. His friends received a card typed and signed by him as follows:

> Raymond Bridgman Cowles, December 1, 1896 at Adams Mission Station, Natal, South Africa, has completed his tour of duty December 7, 1975, and will now participate in the universal and unending recycling game. This

gives notice that his name should now be removed from mailing lists. (signed November 1, 1971)

The date of his death was inserted by one of his daughters.

I treasure my last hours with him. It was at a meeting of graduate students at Professor Kenneth Norris's home in the beautiful hills near Santa Cruz, California, in November, 1975. Professor Norris was one of his former graduate students. That evening the "Doc" spoke to the group on the subject of overpopulation and its relationship to current concerns over declining energy and mineral resources. He was still sounding his warnings of so long ago. At 79 he was white-haired, straight-backed, and alert. He parried questions with the skill and quickness of a man half his age.

The next morning I drove him up the coast highway and across the San Francisco Peninsula to the airport for his return flight to Santa Barbara. It was a clear fall morning. The natural countryside of seacoast, marsh, and hills was especially beautiful. As always, he took note of the wildlife (ducks and other water birds) and we discussed favorite topics—animal coloration, temperature and its role in evolution—and, despite our resolve to do otherwise, occasionally lapsed into the subject of human population. My most vivid last memory came as we waited for his plane. He seemed sad, but then as he saw a small child toddling nearby, his expression suddenly changed to one of warmth and joy. He seemed to be reaching out to all mankind.

ROBERT C. STEBBINS

Acknowledgments

There are so many individuals to whom I owe so much that merely listing them by name would surely bore the reader and yet leave some omissions. Thus I must refrain from the pleasure of mentioning all those whom I recall most vividly, but in fairness I must acknowledge a few.

I cannot refrain from expressing my personal thanks to Elna S. Bakker who insisted that I resurrect a disorganized record of observations and delegate to her the arduous task of putting some thoughts into literary form. Only her insistent prodding and skillful editorial labor have made the material readable. To Gerhard Bakker, a former student of mine and now a professor of life science, I owe not only the excellent drawings but many helpful suggestions on subject matter.

To Dr. Robert Stebbins I owe an eternal debt of gratitude for his painstaking examination of the nearly completed typescript and his suggested emendations and corrections. I am keenly aware of the time and effort given to the task, and I have flagrantly imposed on him in return for our many decades of friendship.

If omissions or errors remain they are mine and not those of any of these colleagues and friends.

With each passing year it has grown on me that this teacher at least has lived as an intellectual symbiont with his students. This has led me to feel less and less an individual and more and more a composite product of fifty years of pleasant interaction with undergraduates and more emphatically with my graduate students and post-doctoral scholars. Whatever of worth I may have accomplished must be credited to my very great fortune in having been so blessed with the quality and number of students who attended a great and inspiring institution, the University of California at Los Angeles.

My colleagues, too, have participated in my symbiotic mental life. Often by mere chance some casual or even flippant remark has led to a serendipitous start of new lines of thought which in due time grew or were tested and discarded.

Finally I cannot refrain from touching on another topic. Throughout this book and always in my memory, which covers a half a century or more of desert field trips, are the innumerable camp fires and their evening sacrifice of incense from smoldering wood. Now I am sadly reminded that such luxuries, such reverence for the gods of the open spaces are no longer ecologically excusable. Around all the good waterholes and camping places natural firewood has been harmfully gleaned from the desert floor and turned to ashes. Neither termites, wood borers, nor the elements can recycle these once living materials. From now on the careful naturalist and his students must be content to enjoy fellowship and to worship nature around a noisy hissing gasoline stove—for as long as that store of one-time solar energy remains. Too many lovers of untrammeled nature have simply exhausted what was once a bountiful supply.

In my old age I much prefer to remember those camps as they were and plan for some future evening when I will defy good conservation. For one last time I will sit with friends around a fragrant wood fire and speak of days long gone, when we started a long journey that this book now begins to bring to a close.

RAYMOND B. COWLES

Part I:

Survival in an Arid Environment

1: The Ditch Camp

*F*rom where I am sitting deep in the sun-flooded, sandy plains of the Colorado Desert's Coachella Valley, I look westward to the massive array of the Peninsular Range as it turns south from Mt. San Gorgonio toward Mexico. In each of the notches between the craggy peaks, frayed-edge cloud masses are rolling eastward to the desert where they vanish in the warm, dry air. I know without seeing beyond the range that a storm is pressing on its coastside slopes. Sluicing rain is falling in the foothills, and chaparral is suffusing its fragrance to the chill, damp wind. On higher slopes, big-cone spruce and yellow pine drip in the downpour. A snowy coverlet fits over the top of the range, its ragged border lying along the 7,000-foot line of elevation.

As the storm crawls over the crest and conceals the high-

est peaks, it presages a few days of violent winds. They will
sweep down through Whitewater Canyon and across the
sand and gravel wash near Palm Springs. Then they will race
toward the Salton Sea, down into the Imperial Valley and
east across the Mecca Hills to the Colorado River. Almost
without exception these clouds mean sandstorms. The desiccating winds pick up loose sand grains and dust and whirl
them in gritty showers against every obstacle in their path.

The desert is thirsty during these windy times, and any
stray drops of rain would be most welcome. For the most
part, however, these winter-spawned storms from the west
rage around the mountain tops and may toss a sparse sprin-
kling of droplets that pockmark the sand but fail to sink to
the feeder roots below the surface and benefit the drought-
harassed desert plants.

I know of no desert organism that profits by these violent
winds. Animals seek shelter underground or in rocky nooks.
Simple dislike of the driving sand may be the reason. But
when every bit of vegetation is dancing and plant fragments
drift madly in swirls across dune and plain, all creatures that
depend on eyesight for food detection are baffled by the movement of inedible things. For animals that may become food
for others and thus are forced to be vigilant at all times, rapidly moving things obscure the presence of another moving
object—the predator intent on capturing them. Both predator and prey are confused by sandstorms and their whirling
contents, and, incidentally, specimens become scarce for the
grit-battered naturalist. He would be wise to emulate them
and sit out the storm.

Fortunately it is not only from such unpromising storms
that rain may reach the desert. It may arrive in the warm season when the configuration of competing pressure areas,
both highs and lows, permits hurricane-like storms (*chubas-
cos*) to move northward paralleling the Pacific Coast of Mexico. Massive thunderheads thrust up above the mountains
from the Gulf of California to the eastern flanks of the Sierra
Nevada. They often bring torrential, though spotty rain, which
may benefit desert life—and also destroy homes and other

property. In the summer of 1974 dozens of lives were presumed to be lost in a flashflood near the hamlet of Nelson, Lake Mojave, Nevada, that wiped out buildings and vehicles in a muddy rush of water.

These summer tropical storms are accompanied by a combination of high temperatures and humidities. They make life virtually intolerable for man who depends on jettisoning his body heat through sweat and evaporation. Such conditions invading the desert from the Gulf of California were at one time known as "crazy weather," with death for the old and the susceptible young a common occurrence.

While the days are insufferably hot, the evenings and nights can be incredibly beautiful. All along the ridge of the Cuyumaca Mountains, the Santa Rosas, and the crests of Mt. San Jacinto and Mt. San Gorgonio the heaped foam of thunderclouds flickers with continuous lightning for hours at a time. From the far side of the Imperial Valley, where I once worked, these storms were spectacles of such beauty I remained entranced far into the night, watching the flare of blue and sulfurous yellow lightning and listening in vain for any rumble of thunder. The sounds of all but the closest flashes were muffled by the distance and the heaviness of the humid air, which at times seemed almost too moist to breathe.

At the time of these most fascinating encounters with weather I was working on the sand dune side of the "highline" canal beyond the small town of Holtville and toward the old plank road leading to Yuma, Arizona. In both the summers I was resident, temperatures rarely dropped to below 90° F. except in the pre-dawn hours, and daily maxima exceeded 110° F. with monotonous regularity. The dry heat was tolerable, but from time to time masses of warm moist air moved north from tropical Mexico and invaded this area. They brought intervals when both humidity and temperature were high. Life at times became almost unbearable.

During the worst spells I sat quietly in the coolest part of the shack. By leaning forward I could count the drops of sweat dripping from the tip of my nose. They fell at the rate of one every second or so. I had to drink enormous amounts of water

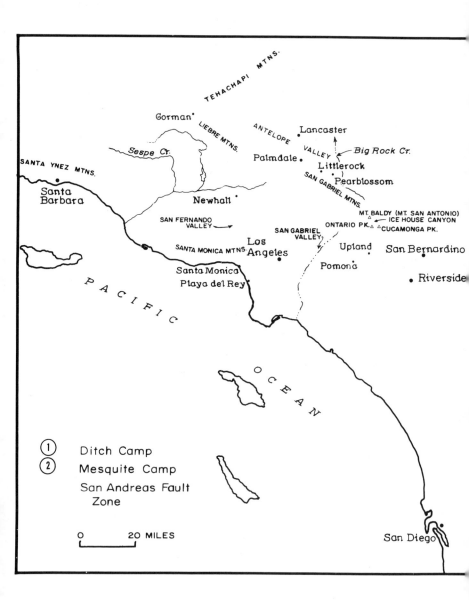

TEHACHAPI MTNS.

Gorman
LIEBRE MTNS.
ANTELOPE
Lancaster
Sespe Cr.
VALLEY
Big Rock Cr.
Palmdale
Littlerock
SANTA YNEZ MTNS.
Pearblossom
SAN GABRIEL MTNS.
Santa
Barbara
Newhall
MT. BALDY (MT. SAN ANTONIO)
ICE HOUSE CANYON
SAN FERNANDO
ONTARIO PK. △   △CUCAMONGA PK.
VALLEY
SAN GABRIEL
Los
VALLEY
Upland
San Bernardino
SANTA MONICA MTNS.
Angeles
P A C I F I C
Santa Monica
Pomona
Playa del Rey
Riverside

O C E A N

① Ditch Camp
② Mesquite Camp
San Andreas Fault
   Zone

O   20 MILES

San Diego

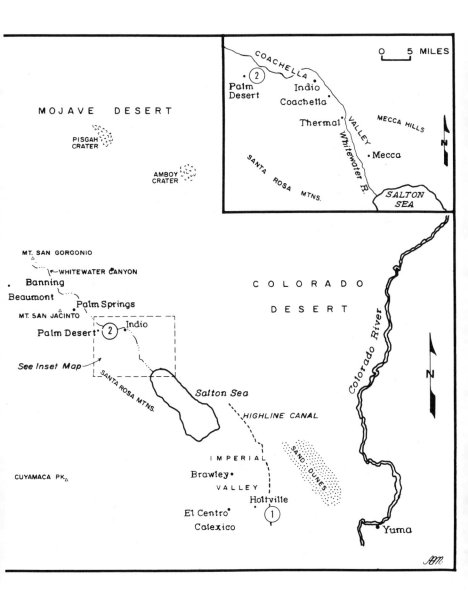

to make up for this continual loss, but there was little relief from perspiration because of the high humidity and the lack of wind.

In the evenings I would sit straining to hear the distant thunder from the tempests raging along the western horizon and to feel any breath of stirring air that would relieve the subtropical heat. Nothing. The only break in the blanket of silence was the sibilant stridulations of night-active crickets and desert toads. At long intervals I could hear the call of coyotes, but in this hottest weather even they seemed to be oppressed by the atmospheric "weight" of the unwonted temperature and humidity.

Day after day my partner and I looked with longing at the faraway storms, hoping for a break in the weather and the coming of heat-relieving desert rains, which—when conditions are right—accompany these meteorological disturbances. The strength of a low-pressure trough seldom was sufficient to overwhelm the intense radiation and the flow of hot air rising from the desert floor. One particular storm, however, did sweep in from the south. With a curtain of wind-blown sand it crossed the border and bore northwestward along the high-line canal. The storm broke over our encampment with an incredible flood of rain. It came neither in sheets nor droplets nor gusts, but in a perpendicular downpour of truly unbelievable proportions. To say that it came by the bucketful is totally inadequate to describe the violence of its arrival. Within minutes streams were rushing down the slopes of the nearby sand dunes, a fantastic sight in itself. They scoured at the canal banks, endangering the farms that lay at the bottom level of these life-giving supplies of water.

The storm passed within some fifteen or twenty minutes at most, and it left behind as far as one could see a most unusual landscape: a desert in which the hollows between the dunes were dotted with thousands of pools of water. The sudden drop in temperature, the fragrance of a newly wet desert, and the sight of acres of cool, swimmable water were too much. We dropped work and ran out to the nearest pond, stripped, and went swimming under conditions that very few

Plate 1. Wind-carved and rippled sand dunes, habitat of some of the most interesting little animals, including the fringe-toed sand lizard.

people can ever imagine. The water was as pleasant and inviting as it appeared to be. We swam, floated, and loafed, carousing like Roman senators in cool, liquid luxury.

We were aware of nothing but the miracle of pleasure until our knees and elbows began to bump bottom. The porous, thirsty sand was soaking up the ponds almost as rapidly as they had been formed. In an unconscious effort to prolong the exquisite sensations of our impromptu dip, we had kept pace with the lowering water level by flattening ourselves parallel to the pond floor. Still attempting to swim we scraped our arms and legs on the rough desert vegetation in the dune troughs, determined to hang on to the last moment of pleasure. Finally we sprawled in the few remaining puddles, splashing a gritty mixture of sand and water over our now chilling bodies. Then the ponds were gone, first one and then another, rapidly sucked down into the earth. Within a very short time one would never have guessed that for a few blissful moments we had had our own private swimming pool, steps away from our rickety shack.

Where canyons extend back into the mountains and widen out into large water-collecting basins, storms such as these within minutes can create cataracts of such force and fury that they roll boulders up to the size of houses as though they were marbles. The waters boom and rattle with millions of tumbling stones, an awesome experience that has to be seen and heard to be believed.

Though I had witnessed small cloudbursts and their effects in canyons in southern California, it was not until many years later that I appreciated fully their nature and possible dimensions. I was conducting certain studies in New Mexico when one of these torrential storms moved in across the mountains near Socorro. I was on the way home after a day of work when the storm broke, drenching the road that ran along a small canyon down to the main highway to town. As the storm struck, I knew from its magnitude that I would be prudent to cross the two or three bridges down canyon before the arrival of the main flood. With this in mind I sped down the road and crossed the first of the culverts or small bridges. The flood seemed at first to be rather moderate in size, and we paused (I had a student with me) to watch the water rise toward the top of the ample culvert. I noted, however, its increased depth and the speed with which it approached the roadbed itself and decided to escape to the alluvial fan at the mouth of the canyon.

As we raced down the slope, the gully beside us had barely been dampened by the lighter rains of the lower elevations, though back higher up it was brimful. We outraced the entire flood and had the rare opportunity of watching it advance as a wedge of water-borne foam pouring out of the canyon's mouth, spreading, dropping to a harmless two- or three-foot depth, and disappearing in only a few minutes' time. We drove back up the canyon to see what had happened, but the flood had vanished, leaving a feeble stream.

To produce swollen rivers, washed out bridges, destroyed cars, and lost lives, one would assume that prolonged, even though torrential, rains are necessary. This is not true for desert storms. From beginning to end, their concentrated fury lasts but a half an hour or so. They may be concealed from view by foothills or mountains, and one may not be aware that more than a drizzle has fallen. Yet the downpour comes with such violence that the soil is scarcely penetrated. Instead, it is torn away and carried with the descending flood to form a mass of muddy water and debris, which often has an abruptly wedge-shaped advance face and a gradually tapering terminal edge. It churns down the winding channels of the canyon bottom, to exit at length and lose its force as it spreads out over the flats below.

My first experience with the desert, its plant and animal residents, its storms, and its high, summer-long temperatures, came when money for a college education was necessary and desert salaries for labor were twice those elsewhere. This economic reality led me to volunteer for work with one of the Imperial Valley irrigation districts.

The district camp to which I was assigned was on the so-called high-line canal, a half mile from the bridge connecting the Imperial Valley with some of the most spectacular sand dunes in the country. The accommodations were crude in the extreme—a clapboard-sided shack with a canvas roof, open-screened sides, and a brush-covered porch. A floor that supported the frame rested on a few bricks. They held the structure some six inches off the ground and provided an ideal shelter for sidewinders, black widow spiders, sun spiders, and various other interesting creatures of the desert.

The camp was lonely and remote, and my major task was to patrol a five-mile stretch of canal bank daily to see that there were no breaks or flooding that might drown and heavily alkalize good farmland. As muskrats were the commonest source of canal damage, we were urged to shoot them as well as the occasional Colorado River beaver that attempted to establish homesites along the canal sides. This was back in 1917 when some of the old-time "bad men" and their victims (those who survived various shooting affairs) were still living. Being near the Mexican border and close to a continuous flow of water that led deep into California, our shack was on a natural approach or escape route for bandits of any nationality. The sides of the cabin were full of holes, souvenirs left by two

escaping criminals when they temporarily sought shelter in it.
Under cover of darkness they fled into the desert, from which
they could strike back toward the canal for water if necessary.
They made the break across the border into Mexico and presumed safety. On another occasion a group of desperados held
up a store or two in Niland, killing one owner. They, too, followed the canal in their escape through the desert. The life line
of water made these attempts possible.

Those were the days of the old plank road, a movable highway of railroad ties that provided traction across the drifting
sand dunes to the east. Although it was inadvisable to use the
route during the summer heat, not a few reckless motorists
attempted it. Every hot season a number of cars broke down,
and their passengers had to walk to the nearest water, which
was the high-line canal. I soon discovered the impersonal ruth-
lessness of the desert climate from my experiences in rescu-
ing those left in marooned cars while the driver sought water
and help. Some made it to safety, but we were often the first
to learn of impending disaster. We contacted farmers, brought
horses to tow the cars to hard ground, and stayed until the
cars started or we could bring their occupants to a supply of
water.

Three people died in an attempt to reach help during the
two summers I spent on this job. On one occasion, three men
from Los Angeles came out to look over the prospect for stak-
ing out homesteads above the canal. Most unwisely, they chose
midsummer for their venture. Two were experienced in desert
ways, but they were overweight. One of the two and his inexperienced companion were overcome by the heat. The third
member of the party, in somewhat better condition, sought
help from a guard station immediately below my post on the
canal. By the time the ditch rider had reached the two left
behind, they both had died. The man who had gone for assis-
tance had to be taken to the hospital, where he was in critical
condition for several days.

In a less tragic instance, a man and his family had been
caught in the sand not three miles from water. Rather than
drink of the scanty supply he had provided for his family, he
started out thirsty and finished his three-mile journey

on hands and knees down the bank of the canal where he drank of the muddy flow. The family was easily rescued, but the man spent some days in the hospital recuperating from the heavy going through sand and his short exposure to the unmerciful heat. 120° F., as I recall it. He was not conditioned to either the heat or the exertion, and three miles or less were sufficient to seriously endanger his life.

Among the common victims of this part of the desert were tramps who followed a line of telephone poles, which crossed the arid plains more directly than did the highway. These unfortunates, apparently, were completely uninformed about the desert and did not carry canteens of adequate size. Many succumbed to heat or thirst or both. On three occasions circling buzzards out beyond my camp led me to the discovery of their remains. Interestingly enough, all three had taken off their clothes and had wandered more or less in circles, no doubt completely dazed and bewildered until they dropped dead to be found by the ever present turkey vultures circling the skies overhead.

Swimming in the canal was, of course, prohibited, but on one occasion, the temperature must have risen to 125° F. in the shade and even higher out on the open trail. More exertion was impossible; I floated downstream resting on a log. Even there, the surface water felt hot to the skin. The only noticeable cooling came from evaporation, and it was a standing joke that when dry, one finished a canal bath by using a whisk broom to dust off the residual grit. Naturally the water left a muddy taste in the mouth, and I drank it only when no other was available.

My own daily experience taught me unforgettable lessons on the absolute necessity of water. A one-gallon canvas water bag, probably containing somewhat less than a full measure and losing more by its cooling evaporation, was my inseparable companion. There were few times when the last drop was not consumed before the end of the five-mile hike through suffocatingly hot stands of arrowweed and over loose sand, and I usually drank an additional quart or more of cool filtered water from the gatekeeper's olla before I began that seemingly endless return to the ditch camp.

2: Limits to Life in a Thirsty Land

*S*oon after I began teaching biology at the University of California at Los Angeles I became reacquainted with the desert. Its great stretches—silent except for the wind singing in the low scattered shrubs—were alive with all kinds of creatures, many of which had already excited my curiosity. I introduced my students to more and more of them as my work with desert animals expanded, and it became natural for me to depend on local desert species for examples of certain characteristics. Not that I was uninterested in coastal and mountain forms. In fact, I became increasingly impressed by the variety and richness of the fauna of southern California.

It was then that I began thinking of our state as a mosaic of often widely contrasting living communities, their inhabitants determined by the physical environment. In so doing I often pondered on the breadth and scope of life itself, that fantastic phenomenon that divides the world into two great kingdoms.

Life is and always has been limited to a small vertical depth over the surface of the earth. It occupies a spacially narrow but very important portion of the geosphere—where air, water, and rock are in contact, producing through interaction the varied topographies typical of our planet. This thin and fragile "living skin" is divided into three layers: the hydrosphere, or aquatic regions of the earth; the lithosphere, rock-derived foundations that support living organisms; and the atmosphere, abundant source of the gaseous elements necessary for life processes.

We may speculate as did a Russian biogeochemist, Vladimir Vernadsky, and add the term noösphere, the area influenced by mental activity. With the advent of man, the other spheres have been subject to conscious manipulation with human needs the primary objective. In a few thousand years of civilization enormous changes have occurred within the biosphere. They have accelerated dramatically as man's numbers have proliferated and as he has learned more efficient ways to control and exploit his environment. Applied ingenuity has become, at times, a strong destructive force.

There are but few places in the biosphere where life does not exist. At present only a very small number of organisms are found at the polar extremes, although in the circumpolar regions, especially in the marine environment, life may be very abundant. Mountain heights from approximately 20,000 feet up to the ceiling of the geosphere—the peaks of the Himalayas and other adjacent highlands—are relatively sterile. At such heights there is no indigenous life though small organisms may be blown upward by gusts of air rising from below. On the highest mountains of California, however, there are forms that live on the comparative abundance of the short, warm summers but escape the rigors of winter either by hibernation or escape to lower elevations.

All life in the biosphere must operate in the very narrow temperature range between freezing, which stops the movement of water, and temperatures high enough to have an adverse effect on the stability of chemical structures. Upper limits range from 110° F. to 117° F. except for some bacteria in underground petroleum deposits and the primitive life of hot pools and springs.

We and all other animals depend on energy from the sun. We obtain it from the plants we consume directly or from other animals that have converted plant energy into protein and fatty tissue. Whether second- or third-hand, all of the energy that allows our cells to function, our nerves to conduct messages, and our muscles to respond to emergencies is derived from the sun.

Because of their unique ability to change solar energy to chemical energy, we must recognize the importance of green living things. Theirs is a primacy of position in the evolutionary story. Only through their chlorophyll can the inflowing energy from the distant sun be captured and transformed into organic matter. Using sunlight and the chemical process of photosynthesis, they lock up energy in forms that can be released either to non-green plants such as California's living flame of the High Sierra, the saprophytic snow plant, or to the vast host of animals that directly or indirectly get their sustenance from nutriment manufactured and stored by plants.

Just as essential as sunshine are chemicals from soil, water, and air. Through the magic of chlorophyll solar energy combines these basic elements into simple sugar, which may then be changed to more complicated carbohydrates and protein. If the whole process had to begin anew from such scattered inorganic elements as iron, magnesium, sodium, and sulfur, and the random gathering of solar energy to bind these particles into a living whole, the biotic world would be most unlike that of which we are a part today.

Southern California is well known for its plentiful sunshine and its rather scanty supply of water. Throughout the long summers surplus energy arrives from the sun, but its conversion into chemical energy is retarded because of the dry earth. Outdoor enthusiasts, except for the seekers of snowy slope and icy pond, seldom look forward to the winter season with its gusting storms and blot-out "tule" fogs. We sometimes forget that these periods of high humidity and precipitation provide the life blood for California's natural landscapes, their inhabitants, and our own unique complex of urban and rural life-styles.

When the first fall rains drift down on the hills, mountains, and plains, a new season begins, one of birth and awakening growth. The dust of summer, thickly accumulated on vegetation, is washed away, and the foliage looks laundry-fresh. The rain-scrubbed air is clear after months of obscuring haze and dust. The sun kindles to a diamond brilliance the rain drops still clinging tenuously to perches on the needles of evergreens or the broad surfaces of deciduous leaves. Morning after morning dewdrops hang in sparkling clusters from spiderwebs spun in dooryard shrubs, another indication of the availability of water in both soil and air.

There are differences in the pattern of rainfall throughout California's great length from north to south. Precipitation is lower and less dependable in the southern portion of the state. The presence of a dry subtropical belt in these latitudes, particularly strong in summer, accounts for some aridity; the offshore position of rain-blocking, high-pressure cells has a widespread influence on both the amount and spacing of winter rains.

These rains are necessary for the blossoming time of spring, March to early June, when the shallow-rooted annual plants produce seed, which drops and lies waiting for another season of renewed life. Perennial vegetation awakens from summer dormancy, stretches its limbs, and prepares to grow new shoots, sprout fresh leaves, and thicken flower buds on stem and twig.

Water from the winter storms seeps slowly down into the soil to renew underground reserves and resupply surface springs and streams. One of the first lessons a young naturalist should learn is that water really does not come from pipes, nor is its appearance as automatic as the gesture of turning a faucet. Its sources are influenced by climate, soil type, and terrain. Water sinks rapidly in coarse-textured, gravelly or rocky soil. Should it meet an impervious layer, it contributes to natural underground reservoirs, perhaps rising in seeps and springs. If the soil is saturated or the ground surface nonabsorbant (*e.g.*, bare rock), run-off collects in flowing streams. Only from those sources, as well as from natural lakes and impounded reservoirs, does water arrive in the conventional and now familiar, artificial way.

In the mountains temperatures are low in the cooler months, and the seasons follow the pattern of the more conventional divisions of the year: a clean-cut winter—with its snow-stinging gales and drifts of icy crystals, often many feet in depth—and a burgeoning spring. The new precipitation indicates only a potential of moisture. Plants cannot use snow directly as a water source; they must wait for its melting. Then water can penetrate to the roots, to be used by plants as they resume the vigorous growth of spring. Slowly the thaw creeps up from the foothills and finally reaches the highest mountaintops. Plants first and then animals respond with a renewed vitality.

The miracle of water and its meaning to living things are never so apparent as they are in semi-arid lands such as southern California. Here the prolonged dry season is accompanied by a period of inactivity or slow withering and death. The summer sunshine and its attendant heat, which in moister regions would stimulate growth, deter plant life. Summer scenery often superficially resembles that of the winter dormancy of cooler lands.

The climates of the Pacific Coast are intimately associated with the ocean to the west. The vast stretches of this great sea yield their moisture to surface winds, molecule by molecule. During winter the south-shifting stormy westerlies push weather fronts and masses of moist air across southern California. Cooling because of the rise in altitude or confrontation with bodies of cold air, the latent moisture is released, squeezed out by arrival at dew point. The condensing vapor forms droplets, which fall as rain, increasing in size and volume as the water-saturated air is chilled still further. The precipitation from any one winter storm is usually twice the amount at the 6,000-foot level than in the lowlands below.

With the approach of summer, the offshore upwelling current of cold water that parallels the California coast becomes of great importance. Ocean winds pulled inland by superheated desert air ride over this chilled mass of water and are cooled accordingly. What moisture they contain condenses into fog, clouds of air-supported mini-drops, which scuds into coastal basins and up sea-facing hillslopes most sum-

Figure 1. A generalized pattern in the formation of onshore winds and summer coastal fog. Water vapor offshore is condensed to fog as landward breezes carry it over an upwelling current of cold water.

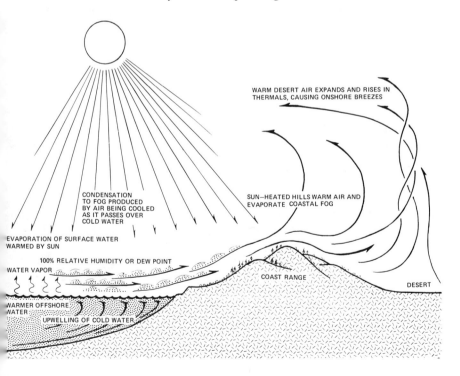

mer afternoons. When sufficiently cooled, the vaporized moisture forms small drops. Drizzly skies and copious fog-drip occur when the marine layer is deep enough, particularly during the cooler hours of early morning.

Proceeding inland the land becomes increasingly warmer than the incoming marine air. The winds change from water-bearing to water-greedy air flows. Periods of great heat occasionally break into the succession of sea-tempered days. The onshore winds become weak, and the high temperatures of interior valleys and deserts spread westward to the coastal basins. Moist air masses, however, often wander in from more humid lands to the south and east. Thunderheads thicken above Lake Arrowhead and Idyllwild, rare rain squalls blow across the desert floor, and even the coastal valleys may enjoy a brief shower.

When ocean breezes reach the mainland in winter and longer nights intensify the cooling of the ground surface, contact with the cold earth reduces the air's capacity for holding moisture. Its water vapor is transformed into ground fog, hindering air and surface traffic. These "tule" fogs persist for several days, lifting somewhat during late morning and early afternoon. In the Central Valley they lie like woolly rugs, reducing visibility to practically zero.

Regardless of these times of storm and fog, sunshine is plentiful, but water is in comparatively short supply. Since

Figure 2. Formation of radiation, or "tule," fog. Thick, ground-hugging fog is frequently encountered in valley floors and other low places during clear, cool nights, particularly in winter.

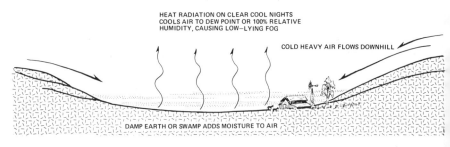

HEAT RADIATION ON CLEAR COOL NIGHTS
COOLS AIR TO DEW POINT OR 100% RELATIVE
HUMIDITY, CAUSING LOW–LYING FOG

COLD HEAVY AIR FLOWS DOWNHILL

DAMP EARTH OR SWAMP ADDS MOISTURE TO AIR

moisture must be available for both plants and animals, enormous numbers of living things compete with each other for this limited resource as well as struggle with a stern environment. In addition to the adaptations necessary for both survival and reproduction in a dry climate, the *number* of creatures that must in one way or another use water is of prime importance. A breeding population of plants (food for animals) and animals (food for yet other animals) is in never-ending contention for water, essential as it is for metabolic processes.

To persist in this highly competitive world, all things must perpetuate themselves. In the two billion or more years since life appeared on the earth, every single living form that has survived to the present has been forced by the attrition of numbers to breed far in excess of mere replacement. Because of all the environmental forces operating against life, the death toll is predictable and enormous. Only a few survive to maintain the breeding stock.

Competition for energy is intense and usually involves lethal activity. Plants and animals must die so that energy can move from one organism to another. Successful species must have a reproductive capacity that can outbreed disaster. They multiply in vast numbers and, though most are doomed to early death, some remain to reproduce themselves. Without this destruction any one species could displace by sheer mass alone every other species competing for space and nutrients.

Man is just beginning to realize through scientific investigation the intensity of the struggle for life and the odds against survival. He is also becoming aware of the consequences as his own offspring appear generation after generation in prodigal numbers. Man's multiplication is the primary cause of shortages of not only luxuries but even the necessities of life. Only his temporary defeat of high death rates has allowed him to multiply to the point where he must develop the science of population management and the art of conservation. Without man's excessive numbers there would be no shortages of wilderness areas for aesthetic enjoyment and recreation, nor of food, water, shelter, energy, and the other necessities of life.

It is largely, if not solely, because of man's ability to procreate uninhibitedly that much fertile soil has been destroyed and local water supplies have been outrun. By outgrowing the food-producing capacity of the land, he lives in poverty or semi-poverty over much of the earth. Subsistence-level economy is all too common. Unfortunately we tend to place emphasis on excessive shortages and not on excessive numbers of people and their concomitant demand for more and more resources. It is time to recognize the major cause of the disease and its symptoms—man's sheer numbers, ever-growing populations that threaten the things we attempt to preserve and what we should conserve, including the unique and richly varied landscapes of California.

3: California, Land of Change

*F*ew areas on earth are blessed with a climate so benign as that of coastal California. Month after month and often year after year the weather patterns continue to be mild and beneficent in the manner that old-time Californians have come to expect. Summer changes to winter by almost imperceptible degrees, a fact that distresses those who look forward to changing seasons and their drama of color and storm.

As spring advances it gradually becomes warmer week by week until the full heat of summer settles on the land for an almost unbroken stretch of three to four months or more. In valleys sheltered from the tempering sea breezes heat may become excessive, but the slow change usually inures one to the torrid hardship to come. Through even the hottest of days ranch laborers work out in the fields, tending crops or harvesting the product of summer effort in bakingly dry autumn weather.

In fall, especially during the Satana winds* that bring superdry air to the valleys, mountains fifty miles away seem less than half that distance. The landscape is one of brilliant light and, by contrast, dark shadows. Even the heat can be exhilarating. With dry moving air, evaporation is so rapid that uncomfortable sweating is rare.

Soon high cirrus clouds give warning of the first cold front marching down from the Arctic. Now the rains begin, moderately at first, and then intensifying until the winter storms roar over crest and summit. Showers of warm rain, at lower elevations, replenish the earth, starting the life cycle anew though winter is still to follow. Fields quicken with sprouting verdure, then turn gold with mustard. The untilled land, now grazing range for numberless head of livestock, was once covered with a multitude of native wildflowers such as the delicate shooting star, one of the first to appear, and numerous bulbs—blue-eyed grass, blue dicks, soap plant, chocolate lily, and the like.

The warmth of spring clothes acre upon acre in the vivid orange of California poppy. The once vast displays of these spectacular plants have diminished as a result of overgrazing through the years. In places, however, lupines still spread lakes of violet or sky blue, margined by the rosy-red of owl's clover or the golden-yellow of fiddleneck and many other species, each in its way an enchanting spread of color.

The southern parts of the state are occasionally beset by radiation frosts when the earth's heat passes unimpeded out into nighttime space, and temperatures drop to freezing or below. Such frosts occasionally endanger subtropical crops— citrus, avocado, and others. They are sufficiently intense

*Also called Santa Ana or its abbreviation, Santana, which probably are corruptions of the original Satanas, or devil's winds.

in localized frost-prone areas to cause damage if not offset by man's various devices for pushing temperatures several degrees higher. These include the effective but expensive and obnoxious smudge pots. Oil is burned to create updrafts that bring in a flow of somewhat warmer air. The pots themselves radiate heat, protecting the citrus trees from damage to fruit or foliage. In other areas powered propellers mounted on towers sufficiently mix the warmer overlayer of air with the cool air collecting in depressions and valleys and thus modify the local drainage of cold air down into pockets and hollows. At times real freezes invade southern California. These may strike even the elevated ridges and slopes where crops are usually safe from cold.

Though the region is famed for its "Chamber of Commerce" climate, only the coast and adjacent hills and valleys enjoy its cool summers and mild winters. Interior valleys, away from the tempering influence of the sea, have longer and hotter summers. The coastal fogs do not penetrate far inland, and neither do the cooling sea breezes.

Relief features greatly influence climate, and the mountains of southern California are classic examples of the dramatic differences in both temperature and precipitation at higher altitudes. The mountaintops are populated with species of plants and animals having their closest affinity with the Arctic. The deserts to the east and north of the mountain ranges have yet another climate. Though only a short distance away, in terms of miles, the warmth and dryness of the Colorado Desert, in particular, are in great contrast to the cool, relatively moist coast. Santa Monica and Indio are no more alike than Lisbon and Timbuctoo. The low-lying deserts abutting on the Mexican boundary have many species that are essentially invaders from dry subtropical regions to the south. In the Owens Valley and arid regions to the north and east, much of the flora and fauna shows greatest resemblance to that of the Great Basin.

Because of this climatic diversity, a study of California's wildlife requires the division of the state into at least four wildlife regions, each of which deserves a lifetime of study:

brush and woodland, grassland, conifer forest, and desert scrub.*

These regions can be further described by habitat: 1) streamside woodlands and brush featuring water-requiring plants; 2) grassy fields fairly heavily dotted with oaks of various species, most of which are endemic (confined) to California; 3) savannas shared by grass and a few shading oak trees; 4) inland valleys dominated by grasses and numerous annual species; 5) the elfin forest or chaparral of the foothills and coastal mountains; 6) the forest belts lying between the chaparral and the frigid mountaintops; and 7) the various scrub communities of the desert. I might well emphasize at this point that in gaining an understanding of whatever wildlife region one may select to visit or work in, tastes and interests vary. Some are content to increase expertise in the sight identification of species, amassing them much as a stamp collector assembles and learns to recognize the stamps of the world and their dates of issue. This is a delightful though somewhat elementary pastime. For deeper understanding, and I feel that this is of great importance to human welfare, the basic principles of interdependence and diversity through evolution should be kept in mind.

The adaptations of plants and animals to their differing environments, for example, raise the fascinating story of the origin of life forms. Environment in company with genetic diversity shapes the raw material of life to meet its demands. Reproductive superfluity, the bearing of more offspring than can possibly survive for more than a few generations at best, supports the process of genetic change. It provides a rich harvest of food for predators and herbivores. It takes the brunt of disease and disaster, ensuring a chance of species survival, and in the end selects the fittest.

Scenic California attracts millions of casual visitors each year. Among them are many whose main interest is enjoyment of wildlands, their beauty, and their marvelous ability to relax the nervous tensions of urban living. Increasing

*Or Vinson Brown's classification: Pacific Coastal, Californian, Sierra Nevadan, and Desert.

numbers within this group find keen pleasure in learning to understand natural landscapes. They attend outdoor-experi- ence workshops and field courses offered by many sponsor- ing organizations throughout the state. One's point-of-view cannot help but change after exposure to such enrichment, particularly if emphasis is placed on ecological interpretations. Scenic values are much enhanced if one learns *why* things behave and look like they do or live where they do, in other words, the *how* of survival.

For such understanding the use of wildlife regions is con- venient but often too broad to be fully adequate. One of the most commonly used basic geographical units in biological study is the natural community. It is the assemblage of plants and animals, with their special requirements, that live in a definable habitat: for example, tide pool, permanent pond, sand dune, and yellow pine forest. Factors of the physical environment—mainly climate and soil—control the nature of the organisms living in such communities. Relationships between these organisms are structured upon the basic needs of food, water, shelter, and reproduction.

Recognizing a specific natural community may take some skill. Changes within the community can mask its real char- acter. Is a certain grassland a true piece of natural prairie? Or was it originally brush or forest and its present plant assem- blage the result of fire or other means of tree or shrub removal? The broader the category the easier it is to identify signifi- cant characteristics. The conifer forest on the western slope of the Sierra Nevada is readily recognizable, particularly in contrast to the neighboring oak woodlands of the foothills or the sagebrush-covered plateaus to the east. It is far more difficult to identify the various associations of cone-bearing trees within this great tract of forest and the reasons for their distribution. Why white fir and sugar pine at this bend of the road and red fir and lodgepole pine three miles away? Such mosaics of vegetation are common over much of Cali- fornia, including its vast deserts.

Often these smaller variations within the larger habitat can be easily accounted for, with a little thought. Canyon bottoms—

shielded from the full impact of sunshine and wind, cooled by down-flowing air, and watered by perennial streams—disrupt the brushy cover so typical of the hills. We immediately recognize that the tall, large-leafed trees clustered along the lower sides of the ravine are very different from the scrubby growth just above them. Users of great quantities of water, they are able to grow there because of a moist environment.

Permanent water in the desert supports an assemblage of plants totally unlike that of arid plain and slope. Flooded river flats and swamps along the Colorado River abound with groves of cottonwood trees and thickets of tamarisk, or salt-

Figure 3. The north- and south-facing slopes of a canyon, particularly if east-west trending, may have markedly different types of vegetation. Amount of solar radiation and soil depth are contributing factors. Streamside growth is characterized by plants dependent on year-round water availability.

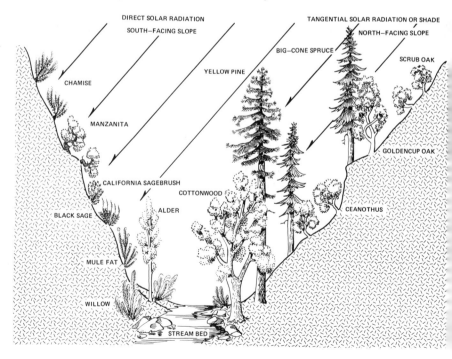

cedar (originally from the deserts of North Africa and western Asia), arrowweed, giant bulrushes, and mesquite. For the most part, these collections of freshwater plants are unlike those inhabiting the "alkali" sinks and seeps of the desert floor. The former are water spendthrifts, having little need to conserve this precious resource. The latter must accommodate to a water deficit made more serious because of the moisture-robbing nature of saline soils.

Such a multiplicity of local variations within a specific biotic spectrum can be complex indeed. Some years ago problems of this nature were attacked by a group of interested biologists. As many as seventy-five California plant communities were recognized, based upon a bewildering number of criteria. This was bad enough, but then it was pointed out that if one included the chemical effects of differing soil types plus water availability in terms of time, amount, and other considerations *plus* altitude, a much larger number of communities would have to be recognized. Clearly, things were getting out of hand. It was finally agreed that only some thirty communities would be on the basic list.

Once established, plant and animal communities may remain stable for centuries until the next major change in climate, but for two periodic occurrences: fire and flood. Modifications initiated by such forces occur through a dynamically operating succession of plant and animal species taking place over a series of seasons. In a perceptible but complex sequence, one assemblage appears, becomes dominant, and then gradually dies out to be replaced by still another assemblage of flora and fauna. At length, what is known as a climax community is produced. It is relatively stable, adjusted to its physical environment. Little else will replace it unless another catastrophe overwhelms it or there are basic changes in the region's climatic patterns.

In California, where fires have always been frequent and extensive, it is often difficult to tell what the climax community actually may be or for how long, if ever, it will remain a "final" biota. The same is true when periodic floods sweep down through canyons, uprooting alders, sycamores, and lesser vegetation, scraping channels clear to bedrock, or leaving nothing but jackstraw tangles of logs lying here and there among heaps of clean, rounded boulders. Unfortunate animals living near the streambed are swept away or buried under sand and gravel. Such newly formed "deserts" require years for their total rehabilitation. California is dynamic country. Through fire and flashflood, upheaval and erosion, its vegetation typifies the eternal constant, change.

4: California, Land of Contrast

*T*hroughout its length California is characterized by long mountain ridges interspersed with peaks and passes. Separated by these ranges, the lower elevations of the state vary from the deserts east of and below the Sierra Nevada and other fringing ranges to the agriculturally rich central valleys of the San Joaquin and the Sacramento rivers—now virtually covered by irrigated crops—to smaller valleys and a narrow plain west of the Coast Ranges in southern California.

During the cooler months the visitor or resident of the warm, lowland valleys can enjoy, perhaps wistfully, the sight of looming mountain masses covered with snow. It lingers almost year-round on Mt. Whitney, high above the Owens Valley in eastern California. For several winter months and those of early spring it masses in steep ravines and frosts the tops of Mt. San Gorgonio and Mt. San Jacinto, tall ramparts behind Palm Springs and its satellite communities.

Time and again in my forty or more years of teaching, research, and living in the desert during the summer months I have looked longingly to the deliciously cool heights and wondered how I became committed to work with reptiles. These creatures are not only so much more prevalent and varied but reveal so many more intriguing features in the hot, dry lowlands than in other habitats. At times the desire to take a short recess from my research was too strong. I would flee the heat-quivering hills and coke-oven washes to grind up the grade that traversed the slopes covered with chaparral and pinyon-juniper woodland, which separated the first ranks of yellow pine from the desert floor below. In doing so I crossed many finger-like projections of the cool and moisture-requiring conifer forest that penetrate downward in canyons, particularly those that are north-facing or have permanent streams.

I drove from the searing heat of the desert to pine groves dim with pleasant shade in only thirty-five to forty minutes. In that time I went from sea level, or even below near Indio, to 5,000 feet, from date palms and citrus groves to yellow pines and black oaks. To use another system of wildland classification, in addition to those mentioned in the previous chapter, I went from the Lower Sonoran life zone to the Transition life zone. These vegetation types mark broad climatic and biological zones, which were designated by one of the giants of natural history, Dr. C. Hart Merriam, as basic biotic divisions of North America. The zones occupy various altitudes at which they are characteristically found and, for the most part, are named for geographic regions where comparable flora and fauna are typical. Though other systems are coming more and more into use, the life zone concept conveys an important climatic meaning: altitude approximates latitude. By going higher in an area, in a sense, one is also going north. (This is true only in the Northern Hemisphere, of course.) The tundra of the high meadows above timberline in the Rockies is very close in appearance, behavior, and even in species composition to the lower-lying tundra of the Arctic.

The Lower Sonoran life zone has species characteristic of the desert washes and plains in Sonora, Mexico. The chaparral of foothill California, southern Arizona, and northern Mexico all belongs to the Upper Sonoran life zone. The Transition zone (around 4,000 feet to 6,500 feet) is typified by yellow pine, localized conifers such as incense cedar and sugar pine (California), Arizona cypress (Arizona, New Mexico, Texas, and Mexico) and corkbark fir (Arizona), and deciduous oaks. Climatic conditions and plants and animals similar to those of southern Canada are found in the Canadian zone (7,000 to 9,000 feet). Several species of trees are even common to both areas—lodgepole pine, Engelmann spruce, and subalpine fir (the latter does not occur in California, though it is widespread throughout the intermountain West). The Hudsonian zone occupies timberline and just below. The climate and wildlife are like that around Hudson Bay. Small samples of this zone are scattered in southern California on higher elevations where the larger reptiles (*e.g.*, rattlesnakes) are almost missing in the biota of these high, cold sites. Above timberline, the Arctic-Alpine zone occurs on mountain peaks, whose closest vegetational and faunal affinities are with the Arctic of the Far North.

The Transition zone is the dividing belt that separates the warm, dry Sonoran (also referred to as austral, meaning southerly) zones from the cooler, damper regions with their boreal (northerly) relationships. Except for ski and other winter sport enthusiasts who gather at the snowier Canadian and Hudsonian altitudes, most resort activity is concentrated around lakes and streams within the Transition zone. The desert, however, hosts thousands of "winter migrants" as they seek escape from the snow shovels and icy roads of the Midwest and northeastern states or the fog and rain of the Pacific Coast.

It is often difficult for even the experienced Californian to appreciate the sudden and definitive contrasts in climate that accompany changes in altitude, especially the rapidity with which weather at high elevations can shift from warm to cold during the unstable spring and fall months. As a teacher I was aware of this innumerable times. Despite my specific directions to bring camping equipment suitable for both extreme heat and uncomfortable cold on field trips and other outdoor excursions, some students simply did not follow instructions. There were at times hilarious and at times pathetic results.

Not many years ago I took my usual scouting trip to plan the field and camp activities for the class that was to accompany me to the mountains a week later. At 6,000 feet I found that a temperature inversion had resulted in a May heat wave more appropriate to July. The thermometer peaked around 90° F. during the midday hours in my chosen campground. The characteristic reptiles were out in full force—the fence lizard and its smaller cousin, *Sceloporus graciosus.* Birds, squirrels, and chipmunks were abundant and engagingly active, courting, searching innumerable hidden food sources, and skirmishing for territory. Beechey ground squirrels were already investigating the newly dug garbage pits on the periphery of the campground.

On returning to the Los Angeles campus Monday morning, I discussed the forthcoming field trip. After describing the weather conditions I had encountered, I reminded them to be sure to bring three or four warm blankets or a good sleeping bag, sweaters, and windbreakers as the weather could turn cold during this fickle season. I mentioned camping in a snow shower in June at this location several years back. The temperatures on campus during the following week exceeded 75° F. several times. But spring fever was epidemic. Student and teacher alike were bemused by the warm wind, and the scent of fresh mowed grass blowing through the laboratory windows was in delightful contrast to the usual smell of formaldehyde.

Friday morning I partially returned to my senses, and once more I reminded my class that despite the pleasant temperatures of the previous week *everyone* should bring warm clothing and adequate bedding. I also stressed that sleeping on cots would be practically impossible. Everyone should be prepared to spend the night on the ground, but I would see to it that they all enjoyed the luxury of ample beds of pine needles to cushion bones and insulate against the chill earth. In describing at length the spicy fragrance of pine resin seeping out from under their bedrolls, I really made it sound good—comfortable but beguilingly adventurous.

Amid the business of checking numbers of bodies, numbers of cars, and pieces of field equipment I hurried through departure details. As we approached the mountains I could see clouds streaming over their tops and through neighboring passes. A change of weather had indeed occurred. I immediately foresaw the unpleasant possibility of a batch of thoroughly chilled and miserable students. Why hadn't I thoroughly inspected their camping gear prior to leaving?

I chose the most sheltered spot I could find. It was somewhat protected from full exposure to the wind, but gusts were roaring through the tops of the pine trees. Temperatures were rapidly dropping from a tolerable 60° F. to 50° F. and at sunset to the shivering 40s. By taking advantage of the wind-breaking shelter of cars, spread blankets, and the trunks of trees, we all managed a hot meal before gathering around the central campfire for the customary evening of singing, marshmallow toasting, anecdote telling, and the general chatter that makes camping with students so delightful.

I kept an uneasy eye on the falling mercury and the increasing windy gusts. Then I could stall no longer. I had to find out just what kind of bedding the students had brought.

"Sack time, kids! We want to be out of the campground at eight o'clock tomorrow morning." Car trunk doors opened and gear clattered. Despite my little allusions to the delights of pine needle beds, more than half the class hefted out bulky camp cots, one of the coldest and most awkward and uncomfortable devices ever invented. I knew it, I muttered to myself, I knew it! Many of the students in this introductory course were newcomers to southern California, and all were camping novices. Many were from the East and trusted the travel posters more than their professor and his baleful warnings. Fearful they were, but of beasties in the night, not unstable weather.

As they argued, bargained, and shared advice about cot sites, I saw with growing alarm that they had as carelessly ignored my instructions about adequate blankets. Most were as thin as sheets, and they flapped uselessly in the rising wind. Two girls had brought a cotton blanket apiece and settled down on their carefully isolated camp cots, as far from protecting vegetation as possible. They insisted that they were scared to death of the "dangers of the wild," despite the protection of a dozen able-bodied, gallant young men. The two girls, and three others, absolutely refused to double up and share blankets, or to sleep on the needle-insulated ground, or to drive back to campus.

Dawn poked me in the eye and I awoke to fretful complaints. "I've never been so cold in my life!" "Does anyone have an extra sweater?" "Will somebody please start a fire?" The stubborn campcotters hadn't slept at all. Scuttling between bed and campfire, they fought both the need for sleep and the tenacious chilling wind. No wonder this company of misery: when I unscrewed the top of my canteen and held it upside down, frozen slush was plugging it as effectively as a cork!

On another occasion in late May I was conducting research on desert reptiles. Unseasonable and excessive heat drove me to nearby mountains for a brief respite. I left the research site knowing that a change in the weather was due. A winter-type storm was riding the lofty crest. High cirrus clouds spread out like dunes of white sand, and nimbus clustered in the notches above the passes. I prepared for either cold rain or cool winds of moderate intensity.

The pines of the Transition zone would afford some shelter, and I headed for a campsite deep in one of the groves. By early evening I knew what was in store. Flurries of sleet and snow pellets struck the car as if thrown in handfuls by a petulant wind. Temperatures had fallen sharply by the time I organized camp and prepared dinner. Now the gales careened through the trees with an almost frightening sibilance of sound. A really bright campfire was impossible because of the danger of flames spreading to piles of still-dry leaves that littered the campground. Rather than drive back to the desert floor, there was but one thing to do—seek warmth in bed. I snuggled down into my sleeping bag, wrapped in all the clothes I had brought, and tucked the cover around me tightly. Any seasoned camper can tell you that there is always one cold wind that is aimed directly at his neck.

An hour or so must have passed before I relaxed in the growing warmth of accumulated clothes and bedding. Finally I fell into intermittent sleep. Throughout the night the crash of an old rotten pine branch or a belated thrust of wind from the diminishing storm startled me to semi-wakefulness. I appreciated the snugness of my retreat and its contrast with the bitter world howling about me.

The storm moderated sometime in the early morning hours. I dropped into a sound sleep from which I woke only because of the complete stillness surrounding me. As I pushed back the covers to glance about at the weather, the quiet was absolute. Everywhere, even on top of me, was a blanket of snow, and the heavy flakes were still falling, joining the snow already on the ground. Had this been a rain it would have been a cloudburst. As it was, the flakes fell so quickly they had thoroughly chilled the waterproof windbreaker on my bed. It was heavy with snow, which, fortunately, was not yet at the melting point.

I lay there quietly, absorbing the white enchantment drifting silently around me and wondering how to prepare breakfast without becoming wet through. The dawn brightened, and the snow seemed to fall less heavily. Within a half hour patchwork pieces of blue sky floated above the crystal-crusted pines. The storm had passed. I decided to shake the snow from my bed and pack. After dressing I tramped down the snow around the car and began to strike camp. My drive back to the main highway was slow despite a demanding stomach. All went well until I hit a slight incline onto the pave-

ment. The wheels started spinning on the snow. Having no
chains, I had to either back up and take the incline at a rush
or wait until the last of the drifts had melted. My hungry stomach recommended the first solution, and luckily it worked.
Only in the mountains of the West can one drive from lowland heat and then get stuck in snow for two hours the week
before Memorial Day!

The storm was typically local. A few miles downgrade the
lighter fall and rising temperature turned the pavement a
gleaming black. Only a dusting of snow sparkled on the
shrubs of roadside chaparral. As I reached the edge of the
desert, warm drafts gusted upward along the ridges and can-
yonsides. The night's moisture clung in drops to leaf and
twig, brilliant with reflected sunlight.

Though there had been light rains on the desert itself, the
heat of the ground and intensity of the sun had already
brought most of the reptiles to the surface. Here they were
basking, and collecting was perfect. At one point on the
mountainside (at 3,000 feet) tracks of the desert bighorn
sheep trailed everywhere. I learned for the first time on this
"escape" (whether from heat to cold or cold to warm is moot;
at this point in memory they have equal attraction) that these
handsome wild sheep have devised a way to get at the nutritious moist pulp of the fishhook cactus, and probably other
kinds of cactus as well. They paw away at the succulent stalks,
breaking them off, and gnaw or tongue-rasp the thorn-free
end into a cup-like depression from which they remove the
pulp. How I wished I could have lived when the desert sheep
were present in large numbers. They must have been pressed
for food and water at times, and their thirst and hunger surely
affected the abundance of the cactus upon which they fed.

Though knowing that California is a land of contrasts that
lie juxtaposed to each other as in no other part of the United
States, even biologists may be excused for failing to understand fully how so many and such diverse species can live
so closely together. A well-known taxonomist friend of mine
some years back refused to believe the lists of new subspecies of birds compiled by a most knowledgeable western sci-

entist. My eastern friend insisted that such "splitting" of species into the smaller taxonomic units known as subspecies and varieties was wholly unrealistic. His convictions were so strong they almost amounted to outright condemnation.

Despite that criticism, such a division of species into sub-units has subsequently been completely justified. For scientific accuracy it is absolutely necessary and unavoidable wherever different climates are so closely adjacent as they are in many places in the mountainous West. Speciation usually depends upon genetic isolation. Thus climatic diversity stimulates the separation of discrete taxonomic units: first varieties, then subspecies, species, and genera. This is well illustrated by the boas of California. The desert-adapted subspecies of the California boa, *Lichanura trivirgata gracia,* is more

Figure 4. The east face of Mt. San Jacinto supports a number of vegetation belts. Typical plants indicate differences in temperature and precipitation because of changes in altitude. Common birds frequently found at these levels are listed on the right.

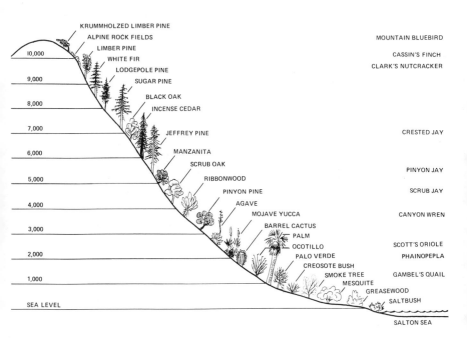

striped than the coastal and mountain subspecies, *Lichanura trivirgata roseofusca,* which is a denizen of the chaparral, oak woodland, and rock-strewn grasslands. A marked difference in habitat characterizes the ecotone, or border, between the upper edge of the chaparral and the lower edge of the adjoining coniferous forest. The ecotone separates the California boa of the chaparral from its entirely different relative, the rubber boa, *Charina bottae,* of the forest. This gentle creature is sluggish in behavior and has a rubbery skin, gunmetal gray in color, and with its blunt tail it appears to be two-headed. Not only does it look quite different from most boas, but it dwells in a climate—cool in summer and cold in winter—seldom associated with boas and their relatives, the pythons. All three of California's boas have strong habitat preferences, differ in appearance, and yet can be found within miles of each other. California's diversity is a wonderful challenge to curious naturalists.

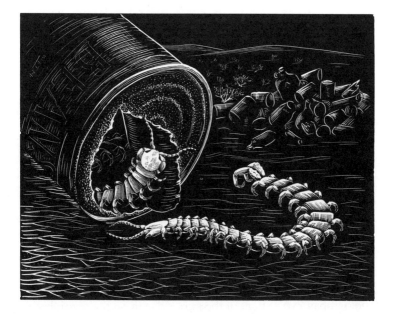

5: *Around the Campfire*

Nightfall is an interruption. Regardless of where
we are and what we might be doing, we are
usually aware of its approach. Time to quit the job and go
home. Time to start dinner. Time to check out the children,
get ready for a play or a party, watch the evening news. There
are certainties about nighttime. It will get dark; part of it will
be spent in sleep. Something, however, happens beyond
the simple setting of the sun. Life shifts gears, changes direction, even if slightly. Things are done that seem somewhat
out-of-place during earlier hours. It is time for a cocktail,
to review perhaps more objectively any disquieting events
of the day, to take stock of the state of the world, to plan for
a more realistically conceived tomorrow.

A tasty meal, an evening's relaxation or entertainment—

these are good hours ahead. Though the shock of morning may be more dramatic, the day ahead is uncertain. It usually means work, often worry, perhaps distress, or exciting new discoveries. Night, on the other hand, is a pleasant companion—rest and laughter, a cherished hobby, an engrossing book, a warm friend, a cool wind, and a muscle loosened that was tense before.

In the world of the wild the departure of the sun is an occurrence of major importance. Plants cease to photosynthesize, though they continue other physiological processes, and animals either settle to rest or awaken to activity. As diurnal species give way to those nocturnal, the machinery of nature shifts its gears as well.

Almost every afternoon in the warm season, coastal fog, held at bay by the heat of the sun, rides in on the ocean breeze toward the seaward bluffs, envelops the surf-ruffled shore, and creeps ever so quietly up every valley of the bordering mountains. Then, dammed up, it rises higher and higher along the flanks of the Coast Range, veils the trees in cool, wet, floating mist, and muffles distant sounds so that the drip of moisture from leaf tip and branchlet often becomes audible.

Fog is a frequent companion of the summer night, and in the cool months of late spring and fall it may occur during the day along the entire California coastline. From Point Conception north it fosters many kinds of trees, which reach up into the moving screen of fog, collect the moisture, and return it to the soil in a nightly shower that keeps the soil damp and favorable for growth. Although fog is composed of odorless and tasteless droplets of water, it stimulates the tissues on which it settles so that one is often aware of a pleasant, almost spicy, odor as the fog arrives each night.

According to research by Don Mullally in the tree groves along Skyline Drive near San Francisco, precipitation from fog drip amounts to double that of annual rainfall. Fortunately for the vegetation, fog is most prevalent during late spring and summer after regular precipitation has ceased. Thus fog climatically "bridges" what would otherwise be an extremely dry season with ample moisture for plants that can collect and use it.

Redwoods, Monterey cypress, Monterey pine, the native sycamore, and to a lesser but still observable extent, oaks, some species of the introduced eucalyptus, and many other types of coastal vegetation collect and drip this moisture. I have noticed that the European plane tree, close relative of the California sycamore, but originally an inhabitant of areas where moisture is far more abundant, seems totally lacking in the ability to attract fog droplets. The two species, European and California, when growing side by side over a pavement demonstrate this difference.

Nocturnal visibility is characteristic of desert regions. In heavily vegetated areas, particularly in dense forest or woodland, most or all of the light from stars and the night sky seems to be lost by absorption or random scattering. The nights are very dark, and artificial illumination is necessary for even the simplest of activities. On the contrary, California's deserts consist of light-colored soils varying from pale buff to soft pink, and their plant life is so scanty it throws few shadows. All the natural light from moon, sky, and star, vivid in the clear air, remains to aid one's vision. Just a few minutes without artificial light and with automatic ocular accommodation, one can find one's way across strange terrain with remarkable ease.

In high mountains night visibility is intermediate between that of the humid coast and the sere desert. Judging by my own eyes and their ability to accommodate, nights do not seem as dark at higher altitudes as in the heavy forests of the Pacific Northwest nor as bright as in the desert.

There is another feature that mountain nights have in common with those of the desert—or did have in less smoggy times. That is—or was—ultra-clear air extending out uninterruptedly into space. Shortly after sunset heat is rapidly radiated into the sky, and the temperatures of both air and ground drop quickly. Night, unless there is a temperature inversion layer, may become quite cold.

From about 5,000 feet upward the evening chill becomes

more exaggerated. People unaccustomed to clear mountain air and skies and the consequent quick loss of heat to space are often caught without adequate clothing and suffer accordingly. I have learned to expect a scurry for coats, blankets, fuel, and a good fire around sundown after a day in the mountains with my students.

Nightfall on the desert is remarkably different from that event in other regions of the world. In wintertime the almost balmy temperature and gracious warmth of the setting sun are replaced by increasing and often piercing cold. The change is so abrupt that one feels it almost immediately as the heat departs into space, and the dry air, unable to hold the re-radiated heat, becomes sharply and uncomfortably cold. In summertime, while nights at high altitudes cool swiftly, those in the desert do not. Weeks of long, super-hot days and the heat accumulated in soil and rock under intense solar radiation keep desert nocturnal temperatures relatively high. The approach of night, however, signals at least partial release from the tension of burdensome heat. Temperatures as high as 90° F. are most welcome after 120° F. in the shade.

In the Colorado Desert moist, warm air occasionally drifts northward from tropical storms originating south of the Gulf of California, preventing the escape of the day's accumulation of heat. Under these conditions even the nights remain excessively hot.

In these so-called temperate latitudes nighttime temperatures may remain for hours far above those ever encountered on the hottest days on the Equator, and one can expect temperatures of 100° F. or more as late as midnight.

The sunset skies of the desert have scenic effects that are practically unknown in other climates. The sky blazes behind the peaks clustered to the west. This brilliant color changes from lemon to gold to orange, and eventually the sky becomes deep violet. The absence of clouds confines the warmer colors to a fan-shaped glow, which slowly fades until all above is inky blue and the mountains become sharp-cut silhouettes of black velvet. In more humid climates, dust, moisture,

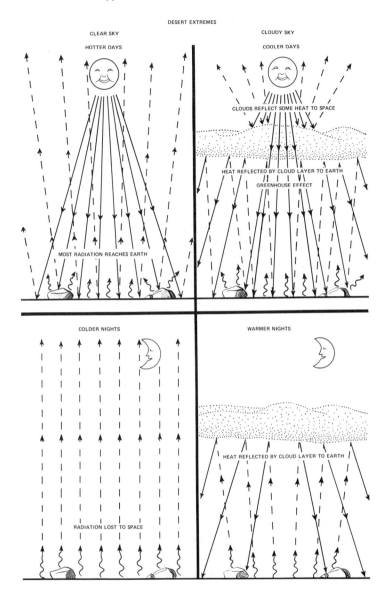

Figure 5. Comparison of clear and cloudy skies in a desert climate. Day or night, a cloud layer creates a "greenhouse effect" by returning to the earth much of the heat radiating from its surface.

and other microscopic flotsam scatter the remaining rays and soften the harsh contrast characteristic of the desert.

Summer or winter, there is something special about sundown and the oncoming night, and my desert camps were no exception. Not the least was the cessation of work, return to camp, and, in those years of fewer people, the gathering of scanty firewood. I often used cactus skeletons and the roots and stems of stunted shrubs. Soon my camp was rich with fragrance. Food cooked in the aromatic smoke from desert wood has a tang in this clear, unpolluted air unknown outside the arid world. Long before the summer sun has set, the first flight of bats commences, most often the little canyon, or pipistrelle, bat with pale silvery body, black wings and ears. Along the Colorado River they flicker across the sky, bent primarily on reaching water where they can replenish the moisture lost during the day, even in their relatively cool rock-crevice retreats.

In the same locale nighthawks by the hundred appear soon after the heat begins to abate. They flutter and sail toward the river for the first drink of the day. During May and June when many are still incubating or hovering over their eggs to protect them from the sun's increasing heat, this first intake of water precedes feeding. The birds nest, or more accurately, lay their eggs, on the exposed ground. Throughout the day the relentless sun beats down. Air and ground temperatures may exceed 120° F. for hours on end; the direct heat of the sun contributes to what for most creatures would be unendurable conditions. Insulated against heat by its feathers, each nighthawk sits in a self-made patch of shade and comfort. Plumage is as effective in shielding the skin and blood vessels from high temperatures as it is in containing body heat during cold weather.

From time to time they open their enormous mouths and flutter their gular pouch, evaporating some of their small supply of water to keep blood and body temperatures below damaging or lethal levels. But water is so scarce and the day so long that excessively prolonged cooling by this means would dehydrate the birds. I know of no other animals, however, not even the supposedly sun-tolerant lizards (that possess no feathery insulation), that can remain in direct sunlight for so long a time. Many of the smaller lizards will die in minutes under such conditions. Yet the nighthawks, warm-blooded, heat-generating birds, complete their incubation period and care for the young in the unrelenting heat of the desert until all can take flight to a less strenuous environment.

These crepuscular (dusk and dawn) flights of bats and nighthawks are generally silent. The bats seldom twitter, and the prolonged croaking warbles of the nighthawks are very rarely heard after the close of the mating season. That particular call and the roaring courtship dive are usually reserved for cooler hours and, if possible, after a drink.

The mating cry of the nighthawk (sometimes called a bull-bat, though it is not a bat at all) is a common spring sound on the desert. When it is first heard, those unfamiliar with nighthawks often look in vain for a noisy amphibian, particularly around an oasis or a farmer's reservoir. The other characteristic sound made by the nighthawk is produced apparently by its vibrating feathers at the end of a steep dive at maximum speeds. Such diving is most common during the breeding season. The source of this sudden, vibrant buzz is easy to detect, as the birds are often visible against the sky.

Other sounds belong to the dusk—the thin whistling of a Say phoebe, a hardy desert flycatcher, and the faint calls of a rock wren near rugged slopes and boulder-strewn hillsides. Desert sparrows chirp in the thickening shadows. Though there appears to be a scarcity of life on the desert, nonetheless it is there, and one can gain an inkling of its abundance by listening to the sounds of dawn and dusk.

One of the delights of camping in the unspoiled desert is the nightly scurrying of the several species of the attractive little rodent, the kangaroo mouse. These kangaroo "rats," as as they are usually called, bear a rough resemblance to their namesakes in the length and power of their hind legs and their bipedal locomotion. In starshine, moonlight, or camp-fire glow, their dancing shadows flutter at the far edge of vision. And it is their shadows, not their bodies, that are visible on these rare occasions of abundance and great activity.

This is also true of other desert ground-running, nocturnal creatures. The remarkable concealing coloration of desert animals is probably amplified in our perception because of our limited noctural vision, but it also serves to conceal them from nocturnal predators. The pale fawn grays and browns of their upper surfaces become virtually invisible. In the tangential light of fires or a rising moon they cast sharp black shadows against the pale desert sands that are far more conspicuous than their bodies. Their activity is indeed a shadow ballet attended only by those who dare the silent infinitude of the desert wilderness.

My camp, where I conducted research in animal temperature control, was located near mesquite thickets, often in the lee of a mound of wind-drifted and compacted dust and sand through which ran multitudes of burrows of arthropods and rodents. Arthropods are the insects and numerous other species of backboneless creatures with jointed limbs. They include scorpions, which may be as long as three inches, and the harmless (to human beings) but speedy solpugids, known also as hunting or sun spiders. These long-legged, ghostly creatures, about the leg spread of a quarter, emerge on warm nights, as they had at the ditch camp where I first met them, to dart over the ground in search of their victims. Their swift shadows caught my attention night after night in late spring and summer as I rested in the mesquite grove.

Scorpions appear to be more shy and conceal themselves by remaining still. I rarely saw them unless I was hunting for them. This I did by following their distinctive tracks, as the animals themselves are difficult to see. Pale straw in color, they match their background, and their quiet habits render them invisible. I collected a number of them, however, with a portable ultraviolet light. Then they became spectacular. They glowed with an eery light that reminded me of animated constellations gleaming on the sand. Under the most fortunate conditions I have seen as many as six small scorpions within a single field of light.

To those who love the desert—and judging by its spread-

Plate 2. This large scorpion is formidable in appearance, but actually it is not as venomous as its smaller amber-colored cousin.

ing urban communities it has a strong appeal—night is a time for deep enjoyment. The dark is not to fear but to explore. Star glow and the faint shimmer of the night sky brightened my camp and its surroundings. Stretched in my sleeping bag and relaxed after a good meal and a vigorous day of exercise and work, I watched for the occasional meteor and listened for the comforting sounds of night—the distant bugling of a coyote, whose wailing bark belongs to the wilderness, and the mellow, dual-toned hooting of a mated pair of horned owls as they went about their night's business of defending territories and hunting unwary rodents.

In summer, especially, work began well before full daylight. I awakened to the first of the mountains darkening against the eastern sky. Then the light spread over those still violet-shadowed to the north and south. Finally, the horizon glowed as if afire just before the sun burst above the edge of the world.

What is left of the unspoiled desert spaces are the last fragments of virgin nature remaining in many parts of the Southwest. They are hospitable to those who accord them due respect and who have the knowledge to enjoy their intimate little canyons, their wide sun-drenched plains, and the plants and animals that live there. The desert has unique aesthetic and scientific satisfactions. It is as deserving of preservation as forests, lakes, and coastlines. Its future merits more than a scourge of off-road vehicles and a population encouraged to growth by irrigation from desalted sea water and other costly sources. Unless we act now we will surely lose these once almost inviolate refuges, which not only serve to harbor wildlife, but which provide valuable sanctuaries of escape from the multiplying pressures of the human world today. Even their heated air currents are essential to sustain patterns of atmospheric circulation that draw in cooler and heavier air from the sea and stabilize the climate of coastal California. We have a number of reasons to be grateful for those "wastelands" east of the mountains.

Plate 3. The Jeep and the desert quail were first, and the mouse and shovel-nosed snake arrived later, though not necessarily in that sequence. The higher banked curves of the snake's track are clues to the direction of body movement (right to left).

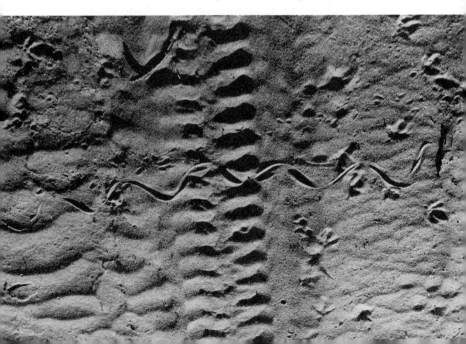

6: The Fire Factor

One of the most widely held beliefs in southern California is that floods always follow fire. The truth of this assertion depends on several factors: the porosity of the soil; the steepness of slope; the intensity, amount, and duration of rainfall; and even the season of precipitation. A burned-over hillside may erode much faster than one that has a dense cover of protective vegetation, but there are too many variables to permit unchallenged the flat statement that floods and erosion without exception follow a chaparral or brush fire, and especially the conclusion that no other plant cover could be as effective in controlling rapid runoff.

There are scores of places in the mountains of California that have been burned in the last thirty years. They frequently

demonstrate that disaster by flood is by no means the ines-
capable result of disaster by fire. Usually within a few months
after a burn there is a remarkable recuperation of various
types of plant and animal life. Though their leafy twigs and
stems may have been completely destroyed by fire, chaparral shrubs actively react to this destruction in one of two
ways. In some species new shoots almost immediately begin
growth from the top of the root, or its "crown," even before
the winter rains have begun. These are the "crown sprout-
ers." Others have seeds that only when stimulated by heat
readily germinate. These small but stubborn new shoots,
plant counterparts of the mythical phoenix, are joined by a
host of herbaceous plants, some of them so disaster dependent they never appear except in disturbed soil or after a burn.

The mixture of grass and wildflowers that is the first stage
in fire recovery is lush and dense. The ash provides nutriment, and the full flood of sunlight encourages plant growth.
The green cover will dominate several spring seasons until
the shrubs become tall enough, once again, to shade it out.
The nature of the rains, the time of their arrival, and the stage
of plant renewal or regrowth determine to a considerable
degree the amount of damage inflicted by them.

The supposedly invariable sequence to chaparral fire—
erosion or gullying—is certainly not inevitable. It is perhaps
ironical that I first noticed this while attempting to get docu-
mentary photographs of a predicted wash-off and its ensuing
flood and channel clogging. Most of my efforts to get evidence
of such damage after several extensive fires in the nearby
Santa Monica Mountains had been frustrated either by the
perversity of the rainfall or the very rapid growth of annual
and perennial vegetation following early fall rains. Elsewhere
within the same time span there had indeed been local floods
and mud. Obviously the facts were not in agreement with the
popular notions then being taught, and this was the beginning of some studies undertaken only to satisfy my curiosity.

While I was seeking those pictures, there were several
storms of nearly flood proportions. In places they were accompanied by massive erosion, but, confounding my expecta-

tions, damage was also remarkably heavy where there had been no local burns. Cloudbursts are often extremely restricted in mountainous country. Without rain gauges in the right place at the right time, deductive conclusions about rainfall amounts may be very misleading. I learned to my surprise that even unburned areas may suffer from flood erosion and damaging mud flows if the local rainfall is large enough.

That fact would not have surprised me if I had stopped to think. In one cloudburst episode I had seen chaparral bushes, hundreds of streamside alders, large oaks, and sycamores uprooted, their limbs amputated, their trunks dismembered, and the debris ultimately piled in massive rows of flotsam down canyon.

I turn to two other misconceptions: (1) it is chiefly the roots of woody plants that hold soil in place, preventing flood injury and erosion, and (2) we should reject the policy of controlled chaparral burns as they encourage grass which is ineffective as an erosion control. The protection against rapid runoff is largely a matter of screening the surface—the skin or finely powdered soil on top of the ground—against battering by heavy raindrops and the subsequent movement of water and soil over the surface. The flow of mud seals off small holes and crevices, making the surface almost impermeable. Breaking up the impact of large raindrops is the primary protection against topsoil damage, and the help of roots and rootlets is secondary in importance. When the soil is deeply sodden and water-filled, the tangle of underground roots may prevent downward slumping of the soil, a land- or mudslide, but frequently an entire, thoroughly wet slope bearing chaparral or even large trees slides downhill despite the plants' interwoven substructure. Masses of soil simply cut loose and slide off down slope in response to gravity and the lubrication of water.

New understanding of the retardation of runoff indicates that it is caused, not so much by the underground network of roots, but the overhead cover of leaves, stems, twigs, and other plant material. Such cover breaks raindrops into a fine spray, and the vegetation that best shatters or disrupts raindrops is the most effective defense against surface flow, flood, and sudden heavy erosion. Annual grasses, so abundant after fire, form an adequately dense screen for this purpose, and may be as efficient, if not more so, as mature chaparral. Their tall, perpendicular stems shatter raindrops efficiently, and the myriads of thickly packed, vertical stems prevent an unimpeded downward flotation of debris. They hinder water movement from accelerating, giving it time to penetrate the topsoil, and reducing the damage it is capable of inflicting at higher

Figure 6. Erosion is accelerated where rainfall hits soil that is not protected by a plant cover. Grass is as effective—if not more so—as chaparral in deterring destructive erosion.

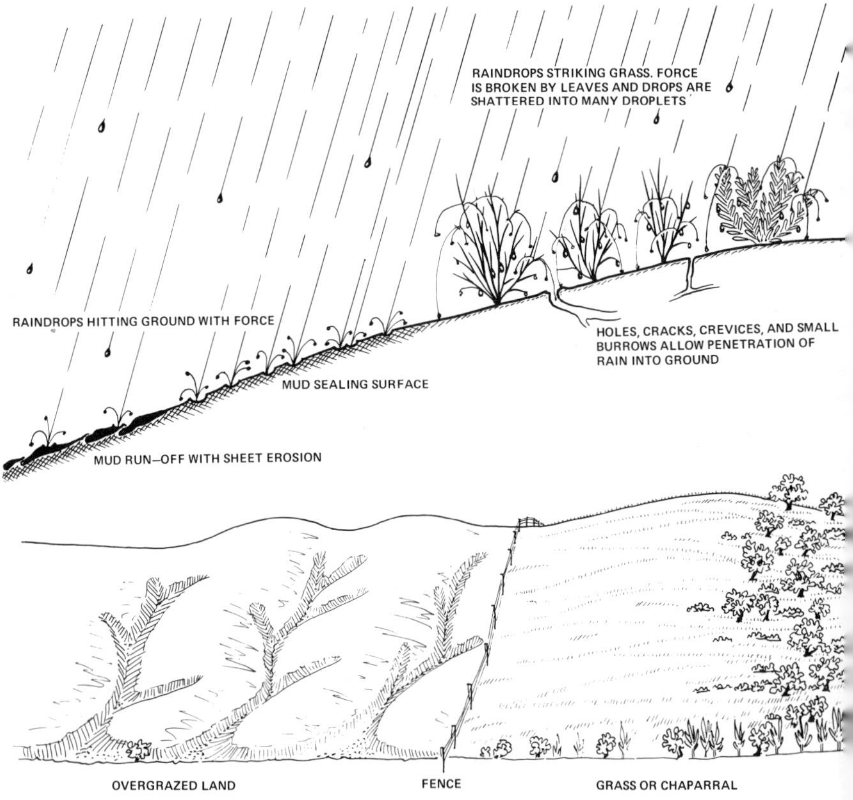

RAINDROPS STRIKING GRASS. FORCE IS BROKEN BY LEAVES AND DROPS ARE SHATTERED INTO MANY DROPLETS

RAINDROPS HITTING GROUND WITH FORCE

HOLES, CRACKS, CREVICES, AND SMALL BURROWS ALLOW PENETRATION OF RAIN INTO GROUND

MUD SEALING SURFACE

MUD RUN—OFF WITH SHEET EROSION

OVERGRAZED LAND   FENCE   GRASS OR CHAPARRAL speed. Their habit of remaining erect after death is also in their favor. Unless they are unduly softened by rain, they form a surface mat through which a new crop of seedlings will spring up after the first winter storms.

I have reason to believe that under most, if not all, intensities of rainfall, grasses retard this movement of water even more effectively than the accumulation of detritus under chaparral. After a number of storms I have crawled under stands of ceanothus, or California lilac, and noted for myself the collections of curled, dry, floatable leaves, small twigs, and flakes of bark. This material can be easily lifted from the ground and carried away by an intense downpour. The rooted grasses, on the contrary, remain anchored in place. If overwhelmed, they collapse and form a pad with the stems lying in the direction of flow, protecting the soil surface from damage.

Experiments conducted by Dr. Harold Biswell and others at the University of California on slopes of 10 percent grade or less have clearly shown that a grass cover is fully as effective as the shrubs of the brushlands in soil protection. Detailed analysis also indicates that grasses may aid in the conservation of underground water, because they die soon after the winter rains have ceased, unlike the chaparral, which continues to draw water from underground through much of the year. Dr. Biswell has even reestablished stream flow and salvaged wells that otherwise would have been dry simply by eliminating chaparral and its drain on moisture by transpiration. California's native scrub is composed of plants that, though most active during the times of optimum temperature and soil water, are semi-dormant in the warm dry season. They do, however, maintain a steady drain on subsurface moisture, tapping with long, probing roots into deep, underground sources until the reserves are depleted. If those who oppose controlled burning of the chaparral continue to maintain that it is the best cover for watershed and the most effective check on erosion and flood, I can answer that there are enough exceptions to their rule to require further unbiased experimentation and research. Only this will end the controversy.

Since dry grass is very flammable, what of the fire hazards wherever grass may be substituted for chaparral? It requires about the same amount of heat to set a grassland afire as it does to kindle the accumulated debris of brush. The dangers to personnel fighting a grass blaze are far fewer than those threatening the crews manning the hoses, bulldozers, and scrapers needed when fire is racing through the chaparral. A grass fire is far more easily quenched, and a garden hose that can douse it with little trouble could not possibly stop the onrush of a full, wind-driven brush blaze. Under identical conditions, one tank truck of water is able to put out a far larger fire front in grassland than it would in chaparral. Grass is mere inches in height, whereas the shrubs of brush country are measured in numbers of feet. In addition, there is far less bulk and weight of fuel per acre. As grass is not only short but forms a comparatively thin cover, it is easy to move through and is much safer to work in during fire control than in head-high or taller chaparral.

It now appears that the evidence supports the arguments of those who prefer periodic and manageable fires, when the debris is light, to the inevitable and uncontrollable holocausts that rage through the coastal mountains and foothills when the fuel build-up invites them. Though I tend to disagree with the policy of total fire supression, for the time being I prefer to maintain an uncommitted state of mind. Surely, the story is not as one-sided as was assumed a number of years ago before large-scale experiments indicated that many small repeated fires cause less damage to large trees than do holocausts. For ages before man introduced fire restraint, trees have successfully resisted scores of natural fires.

7: Back at
the Ditch Camp

My first experience with the little horned rattle-snake, or sidewinder, occurred at my canal tenthouse camp. I had heard of the creatures almost immediately after arriving in the desert, but I did not have the vaguest idea of their appearance or their method of locomotion except to know that they were small and crawled about "sideways," a peculiar type of travel for reptiles, at any rate.

As the tenthouse, flimsily constructed though it was, interfered with air movement and held the heat longer than the open, I at once set about making a hammock out of gunny sacks and wires. I strung this under an open-sided shelter,

or ramada, made of brush and arrowweed. In this somewhat
crude but comfortable and well aerated bit of furniture I rested
during the day and slept at night. Clothing added so much
discomfort to my heat-tormented skin that, despite the harsh-
ness of the jute mesh, I frequently stretched out on my hammock wearing nothing or the barest minimum. Even in those
less permissive days such a practice was perfectly seemly,
for only once or twice in an entire summer did someone drop
by, and only once in a total of two successive summers did
a woman come anywhere near the shack. She was riding a
horse along the canal banks some thirty to forty yards away.

Awakening the first morning at the camp, I dropped my
legs over the side of the hammock and discovered all around
my feet and under my "bed" curious crisscrossing marks,
obviously those of a snake yet unlike any snake track I had

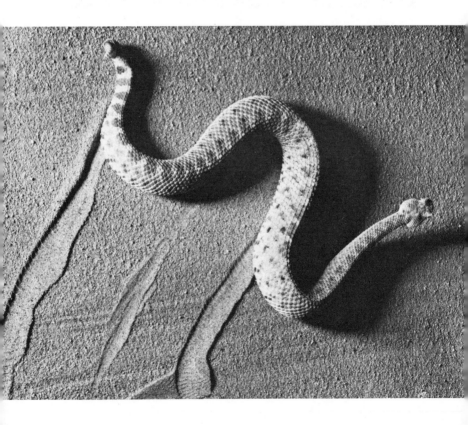

Plate 5. Sidewinder tracks on top of those of a car. Both roll and so leave tread marks.

Plate 4. Sidewinder making tracks whose imprints are proof that movement is by a rolling rather than a sliding motion. Note the J imprint of head and neck.

ever seen before. The maker was nowhere in sight, having retreated under the house where shade and shelter were adequate during the potentially lethal heat of a desert summer day, though at the time I was unaware of this limiting factor.

Strangely enough, I never did see the originator of those odd tracks. Each mark bore the crosswise print of the belly scales, and it was to be years before I learned the obvious reason for these treadmarks. I should have discovered for myself that to leave such a pattern the body of the snake was being laid down and rolled rather than moved horizontally along the ground, but, novice as I was at that time, the significance was lost in simple curiosity and the fear of the reptile itself.

For most of the summer almost every morning the trails of sidewinders appeared around and under my hammock. That their presence led to my extreme caution when I arose in the morning or at night goes without saying. Throughout the day, however, our activities never coincided. As far as I know, never once in the course of this total six months of summertime did my sidewinding neighbors venture out in the daytime to visit the shade of the ramada, the locale of their nocturnal wanderings. Was this because of excessive temperatures or simply the presence of an active human being? I do not know.

Here at the ditch camp I made my first acquaintance with one of the fabled and greatly feared, though actually harmless, desert denizens—the solpugid, or sun spider. When I lit the lamp at night to read or make admittedly desultory efforts to tidy up that miserable little shack, the feeble light attracted literally thousands of winged and creeping arthropods. At times the screens near the lamp were concealed beneath hordes of insects ranging from gnats and mosquitoes to handsome moths and even an occasional praying mantis.

Because of the position of the built-in table where I typed letters or read, I usually had my back to the screen and sat facing the light with the rest of the cabin more or less in darkness. One evening I felt a movement on top of my head. I reached up, and in shock, placed my hand on a large sun spider—an inch long and with a girth equal to that of a lead pencil. My reflex action dashed it to the floor. I carried the lantern to the corner in which it landed and was amazed to discover four immense fang-like jaws, shiny little beady eyes, and an apparent set of ten legs, the two foremost of which I later discovered were pedipalps, largely sensory appendages that the creature holds above the ground as it scurries about in search of prey.

These fascinating distant relatives of true spiders are found throughout the world in temperate or hot deserts, both north and south of the Equator. In many places they are reputed to be poisonous to humans, which is not true, and savage, which in a sense is true. In fright they react with feinting movements and displays of pugnacity. Actually they are, in their way, beautiful creatures, very swift for their size, colored to blend in with their sandy-soil backgrounds, and wonderfully equipped to survive in this seemingly harsh environment.

Later I captured one and placed it in a Mason jar. I fed it grasshoppers, which it attacked immediately, extracting every shred of digestible material before discarding the carcass. Even with the slight knowledge that I then possessed, it was apparent that the solpugid had punctured the heavy, chitinous, femoral sheathing of the grasshopper's legs. Its jaws were still inserted when it started pumping movements with its abdomen, followed by pauses as it ingested and absorbed the nourishing juices it had sucked out through the grasshopper's wounds. At the same time the digestive fluids in the sun spider's venom were dissolving the tissue in situ—a masterpiece of efficient extraction. My further encounters with sun spiders were around campfires. There, their concealing colors proved so effective that I learned of their presence only by watching their fleeting shadows pass over the rippled surface of the sand.

Although many animals of the desert may be turned up under almost any pile of trash, logs, or flat stones, the dangerous black widow spider—a threat to human life in the aged and very young—is far less frequently observed though probably equally abundant. Black widows are more secretive and appear to remain in their fixed abodes once mature. They are usually found in deep crevices where they can spin a ragged web over the mouth of their shelter. They commonly occur in the standpipes around irrigation fields, where a combination of moisture and abundant insect life enables them to thrive in the humid darkness and the safety of these concrete, ready-made spider houses.

I was unaware of their presence around the shack; in fact, at that time I was scarcely aware that a dangerous spider existed, but I made their acquaintance immediately after the encounter with the solpugid. As I lifted the lantern from the floor where I had been inspecting the sun spider, a glint of web under the table where I customarily worked caught my eye. I found two black widow spiders inhabiting opposite ends of the bench-like table! These were, of course, dispatched. I continued the search which revealed a total of nine such spiders occupying my premises. They had probably been there for weeks, living in complete amiability with their human co-occupant.

While making inquiries about the black widow's venom, I came across a wealth of stories attesting to their aggressive disposition, wholly unwarranted by my experience. I also found information on their favorite shelters, which, fortunately in the freedom of the open spaces, I had not had to use—outdoor privies with their congregating flies, darkness, and opportunities for concealment. The number of tales about the frequency with which users of privies have been bitten in the most vulnerable, exposed, and sensitive part of their bodies led me to believe that danger lurked in every outhouse. The incidents are by no means common, but there are well authenticated instances of men using these outdoor facilities, being bitten, and suffering the most excruciating pain. Avoiding the outhouse, I continued a wary relationship with the spiders, but I was less tolerant than they. After the first experience, I made frequent searches of the premises. I turned up only an occasional spider that had grown to maturity in some obscure crack or cranny in that frail structure and had escaped attention until it moved into a more obvious home.

Much later I learned that although the pain of a black widow bite is intense, affecting the abdominal muscles and giving rise to symptoms resembling appendicitis, recovery follows within a few days if the victim is in normally robust health. Dr. William Berg, experimenter with poisonous arthropods, was misled into thinking the black widow spider was relatively harmless. When he allowed a spider to bite him, he suffered agony for several days. He informed me that although he used everything then known, including opiates, in an attempt to alleviate the pain, nothing seemed to serve. For months afterwards he had recurrent nightmares in which he was once again bitten and experiencing the pain. Clearly, black widow spiders are not to be trifled with, but in general they are shy creatures and only very unusual circumstances can induce them to bite.

The only place in the desert where I found the spider exceedingly abundant and relatively conspicuous was in the lava beds around Pisgah Crater in the Mojave. On one occasion, probably at the peak of abundance, I noted black widows in every deep crevice in the lava. Here they spun their ragged webs. Though all withdrew upon being approached, they were a danger to visitors who might have dispossessed them of their retreats in nearby campsites. These were the largest and healthiest black widows I ever encountered. When I returned to the same area a year later there were very few surviving individuals. Today they can still be found but it requires fairly diligent search.

In addition to the sidewinders dwelling below the floorboards in my Imperial Valley shack, a large, robust, and highly nervous desert diamondback, known technically as *Crotalus atrox*, once made its home. This species of rattlesnake is most abundant in mesquite thickets and in the arrowweed-willow growth hedging the Colorado River, a plant association that also flourishes near irrigation canals and around the seepage pools below them. Along the trail that constituted my daily beat, I occasionally saw their tracks, but several months passed before I discovered my very first desert diamondback, a large specimen approximately five feet long. I had been riding my horse through the tall arrowweed bordering my pathway from camp to headgate when I heard the unmistakable sound of a rattler on the opposite side of the canal. I retraced my steps, crossing the bridge, and found the reptile only to destroy it with considerable feelings of triumph.

Since these formidable reptiles are unusually timid and retreat rather than commit the error of advertising their whereabouts to a human being, I can only guess that it had seen my head protruding above the arrowweeds as my horse trotted shoulder-deep in the brush. For the rest of my six months of summer living spent in a habitat where these rattlesnakes are fairly common, I had no other face-to-face meeting, a testimony chiefly to the timidity of the rattlesnake and its peaceful disposition rather than to my powers of observation.

A possible exception to that statement occurred one night when an unusually large head of water poured into our irrigation canal. Headquarters warned us to be on the lookout through the night for a possible break through the ditch walls. The water rose well above the berm, which was covered by streamside vegetation over much of this distance. This rise in water drove some of the resident rattlesnakes from their retreats up onto the higher and drier land where the footpath lay. I saddled my horse for the ride along the canal, only to discover that the animal, out of nervousness or fear, had dropped its head until its nostrils were barely clearing the path. Then it paced slowly down the shadow-blackened trail. Though half-expected, that first muted clatter—"dried beans poured into a tin can"—thrust fingers of fright up my scalp. But, most extraordinarily, it did not alarm the horse at all. As if ignoring the buzz it took the bit in its teeth and kept plodding forward, head still held low and within easy striking distance of any large rattler. Admitting to some panic, I finally brought my mount to a halt. At that moment I heard a rattlesnake rattling in retreat as it slid down the bank toward the canal.

Inexperienced and alerted by Headquarters to the dangers of spooked rattlesnakes, ditch cave-ins, and breakthroughs, I certainly did not want to dismount and continue the patrol on foot, but when I tried to force the horse forward once more, it gave the same performance, endangering the capital I had invested in the brute.

Since money, or rather, the lack of it, loomed so large in those early student days, I tied the horse to a willow tree, cut a long shoot for myself, and *walked* down that path, pushing the willow twig ahead of me. I don't remember if I muttered some prayerful profanity at the same time! Fortunately, no more snakes came my way. If they were present, they may have been forewarned by the moving branch and have left the path without alarming me. At any rate, the adventure proceeded without further excitement, and when dawn patrol resumed, there was sufficient light to reveal any reptilian threats.

I stress this episode because it is so commonly believed that horses will panic at the sound of a rattlesnake and often suddenly bolt, even throwing their riders. This may be true. Perhaps my particular beast was unaware of equine protocol.

Whenever water reaches desert soil, usually vegetation flourishes and with it a whole succession of animals from insects to mammals. Canal or ditch banks, unless cleared of their encroaching brush, become virtual oases for many types of animals that otherwise would not occur. Coyotes ranged the open desert near my camp, and, judging from their tracks and sounds, made repeated foraging trips into the irrigated sections in search of items of their "normal" diet as well as turkeys, chickens, and even lambs. Occasionally they traversed the one bridge in a ten-mile stretch of canal, but at other points they plunged in and swam across with no apparent difficulty.

I first became acquainted with wild coyotes in those six wonderful, though at times trying, months of desert ditch patrol. I saw one sitting in open daylight on top of a mesquite-covered sand dune, recklessly bugling his call at a time when most of his species are usually out of sight and silent. He was so engrossed in this activity that I was able to ride up to within fifty yards of him before he became aware of my presence. He rose to his feet, watched me with alert dignity, but made no move even when I pointed my arm at him as though about to shoot.

On another occasion, an adult female and her three pups had apparently been waiting for a favorable moment to attack a beaver (they occur along the Colorado River drainage, even invading its irrigation system) that was slicing willow shoots only a few feet below the top of the canal bank. I had ridden to within less than fifty feet before they saw me. Mother and pups promptly fled across the desert expanse, still in plain sight. The largest, and thus presumably the parent, was so imposing that it may have been a dog-coyote cross or one of the very rare wolves that occasionally ventured up from the wilds across the Mexican border. In the dimness of early dawn and with my degree of unfamiliarity with either coyote or wolf, it was impossible for me to tell which they were. Certainly the adult was a far larger animal than the one I had seen howling on the dune.

Imperial Valley lies in the flyway of migrating waterfowl. Though some may have difficulty in associating a desert, even irrigated, with large numbers of wild fowl, they are extremely abundant and use the canals and the copious seepage pools along their route. As early as August migrating ducks put in their first appearance. Since ditch riders were expected to supplement their diet with whatever game they could procure—quail, rabbits, dove, and, when possible, ducks—their advent was most welcome.

In those days the birds were so numerous I lived on fresh meat two or three times a week (no refrigeration in my ditch camp!) without having to spend extra effort in actual hunting. Quail flushed from the path ahead, and doves were everywhere. When the ducks arrived, their habit of following the canal made them easy targets. When I sighted an approaching flock I stepped out of the shack, waited until they were overhead, and dropped a bird within a few yards of my tent-house door. Market hunting had been terminated only a few years prior to my arrival on the desert, and one of the old-time hunters told me of killing several dozen birds in one shot by using big, swivel-mounted, "four-bore" shotguns in the bows of their boats.

Now, the irrigated lands have spread out like waters of a rising reservoir. There are far fewer neglected seeps along the canal. And with the increased hunting pressure along their migration routes, ducks have become much scarcer than in those early days. Unfortunately, most wildlife has not withstood the encroachment of urbanization, agriculture, forest cutting, weed clearance, and annual hunting seasons.

In my ditch camp days this was pristine desert, bordering the lush bottom lands of the Imperial Valley. Aside from the heat, or even despite it, life was rich for a youngster already infected with the enthusiastic curiosity of a naturalist. There was no lack of opportunities for daily discovery of biological facts, beauty, and appreciation of the desert's own and very special allure.

8: Living Thermometers, Part I

We seem to have an implicit recognition of kin-
ship with warm-blooded animals, to a greater
extent with mammals and a lesser one with birds. This feeling is expressed in admiration or even love of the attractive-
ness of furred and feathered creatures. We have also acquired
an amazing amount of facts about their lives. Although a
sense of relationship to birds may be misplaced on a scientific
basis since they are more closely allied to the cold-blooded reptiles than they are to mammals, nonetheless their handsome
plumage, their flight, for a long time envied by earth-bound
men, and, of course, their songs, which were interpreted as

a language of love—all contributed to the sentimental attraction, drawing poets as well as scientists to a study of these animals.

By concentrating on the warm-blooded creatures, those with some type of thermostatic control over their temperatures, we missed some extremely interesting characteristics of what we call cold-blooded creatures. Though all warm-blooded animals evolved from cold-blooded forms, we have ignored the biological importance of the cold-bloods as we sought to understand how warm-bloodedness came about.

For the past thirty years or so a few biologists have been exploring the problems of temperature and its control in insects, scorpions, spiders, ticks, mites, and other land-dwelling arthropods, as well as in salamanders, toads, and reptiles. Through such studies we have learned that cold-bloodedness is by no means a simple, helpless submission to environmental temperatures. On the contrary, through behavioral adjustments to the environment and physiological changes that promote rapid heat gain or prevent too rapid a heat loss, the cold-bloods can exercise some degree of control over their body temperatures.

There is a multitude of common questions that can be answered only by reference to the temperature of the animal and of its environment. How fast can an ant run? The answer can be determined only by knowing how fast it can move at any given temperature. We are entitled to say that under optimum heat conditions it can run at a specific speed; when it is much cooler it can scarcely move at all. In very cold weather it is helpless, and in a warm environment it is very active. The pitch or note produced by crickets is also regulated by temperature since their muscular movements are controlled by this environmental variant. The tempo of their stridulating, or frictional, music-making depends on the speed of muscular movement.

There has been much controversy over how fast insects can fly, but anyone arguing his case must qualify speed records by adding, "At optimum temperatures they are capable of. . . ." Only in this way can one be accurate in reporting such interesting tidbits of nature lore. Bees, in particular, provide fascinating examples of temperature regulation. They can generate a certain amount of metabolic heat by rapidly moving their wing muscles. Thus they are able to leave a warm hive on a moderately cold morning and during flight sustain both body temperature and speed. If they arrive at flowers in which the nectar is still cold, however, then between their drinking of the chilled liquid and the slower movement of their wing muscles, they become gradually colder, and some may fall to the ground. The contact with the cold earth robs them of heat more quickly than it can be generated.

Under winter-blooming eucalyptus trees on a cool morning, I have seen scores of bees struggling to get back into the air away from the soil surface. Knowing they probably would not sting me, I allowed them to crawl up onto my finger, which I then held in the sunshine. After they had been warmed by the sun, as well as the heat from my finger, they regained flight capability. At first they remained almost motionless on my finger, but as they warmed up they undertook an almost ritual-like cleansing of their eyes, wings, and body and a removal of any pollen held in the pollen baskets. If they were intelligent creatures (that is, not dependent on instinct), one would say that they recognized the necessity for improving their aerodynamic chances by removal of dirt from their flying surfaces, and that they realized the weight of the load of pollen clinging to their legs would be a handicap. "Always" and "invariable" are usually unsafe terms to apply to animal behavior; nevertheless in this case I believe I am secure in saying that these preliminaries to flight are invariable. They always precede the next steps to regaining competency in the air.

Following this careful grooming and unloading of the pollen baskets, a bee buzzes its wings in brief bursts. Then it continues with still more vigorous cleaning, alternating with rapid wing movement, and finally it is ready for takeoff in normal flight. Depending on the temperature of my hand, the air, and the amount of solar heat, I have seen the whole procedure take place in from two or three to six or seven minutes.

Plate 6. The sidewinder habit of nudging sand out from under its coils in order to make a shelter is well known, but the fact that it also uses its head and chin to partly cover more of the body is almost never noted. Thrust under its body is a thermometer which showed that the snake was still resting on deeper, cool sand and so cooling its body.

Unfortunately for grounded bees, the flat-bodied, heat-absorbing horned lizards (erroneously called horny toads) often profit by the bees' helplessness. They scurry around picking up bee after bee, give them a crushing bite or two, and then swallow them. Oddly enough, such foraging horned lizards may have a row of bee stings just inside the margin of their lips. Yet they show no sign of being affected by the venom.

I have no doubt that, second to the role of water, temperature is of utmost importance for all physiological functions. That it is essential to an animal's ability to survive is equally clear, as it determines, among other things, speed of movement. If creatures are immobilized by cold, they are more susceptible to predation. On the other hand, they can be dangerously damaged by excessively high thermal conditions. The chemical action involved in digestion is also influenced by body heat. That it has a role in the successful competition for food is also probably true. Other things such as size and limb length being equal, the warmest animal should get to the food first, depriving its competitors while at the same time profiting by its advantage.

Temperature also alters the disposition of many animals. The poisonous Gila monster (a large lizard of Arizona, New Mexico, and Mexico) can be handled with comparative impunity under normal room conditions of cool air and no warming sunlight. Then they are so lethargic that they cannot move fast enough to grab and bite a finger or a hand. They also give the outward appearance of amiability or, perhaps more accurately, docile torpidity. Take these animals, however, out into the sunshine and allow them to soak up solar energy, which they do very rapidly, and their whole aspect changes. They are very likely to become irritable. Safe handling of most reptiles becomes a matter of skill and knowledge of their predictable behavior.

Some as yet inconclusive experiments also suggest that temperature has an important role in dominance, the ascendancy of one animal over others of its species. The reptile able to pre-empt a place where it can maintain a higher body heat than that of others in the same cage will be dominant for as long as it can keep its higher temperature. If it vacates its warmer post and another animal takes over, the pre-emptor gains ascendancy over those not so favored. Presupposing that such changes in behavior and dominance occur in wild populations, as they probably do, then temperature changes, or the accident of such shifts in combination with other factors, could determine which males are most successful in mating and in preserving a territory for themselves, mates, and young. It may very well be that the role of temperature in natural selection is larger than is thought at the present time. I feel strongly that it is of major, though perhaps subtle, importance in evolutionary processes.

Among the questions about animal speed most commonly

asked is: "How fast can a snake crawl?" This quite often really means: "How fast must I be able to run in order to escape a pursuing snake?" On very cold mornings snakes are barely capable of movement. They may even be totally immobilized and unable to crawl at all. If a hiker encounters a rattlesnake on a morning of near-frost, he can approach to close distance and, with a stick, test its ability to move or strike. When its temperature is low enough it is virtually helpless. Snakes like many other creatures, however, can rapidly absorb heat. When heat has been distributed throughout its body by the blood system, a rattlesnake can change from torpor to dangerous behavior in a matter of minutes. At optimum body temperatures of around 80° to 82° F., the top speed of a diamondback rattlesnake is about one to two miles per hour. This can be sustained only for short distances. The fastest desert rattler anywhere in the American West is probably the sidewinder, characteristically found in open country where vegetation is spaced far apart. I have been unable to get satisfactory short sprint speed records of the sidewinder, but I assume that it is three or four times that of the diamondback— only, however, at optimum temperatures of around 85° F. or slightly higher.

In studies of the speed of a rattlesnake's strike, synchronous split-second photography suggests the snake can move its head at a bare five miles per hour. The work was done ingeniously, and the speed was correct for the room temperature at which the photographs and time measurements were made. The investigator, however, reportedly paid no attention to the temperature of the animal, and it is highly possible that five miles per hour is far too slow compared with the speed under optimum conditions. I base this skepticism as to speed on the realization that room temperatures are usually maintained at 68° F. to the low 70s. But as the preference of rattlesnakes is for the mid-80s, one might safely estimate that at optimum temperatures snakes can strike at least twice as fast as stated.

I am often asked about the speed of lizards. The answer again depends on which type of lizard and its body heat, for they, like snakes, are almost immobile on a cold morning. Even at 60° F. many desert lizards become comatose. By mid-morning, the temperature of the lizard's body may have risen from around 100° to 110° F. (depending on the species), and its speed may be six to seven times faster than what it was earlier in the day.

A number of years ago a famous woman herpetologist (a specialist in the study of cold-blooded vertebrates), and one of the best informed on the handling of venomous snakes, was demonstrating a cobra's strike. She was using her hand to stimulate them into performing for a photographer. Though she had done this many times, on this occasion the animals had been taken out into the sun for better color photography. Mrs. Grace Wiley quite dexterously avoided the first few strikes, but the next stroke caught her hand, and she died from the effects of the venom. The reason for that tragic episode will never be completely known, but it seems quite possible that the snake had been heated to its maximum muscular and nervous pitch, and it moved faster than Mrs. Wiley had expected, causing her death.

The number of questions that can be asked about the role of temperature or body heat in the survival of both cold- and warm-blooded vertebrates, at present and in the past, is almost endless. When we know all the answers to the questions, if ever, we will have a far better perspective of past climates, the changes brought about by continental drift, and greater knowledge of evolutionary history and the final rise and dominance of animals that generate their own heat through the use of chemical energy from the assimilation of food.

As these heat-generating animals include man, most of his scientific investigative emphasis has not been on external warming in the cold-bloods—heating through sunshine modified by air and substrate temperatures and the activity of of the animal—but on the far more efficient but spendthrift processes of chemical heat generation and regulation. It is probable that by neglecting the study of temperature in the cold-bloods we have missed a very important chance for insight and understanding.

A number of questions are of practical concern to zookeepers, professional and amateur students of cold-bloods, and the terrarium fancier who keeps reptiles because of their beauty and fascination.

I am repeatedly asked: "How often should I feed my reptiles?" This is undoubtedly of consequence because no one wants feeble or sickly animals for pets. It is particularly important for laboratory research workers. If their reptiles are not in the best physical condition, their observations might lead to false conclusions.

The answer again depends on temperature. Since the speed of all enzyme activity, digestive and otherwise, is influenced by temperature, abnormally low readings will leave reptiles virtually incapable of digestion. Excessively high temperatures may also sicken them or prevent their feeding. Very rough rates of their metabolic requirements, depending on gross body size and temperature, vary from approximately one-seventh to one-thirtieth that of a number of mammals, especially those whose thermostatic necessities demand continual refueling from the food supply. Compared to the warm-bloods, the reptiles waste little energy in generating body heat, but they need nutriment for other processes.

There is no precise answer as to how often reptiles should be fed, but it is safe to assume that so long as they will eat and digest food they are not wasting it. It is not wise to maintain them at lower than normal temperatures to economize on food, however, and anyone who has kept snakes has experienced the disgustingly nauseating odor of putrefaction that comes from a cage when a rattlesnake has failed to digest its food as rapidly as the putrefactive bacteria have multiplied, making it either poisonous or unpalatable to the snake. At any rate, where carnivorous snakes are kept in an unhealthily cool environment, they usually regurgitate their meals. The symptoms of inadequate temperatures in lizards are not as obvious; though they eat regularly, they may lose weight gradually and die.

In my laboratory we found that infrared light bulbs having a yellowish rather than a red hue provide a very satisfactory heating source. If the light and heat are concentrated at one end of the cage, the reptiles can move in or out of the heat circle as they wish and as their needs dictate. They will do a far better job of temperature regulation than even the most sophisticated thermostats and best human judgment. All of our animals, for instance, thrived when they depended on their own control but did less well when we tried to provide them with "optimum temperatures."

The availability of drinking water becomes of much more moment than heat to reptiles when they can maintain their own preferred body temperatures—which, incidentally, are usually higher on the average than I had supposed them to be but lower than the uninitiated expect it to be. Dishes of water should be always available for caged specimens. This is true even of desert reptiles, which, in nature, probably never drink from generation to generation but live, grow, and bear young or lay eggs without the benefit of a single drop of free water.

Some captive desert reptiles learn to drink water as though they had done it all their lives, and they are no problem. Others such as the chuckwalla and the desert iguana (northern crested lizard) can die a death of slow dehydration without using the water provided for them. The best way of inducing those novices to consume water is to allow drops to splash into a petri dish or other shallow receptacle to create ripples. Apparently the stimulus of motion leads them to the water. Then they usually plunge their noses into the water and discover for themselves the delights of satisfying their growing thirst.

In nature, desert reptiles apparently spend much time under ground where water vapor pressure—the humidity at any given temperature—conserves respiratory water losses so effectively that the moisture extracted from food and as a by-product of the breakdown of fats provides the animal with all of its very moderate needs.

I have also been asked how long it takes to hatch reptile eggs. This is determined by the species as well as by temperature, which influences incubation time and development within the egg. A span of sixty to eighty days at temperatures in the mid-80s appears to be the rule for the common reptiles of the Southwest. In the northeastern states, however, the eggs of snapping turtles and possibly some others are laid in the summer, and some of the eggs may not hatch until the next spring, an extremely long period of incubation.

Some tropical reptiles, such as Africa's monitor lizards (all in the genus *Varanus*), usually require from six to seven months. However, the Nile monitor, which, in South Africa at least, lays its eggs in termite nests, requires as long as eleven months for its eggs to hatch. We still need much more information, nevertheless, before we can speak confidently about the influence of temperature on the development of the embryo.

There is a widespread belief that one can tell the age of a rattlesnake by the number of its rattles. This is based on the assumption that the snake adds one rattle per year. Studies conducted by the University of California on the San Joaquin Experimental Range indicate that the belief has some validity for that particular area even though it may be untrue elsewhere. In the San Diego Zoo, however, where animals are maintained under the best possible conditions, rattlesnakes have added as many as eleven rattles in a single year. A new one appears each time the outer surface, more correctly called the stratum corneum, is shed or sloughed off. This is not the true skin, without which the animal would die immediately. Since shedding is at least partially dependent upon temperature as well as quantities of food and water, it is probable that the environment, as well as species, determines how many rattles are added in the course of the year.

Because mountain and canyon streamside camping is primarily a summertime activity when snakes are locally most in evidence, I am often asked, "Is it safe for me to camp out and sleep on the ground?" Without hesitation I always answer, "With the most elementary precaution, one is always safe while camping out." Hundreds of thousands of people spend as many more hundreds of thousands of nights sleeping in the open in rattlesnake-infested country. If there have been instances* of rattlesnakes crawling into an occupied sleeping bag or blankets for the sake of warmth and biting their unwitting host, they have never come to my attention. To be honest, I have frequently wondered why it has not happened.

In my many months of camping where western diamond-backs and sidewinders were very common, I refrained from killing any of the individuals I found near my camp, but every morning I would explore the sand surrounding my sleeping bag for signs that rattlers had approached within dangerous distance. The closest any rattlesnake track ever came to my sleeping bag was about six feet. And, from the signs, the reptile was frightened off, either by my movements while asleep, or more probably by detecting the odor of a human being.

Here, however, I must cite again the contradictory experiences of many years ago in the Imperial Valley when I was sleeping under the brush ramada in my hammock slung between two poles. Connected to my sleeping quarters was that shacky tenthouse whose floor was propped up some four inches above ground level. The sidewinders that found shelter and concealment under the shack's floorboards would make sorties out from under the house and crawl directly under my hammock, which was not more than two feet off the ground. Presumably, sidewinders have just as acute chemo-reception (odor detection) as their larger relatives. They were capable of detecting my presence, yet they did not avoid the vicinity until weeks later. I doubt very much, however, that had I been sleeping on the ground I would have been in much danger from my reptilian neighbors. No one can guarantee that snakes will never crawl in with sleeping campers, but some 500,000 army men during World War II spent months camping in snake country from Palm Springs to Blythe, and

*Some years ago a group of my friends and ex-students did have the experience of finding a speckled rattlesnake coiled up on a sleeping bag while camping in Pushawalla Palms, north of Indio. However, the bag had been in the sun all day and was not occupied. This may explain the seeming exception.

no such verified episodes occurred. Considering all the actual evidence, as opposed to hearsay, I am certain of safety.

Because of low temperatures, rattlesnakes usually do not move over the ground surface between late November to around the first of March. At other somewhat milder times of the year they may be partially and temporarily active in daytime, or crepuscular. When summer comes to the desert, the surface of the ground may be repellingly hot to these snakes on evenings between July and early September, even as late as ten or eleven o'clock. Daytime ground temperatures out in the open beyond shade are often far too hot to be tolerated by rattlesnakes, although they occasionally make brief excursions or traverses between one patch of shade and another, even in very warm weather. Usually, however, they prefer to remain in shelter, postponing the search for food until cooler hours.

Insects, like reptiles, are sensitive to temperature extremes. A most surprising recent discovery concerns a finding brought to light by new techniques of thermometry. Some of the instruments employ thermocouples, bimetallic contacts, that generate a measurable electromotive force (EMF). Other instruments use thermisters in which an electric current is passed through a ceramic bead where changing resistance regulates the flow of current in accordance with the bead's temperature. Using these devices, researchers have found that even small moths and other insects, by vibrating their muscles in a manner analogous to our shivering, generate a surprising amount of heat, and very efficiently at that.

The large hawkmoth, so familiar around petunia beds and out in the desert around sand verbena and other blooming plants, vibrates prior to flight and rapidly raises its temperature to 89° F., enabling it to fly with ease. I was not surprised that a heavy-bodied, well-muscled insect like the sphinx or hawkmoth, covered with a dense pile of highly modified hair-like scales, can generate heat and retain body temperatures well above that of its environment. I was astonished that much smaller and less well insulated insects can do so. Some workers several decades ago obtained somewhat similar records, but the significance of what they were witnessing was not really appreciated. It was only through the modern experimentation of James Heath and Philip Adams that their observations were proved to have such great biological significance.

9: Living Thermometers, Part II

*A*ll terrestrial backboned animals except birds and mammals, the feathered and furred creatures that like ourselves operate at a fairly constant temperature, are referred to as cold-blooded animals. The term can be equally applied to all the arthropods—that is, insects, spiders, scorpions and their kind—and fish, whose temperatures are always those of their immediate environment, with the exception of those of the very high-speed, energetic tuna and their relatives.

The word "cold-blooded" will probably be used for many years to come, but, in fact, the term is misleading. Its employment contributes to many mistaken ideas about thermal control in some large and important groups of animals. Meaning somewhat the same thing is the more technical word "poikilotherm." The root "therm" refers, of course, to temperature. "Poikilo" means fluctuating, that is, fluctuating with the environment. Both terms, however, are relative. In other words, if you think of these animals as cold-blooded, they are cold in respect to what? Are they cold with respect to you, to the air about them, to the soil on which they crawl, or to the water through which they swim? Similarly, if you use the word poikilotherm, are their body temperatures fluctuating above or below that of the surrounding environment or above or below the observer's temperature? Just what do they fluctuate around or from; and what is the origin of these usages?

Discussing cold-bloodedness first, how cold should creatures be to be cold? Should they be merely colder than we are, and, if so, by what scientific edict do we make ourselves the central point of reference for the living universe around us? Another example of human arrogance and anthropocentrism?

At times, many of these animals do seem to be colder than we are. We place our hands on a captive laboratory snake or lizard. Immediately we get the sensation of coolness and conclude the animal is cold-blooded. Yet, if we touch an adjacent glass or metal object that has been in the laboratory the same length of time as the reptile, such things "feel" as cold or even colder than the reptile (depending on their heat conductivity), and they also "feel" cooler to us than wooden chairs or desks nearby.

Place a piece of cloth on a table; let it come to room temperature. Then lay your hand on it. It will seem much warmer than either a glass or metal object. By actual measurement, using a thermometer, all three will show exactly the same temperature level. How can we be misled into thinking that all of the objects, including the reptile, are *cold* when obviously they are at "normal" room temperature (65°-75° F.)? The reason is, of course, that the sensation of cold is only an indication of how rapidly heat is being conducted away from our fingers rather than a measurement of the temperature of the item. This seems elementary, but it is highly informative to perform these and other tests and learn how unreliable our sensations can be when interpreting thermal phenomena.

All objects that conduct heat away from us are termed cool or cold, depending on the rate of the transfer of heat from us, and conversely, objects that conduct heat to our skin are termed warm or hot. Thus a nonconductor of heat, such as a piece of cloth or wood, will not feel as cold or hot as do efficient thermal conductors. My favorite way of estimating the prospects of nighttime reptile collecting is to place my hand on the metal body of a car where heat flow is much more efficient than in the air. With that method I have learned to guess nocturnal temperatures within 2° F.

Of all the familiar land creatures, the amphibia come closest to being truly cold-blooded, that is, with a usual temperature that conducts heat away from the observer's skin. They seem cold and are fairly cool because they do most of their breathing through their skin. In order to exchange the necessary gases, carbon dioxide and oxygen, through the skin its surface must be kept moist for respiration. Then under almost all conditions evaporation occurs, sometimes in large amounts. As the moisture evaporates, much of the skin's heat disappears. The result is a cold-feeling body surface and cool body temperature.

The optimum temperature for amphibian activity (except when they are estivating during summer's heat and drought or hibernating in winter) varies so widely from species to species that it is almost impossible to generalize what it is. Some salamanders, the lizard-like, though scaleless, tailed amphibians, have been found crawling to their egg-laying sites over snow with body temperatures close to freezing. Some other species of salamanders seem to flourish at temperatures as high as 64° F. during periods of reproductive, feeding, and other vigorous activity. Somewhere in between the two extremes we can estimate an optimum of around 50° F. or slightly above. In captivity—thriving, free of disease, and functioning normally—amphibians, like reptiles, should be allowed to choose their own temperatures. It is wise to give them access to a self-selected colder or warmer zone, as their comfort levels and body needs may change.

Reptiles appear to vary less in temperature preference than the amphibians, but even they may have wide daily ranges according to species and habitat. Again, generalizations may be misleading, but semi-aquatic reptiles may accept drops to as low as 50° F., during hibernation, or for a short time during the warm season. Then they will probably seek a warmer spot. A fairly general temperature level of around 60° to 70° F. may be the average for many aquatic forms. Some tropical sea snakes appear to be most comfortable around 80° F., the temperature of the waters in which they live.

Land reptiles indicate their temperature preference by being either nocturnal or diurnal. Nocturnal desert reptiles seem to be active chiefly between 64° and 89° F. Their well-being may be threatened by sustained temperatures higher than those. In fact, 89° F. is close to the upper limit for continuous comfort for such varied nighttime animals as the little, tender-skinned, pink gecko lizards and rattlesnakes. Though predominantly nocturnal, their periods of activity vary with the season.

Diurnal or crepuscular snakes are generally more sensitive to extremely high temperatures than lizards active at the same time of day. Snakes may be abroad when the temperatures read as low as 50° F. and as high as 89° F., the limit, as well, for the nocturnal types mentioned above. It is of interest and possible significance, that snakes out in the daytime are limited to temperatures acceptable by nocturnal species. On the contrary, lizards active in the daytime have body temperatures of around 80° to 95° F. for the coastal and mountain forms, and from 85° to as high as an occasional and brief 113° F. for some desert species.

From these few broad generalizations, it is apparent that, except perhaps for the cold-blooded amphibians, there is good reason to abandon the older terms. Some are cool-blooded, but others are warm-blooded, and some desert lizards would have to be *hot*-blooded—those that may attain temperatures as high as 113° F., which would be fatal for human beings within a very short time. To add to the confusion, desert reptiles hibernate. Within their winter shelters thermal readings remain around 68° to 70° F. for three and four months at a time. When they emerge and become active, however, some, such as the diurnal lizards, may prefer temperatures ranging around 100° F!

After years of research I devised a new term to apply to these animals which were dependent upon external sources of heat— ectotherm. No matter how much their temperatures may vary from time to time, nor how capable they are of maintaining a constant temperature through basking and retreat, their effective heat is almost totally drawn from sources outside the body rather than being created from chemical reactions within it. It is very difficult to force a lizard to exercise enough to measure any capabilities of generating heat, and we have not succeeded to any detectable degree in our laboratories. As far as we have been able to discover by very carefully eliminating all extraneous sources of heat, the chuckwalla (a large herbivorous lizard), when forced to exercise by regaining its balance or struggling to right itself when turned on its back, simply does not generate enough heat to make up for what is lost continuously through its skin. In other words, this lizard cannot produce enough heat to be of significance when compared with what it gains from the hot sun of its desert environment.

A very highly refined determination of the sources of reptilian body temperature would have to take into account the amount of heat absorbed plus the amount of internally generated heat less the amount lost to the surroundings. This should allow one to calculate the animal's body temperature and its running speed. This is not easy to do, however, for the data accumulated even by the use of delicate and excellent instruments must also be treated mathematically in terms of the animal's total surface area and its volume.

All reptiles gain heat at an astonishingly high rate. The smaller they are, naturally, the faster they will heat up under any given condition. If this is not immediately apparent, con-

sider the length of time it takes to heat a half a cup of water
in a small saucepan against the rate for ten cups in a larger
but comparably shaped pan. A large reptile representing one
to several pints of water will heat to optimum much more
slowly than does one representing a teaspoonful of liquid.
Now consider the difference between heating a volume of
water in a small pan and heating the same amount in a large,
flat-bottomed skillet. The skillet of the reptilian world is the
flat little horned lizard. With practically half of its surface on
top of the body, the lizard can turn its top side either toward
or away from the sun. The other half faces downward to the
ground, against which it can press its underside to gain or
lose heat depending on the temperature of the substrate and
its own needs. Thus this lizard can regulate its body heat to
very fine degrees because of its shape and the kind of climate
in which it lives. On the other hand, this unusual arrange-
ment of surface area renders it extremely vulnerable to overheating or over-rapid chilling.

In addition to temperature control through their surface-
to-volume ratios, all of the reptiles that have been studied

Figure 7. Horned lizards position themselves in accordance with
how much solar radiation they wish to receive. On very hot days
they seek total, or almost total, protective cover.

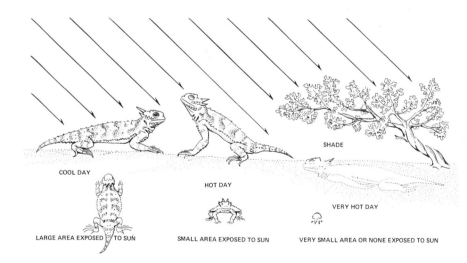

COOL DAY

HOT DAY

SHADE

VERY HOT DAY

LARGE AREA EXPOSED TO SUN   SMALL AREA EXPOSED TO SUN   VERY SMALL AREA OR NONE EXPOSED TO SUN

show the presence of a very fine network of blood vessels lying right under the skin—the capillary "bed" or system. From studies of their total heat gains and losses, it is obvious that reptiles can control the amount of blood flowing through the arteries to the surface by various means. Thus when cold, they begin to bask and flush the subskin area with blood which warms rapidly and then returns to deep-lying tissues through the veins. Heat is carried to all parts of the body in a very expeditious and efficient way, another one of nature's ingenuities.

If, on the contrary, reptiles become too warm, they are able to cut some of this flow of blood to the surface and slow the internal heat gain to some degree. The effectiveness of this device is limited, for all blood transference to these super-heated tissues cannot be stopped without starving the living cells of oxygen, which is needed in quantities proportionate to the heat and metabolic demands of the cells. Many small reptiles, incidentally, are able to change from a dark color to a near-white, which reflects much of the incoming heat.

As a further refinement in the blood transfer of heat, when the source of heat suddenly diminishes reptiles can also reduce the flow of blood from their now adequately warmed interiors to the cooled-off surface. By not circulating warm blood through a cold surface and back to a warm body where it will cool the tissues, they can retain body heat to at least a limited degree. This retardation of heat loss serves them in good stead for short periods of time.

There are some very interesting exceptions to the dependence of ectotherms on external heat sources. Social or gregarious insects often huddle together in an enclosed space sheltered from the wind. An example is the swarming of bees in hives. Each little active body produces a small amount of warmth. When the honeybees cluster together in a hive, the total output from their mass, which may amount to a quart or more of living bodies, is sufficiently large to keep the hive warm even in cold weather. To generate such amounts of heat, however, they must utilize high-energy foods such as honey, which is largely sugar. This they feed on, digest, and rapidly convert to heat, one of the ways in which they are able to maintain a hive at above-environmental temperatures.

A number of years ago I encountered some bushes in the Mojave Desert that were defoliated by hundreds of tent caterpillars. On the day I discovered these infestations it was chilly, and clouds sailed like spinakers before the wind, which rattled the desert scrub. It was altogether a most unfavorable condition for any minute animal to maintain its body temperature. More out of habit than anything else, I inserted a thermometer into the silky tent woven by the caterpillars and to which they returned during this cool spell. I could hardly believe the reading of my instrument and reinserted it into another part of their shelter. No doubt about it, they were definitely not living in the temporary weather surrounding the tent but were enjoying comparative warmth. Part of this heat, easily measurable on a thermometer, several degrees in fact, came from the collective chemical activity of the individual larvae, but some may have resulted from the absorption of infrared heat waves trapped in their bodies and partially retained through the protection provided by their nest.

Another exception to the rule of nongeneration of body heat by ectotherms is the tuna. That large, ocean-going, and vigorously swimming, predacious fish sometimes has a body temperature as high as 10° F. above that of its watery habitat. This is an astounding feat, since water is such an excellent conductor of heat. It may be accounted for, in part, by the rapid generation of metabolic heat within the body through its muscular and other activity and by the insulating effect of the oil in the outer layers of the tuna's tissue.

Finally, there is the extraordinary example of the python which, while incubating its eggs in a compact coil, elevates its own temperature and that of its eggs by some two degrees above that of the environment. It performs that feat through shivers or muscular spasms that pass from head to tail in continuous waves. This was first reported by Francis Gano Benedict in his monumental work, *The Physiology of Large Reptiles,* and has since been confirmed by zookeepers in London and in the United States.

Because the temperature of an animal determines so many other things than just its physical warmth, the study of its chemical effects, its regulation, its sources, and its many attendant phenomena becomes an extremely important and engrossing area of research. Temperature is most certainly a major theme in the evolutionary story.

10: The Mesquite Camp

Du ring the mid-thirties I realized I needed large amounts of uninterrupted time in the desert to investigate what was becoming of almost obsessional interest—how cold-blooded vertebrates survive in a warm, arid climate. I chanced upon a secluded mesquite grove not far from the road connecting Palm Desert on the west and Indio to the east. There I set up what was standard camping gear at the time—a khaki-brown umbrella tent, a "desert rat" water bag whose contents were supposedly cooled by evaporation, a Coleman stove, and a single camp chair. This simple set-up involved little work, but it was certainly primitive when compared to the television-equipped trailers and campers of today.

Though my mesquite thicket was isolated and full of desert wildlife, I was close neighbor to a rancher whose irrigation system supplied me with water, which I needed in plenty but which my air-cooled Franklin did very well without. Once settled in, I put out my cages, low-walled ones for the lizards and high-walled enclosures for the snakes. Then I was ready to snare or capture residents for these temporary homes, and I began the series of observations that would lead, I hoped, to my enlightenment.

A totally unexpected dividend came early in my research. I spent a number of days in testing the upper temperature limits of lizards and snakes by exposing them one at a time to the impact of the sun in their native habitat. And, strangely, they did not seem to be able to stand the heat of their own home. The test required my squatting in daytime heat and allowing the tethered animals to run toward but not reach nearby shade. Watching these supposedly heat-demanding animals quickly die from high temperatures in their chosen home climate was a thought-provoking experience. Here was I, a heat-generating animal with a naked, unprotected skin, surviving even longer exposure while dozens of reptiles were killed in minutes by overheating. Some of the smallest reptiles died within about sixty seconds after being scooped out of their underground shelters into the blazing sun of the surface.

I soon noticed that many of the animals became incapable of motion well before their actual death. Since this condition prevented their escape to shelter, I called it the *potential lethal,* a useful term in those early studies. If I cooled the victim almost immediately after exposure, full mobility was restored, very much like the return to activity following recovery from the torpor of cold. There was one clear difference, however. Temperatures of around 60° F. were required to induce cold coma, and this was some 30° F., or more, below their preferred or optimal temperatures—about 90° to 95° F. In sharp contrast, the crippling effects of heat occurred in the upper 90s (higher for some lizards), a rise above their preferred temperatures of less than a third of the amount required for harmless cold torpor. I surely needed more information to even begin to understand the role of temperature in the evolution of terrestrial vertebrates, but the creatures that had failed in this arena of life were now extinct, no longer around for us to investigate. A bright new area of research appeared to be opening up.

All through the daylight hours the heat was also a test of *my* endurance. Perhaps the most annoying of all the discomforts was the irritating humming of the hungry little eye gnats that hovered or crawled into my ears or around my eyes. These tiny insects were given a vividly apt but unprintable name relating to the source of the staphylococcus infections that caused a very serious conjunctivitis. The gnats carried the bacteria from a special part of the male canine anatomy to man. Nightfall did bring relief, but before falling asleep I kept thinking about those heat-killed reptiles.

There *must* be some significance in the outstanding fact of this far greater tolerance for cold than for heat. There has to be, I mumbled to the desert-bright stars. Then I turned over and continued making observations to the sand bunched under my sleeping bag. This feature of heat-intolerance was so obvious in these modern reptiles that it could not be ignored. But had their ancient precursors possessed similar susceptibilities? And what of the even more cold-tolerant and heat-vulnerable amphibians? Had any of the modern forms any relictual physiological resemblances to ancestral but structurally different early types?

As long as we lack actual knowledge of the thermal limitations of the ancient amphibians and reptiles, our best attempts to resolve these questions must be restricted to deductive logic from the present illusive evidence. The theories that result can be but fumbling approximations, but, for now, they must suffice in suggesting solutions.

Let us assume, for the sake of argument, that the modern forms of land-dwelling, and thus climatically vulnerable, creatures have retained some physiological traces of their ancestry in the same way they display many morphological evidences of relationship. If so, a small increase in solar radiation or a prolonged warm spell probably endangered the ancient forms far more than a pronounced drop in temperature. In other words, what is obvious today about the temperature requirements of amphibians and reptiles could very well reflect similar patterns of the past.

Pondering on these wholly novel problems on another sleepless night, a serendipitous flash asked another question: what caused the extinction of so many reptilian species and the great transformation of surviving vertebrate lines at the close of the dinosaur age? The birds are clearly the descendants of reptiles. The mammals, too, carry skeletal and tissue traces linking them to that long distant lineage. What then happened to the ruling reptiles of the Mesozoic, the Archosaurs, or, as they are more popularly called, the dinosaurs?

At the time I was working in the mesquite camp, enough geological data had been accumulated to give me a general idea of the major climate trends of the Mesozoic Era. Based upon the distribution of ferns, cycads and other plants and marine animals such as corals, it has been assumed that much of the Mesozoic enjoyed a world-wide mild climate. Deserts formed in time of drought, particularly in western North America, and there was at least one period of cooler climate when glaciers occurred in eastern Australia. For the most part, however, the era was characterized by shallow inland seas, marine lagoons, and swampy, sluggish rivers, reflecting general humidity and a mild-to-temperate climate.

Various theories about the demise of the dinosaurs have been considered. One of them suggests that a cooling environment was responsible. Mountain uplift was taking place at the close of the Mesozoic, which resulted in lowered temperatures in various places around the globe. This theory presupposes that the huge reptiles of that time were essentially subtropical and tropical creatures, and any substantial chilling would have weakened them. Another theory postulates intensified mammalian pressure, for this great group of animals was evolving rapidly just at the time of dinosaur extinction.

My growing appreciation of the lethal aspects of heat, however, pushed my thinking along different lines. Could a warm-

Plate 7. The dead pinyon pine is still a landmark at what is now the Salton Sea view in Joshua Tree National Monument. Mt. San Jacinto (right background) and peaks of the Santa Rosa Mountains are among some of the highest in southern California. Most of my heat research was conducted in the Coachella Valley, between the mountains and the hills to the left of the dead tree.

ing trend, even if slight, have contributed to their downfall?

There have been many prolonged cool spells during the history of the earth. The presence of massive glaciers and ice sheets inscribes an indelible record on the earth's surface. But does a relatively minor decrease or increase of climatic heat leave any clear mark on the rocks and topography of the land? If droughts or floods accompany rises in environmental temperatures, a record is left in the form of drifting sand and dunes or as puddingstones and varves from ancient streams, lakes, and riverbeds. It is possible, however, that changes too small to leave a record in the rocks might be sufficient to terminate some lines of contemporaneous land life.

As I reviewed my recollections of college courses and general reading, I could find nothing that might serve as a paleothermometer. If there was, it was buried, as yet unrevealed in the biotic record. I would have to rely on logical deductions based on much (too much!) indirect evidence.

One thing seemed certain—in one form or another large numbers of the ancient phyletic branches of both plants and animals have persisted down to the present, and their taxonomic relationships can be traced by their anatomy. This being so, surely they must also have retained some physiological characteristics as well—perhaps counter-current heat exchange in blood vessels or other evidence from the soft tissues that would provide clues for detecting minor changes in climate. Why reject out-of-hand such a possibility? After all, the salt content in body fluids is readily accepted as evidence of our ancient origin in a slightly saline environment. Cell structure; the mechanisms of inheritance, embryogeny, and reproduction; and the unchanging chemico-physical laws of heat—all are evidence for physiological adaptation to past habitats.

As I accumulated data on living reptiles, other areas of heat investigation suggested themselves. How could the high skin temperature developed under intense sunlight be diffused through the body to its core? From my small knowledge of anatomy and simple physiology, it was obvious that a network of surface capillaries absorbed the heat, carried it to the veins, and finally to the inner parts of the body. I later performed an experiment on reptiles that indicated the blood flow in the skin can be regulated by the animal according to temperature. When these sensitive creatures crawled out to bask in the grateful warmth of the morning sun, this blood vessel plexus, or network, and its regulatory nerve system speeded or controlled body warming. But what happened to this blood flow as temperatures approached excessively high levels? Would it continue to distribute what had by now become dangerously high amounts of heat? Although I found no direct answer to the question, I did notice a slowing of the rise of deep-body temperatures after death, with the temperature gradient from the skin to the interior steepening markedly. From these observations it seemed that the surface circulation, up to some maximum, could change according to the temperature needs within the body. (I later learned that this is true. See chapter nine.)

With a vague picture of the interrelationship between body size and the circulatory system in mind, there rose the related problem of the geographic-climatic distribution of various-sized reptiles from the smallest to the larger species such as pythons, boas, crocodiles, alligators, and large tortoises. Since the surface of the body functions as the absorber of heat and since the proportion, or ratio, of surface area to the volume of the body is geometrically fixed, it was clear to me that large bodies warm more slowly. And in areas where there are sharp temperature contrasts between day and night, such as deserts, they would be less active in early morning and at dusk, when temperatures drop lower than the optimum for such animals. They would have an advantage, however, in that sudden rises in temperature probably would be less dangerous. On the other hand, small-sized creatures would quickly have the speed and alertness required for survival during active hours, but great fluctuations in temperature would affect them more.

I came to what appeared to be an indisputable conclusion: body size in reptiles is an important feature and it reflects an adaptation to local climate. When cold small creatures have physiological and behavioral ways to warm up quickly. When sufficiently warm and fed, they can avoid excessive heating by withdrawal to the shade, and, if necessary, into underground retreats. Modern reptiles can thermoregulate to a fine degree by just shuttling into and out of the sunlight.

A sidewinder occupying one of my ground cages provided a clue to the perfection of this tactic. It thrust most of its body out into the sunshine in the cool morning hours and then, as the sunlight grew more intense, gradually withdrew, diminishing its heated surface area and reducing internal heating at the same time. It retreated entirely into the shade of its burrow from about ten o'clock in the morning until late afternoon, reversing the process in the evening. With a minimum of exposure to the dangers of daytime predators, it could enjoy its optimum temperature while digesting its latest meal. Enzyme action is also linked to heat and has its own optimum and lethal limits.

During all of these studies it became clear that the surface-to-volume (or mass) rule applies equally well to the speed of digestion. In animals with poor masticatory equipment, the digestive juices must go to work on whatever surface areas are exposed. The smaller the food particle, the larger is the related surface to its total volume and the faster digestion proceeds. We and many other animals chew our food and so improve the surface-to-mass ratios and speed digestion. (I am sure your mother must have admonished, "For Heaven's sake! Chew, don't gulp your food!")

While ruminating on these matters some of the puzzles of dinosaur evolution loomed large. For one thing, I could not help but conclude that the widespread progress toward large size must have meant either a warming climate or an evolutionary accommodation to body temperatures lower than those of their ancestors. However, a decrease in body heat meant, as far as I knew, a slowing down of both the digestion rates and of the neuromuscular functions. The disadvantages of that development seemed clear, and hence it appeared probable that growth in size almost certainly matched a warming trend in the environment. Since large bodies warm slowly in proportion to small-bodied creatures, large size for these huge reptiles might well have protected against too sudden or too frequent heating. Small animals are more thermally vulnerable, but they have other heat defenses. They can withdraw into shade, crawl into rock crevices, or dig their own underground retreats. For the large dinosaurs such shelters were unavailable. They survived only because of their large size. It is possible that bony plates under the skin, elongated or enlarged scales, and feathers (the line that led to birds was developing) protected the owners from the immediate danger of overheating. All such safeguards probably extended the daylight hours of foraging, mate-seeking, territorial defense, and other activities.

Back in the 1930s and 1940s the idea of drifting continents

was ridiculed or at most just dismissed with a word or two. However, with no other explanation at hand, I usually referred to Alfred Wegener's theory of drifting continents as a possible cause of climatic change and would conclude a seminar discussion with a wistful, "If only Wegener was right." Now we know that the continents have drifted apart over vast distances and, so far as I have been able to learn, some or portions of the land masses moved into colder latitudes. By logical inference, the ancient reptiles were chilled out of existence. However, considering the notably vast gap between optimum and lethal cold and the very narrow gap between optimum and deadly or damaging heat, I think the question of whether excessive heat killed before cold took over is still open to analysis and argument.

I continued to read extensively in fields that were new to me, and from the accumulating welter of facts I pursued this line of thinking with the hope that some helpful ideas might emerge. One of the insistently recurring ideas was that whatever had happened might well be related to one solid fact: *Every living organism, every descendant from the remote past, must have reproduced in sufficient numbers to have surmounted every disaster and innumerable chronic dangers. Lavish reproduction rather than individual survival might be the clue to species survival and long persistence.*

From this new thought the problem of temperature and its connection with reproduction assumed ever larger proportions until, less by pure chance than from a sensitizing by scattered fragments of information, I looked into the matter and encountered the work of Carl R. Moore and H. D. Chase in 1923 and other associates who amplified the findings. In one of these pioneer experiments wool was taken from a ram, and insulation for the ram's scrotum was devised from it: a simple bag of wool in which the scrotum was fitted. The purpose was merely to prevent this organ from functioning in its role of thermoregulation during spermatogenesis. It appeared that *normal* body temperature alone terminated that process, and the result was total sterility for up to sixty days. But could this experiment have a more general appli-

Plate 8. The desert scaly lizard has scales that are larger than those of most other desert lizards. I saw these reptiles frequently around my heat-research camp feeding on insects. There is good reason to believe that the large scales with air spaces beneath are important heat shields.

cation than for scrotal animals alone? All reptiles, birds and many mammals lack thermoregulatory scrota, so if temperature is a factor in effective reproduction, either spermatogenesis occurs at body heat or there is some cryptic mechanism for thermoregulation such as avian air sacs with cooling air next to the testes.

The migration of the testes in some mammals appears to insure their cooling throughout the period of spermatogenesis, but the exposed position also makes them vulnerable to mechanical damage—a fact reputed to appeal to warring male squirrels. Even their position on the underside of brush-inhabiting quadrupedal mammals, such as the numerous ungulates, exposes them to seemingly unwarranted dangers. Only the protection of the vital and heat-sensitive spermatogenetic processes afforded by the placement of the scrotal sacs, out of the sun and away from body heat, would seem to justify the traumatic risks to reproduction.

In 1965 a review of the available literature on the subject of reproductive sensitivity to heat ("Hyperthermia, Aspermia, Mutation Rates and Evolution." Cowles, R. B. *Quarterly Review of Biology* Vol. 40, No. 4; 341-365) deals with the subject in much greater detail than what would be appropriate here. However, as possibly the most important product of my desert research (in my much-loved mesquite camp of long ago) on such "useless critters" as reptiles, the subject deserves at least some cursory mention in this book.

By reviewing the pertinent literature on reproduction and gametogenesis (production of reproductive cells) I discovered that the genetic sequel to abnormally high body temperatures seemed to be present in a surprisingly large number of tested plants as well as animals. Instances of immunity to such temperatures either have gone unreported or may be exceptional. Of probably even greater importance, however, was the emerging fact that body heat levels below those that may sterilize outright usually cause a notable increase in mutation rates. Furthermore, these critical heat values lie very close to normal body temperatures. An exaggerated mutation rate could weaken the chances for survival of a species even though the mutated individuals survived. The natural question was, could such a phenomenon have led to the demise of the dinosaurs? And if so, what then of the changing paleoclimates that in this subtle way would upset effective reproduction?

The complete story is not yet available, but it seems increasingly possible and even probable that large numbers of susceptible organisms, including early reptilian stock, need not have been exposed to actually lethal temperatures but to a very slight warming of their environment or to increasing penetration of sunlight. The result might well have been a progressive accumulation of maladaptive mutations tantamount to reproductive failure. The needed alteration in the thermal environment would have been too moderate to have left any visible record except in the changing biota. At times it might even have been so gradual and slight that it benignly stimulated mutation rates and led to new and favorable combinations and an accelerated evolutionary rate. Some of the products may even have been what to us would be bizarre but viable forms of life that filled the ecological voids left by the attenuating populations of previously well-adapted organisms.

Reflecting on that first stimulus to a very different and wholly unorthodox view of extinction, many other ideas flooded in. But I needed supportive literature. Quite naturally it was lacking and would remain so for as long as the idea persisted that only increasing frigidity could be responsible for the climatic extinction of fauna. An elementary first step was to determine if modern reptiles might be similarly vulnerable. A simple test would be to subject a local species to overheating and check the effect on reproduction. I therefore collected a number of the little yucca night lizards, the only species for which there was an adequate body of readily available information on seasonal reproductive patterns. Even the testicular cycle had been described and correlated with the months in the year.

In this experiment we exposed the lizards in full reproductive condition to a few days of supranormal but not lethal temperatures and then sacrificed them. As we had hoped, the testes had collapsed and assumed the post-breeding condition that normally was observed later in the year. This preliminary experiment appeared to be proof of heat-induced sterility, but of far greater significance would be heat testing at a slightly lower level followed by experiments with inbreeding to at least a second and third generation. By using modern techniques and microscopy it might be possible to detect and count damaged genes, but as far as I know no such experiments have been conducted on vertebrate organisms, though the mutagenic consequences of heat on the common fruit, or pommace, fly, *Drosophila*, are well documented.

Abnormally high heat is also known to destroy bacterial and viral infections in man and other animals without serious consequences to the host organism. Fever heat also stimulates or speeds the immune responses. In a similar manner scores of plant scions taken for fruit tree grafts from desirable but virus-infected stock are cleansed by heating to levels above those tolerated by the parasite but below those harmful to the scions. Multi-ton loads of infected but otherwise desirable sugarcane cuttings are routinely treated before setting them out in the fields. Whether the responsible organisms are killed outright by the treatment, or the immunogenic responses of the host are stimulated, or whether, just possibly, the mutagenic effect of excessive heat (for the parasite) overloads the reproductive functions with lethal mutations in these short-lived organisms has—as far as I know—never been investigated.

There are increasingly numerous suggestions that in animal organisms normal fevers should be regarded as curative rather than harmful. There is even an intriguing statistical survey done in Germany on women who had had high fevers at some time in the prior five years. It found that they were not victimized by a type of breast cancer that is suspected of being started by a latent virus infection. Is it possible that the antipyretics such as aspirin may knock down a therapeutic fever, permitting a few resistant individuals of the causative virus to retain their deadly potential? These and many other untested ideas have been emerging from studies of the very narrow band of high temperatures that lie just below the lethal for the entire human body.

As for the ancient reptiles and their much altered descendants, we may never be able to know very much about their physiological limitations and which of the present temperature requirements and tolerances are legacies from the remote past. If genetic susceptibility to heat is one such relic, then with due caution we may apply it to our thinking. It could supply us with a tenuous connection between the past Mesozoic events and the present.

The boundary zone between normal temperatures and excessive heating is so extremely narrow that it is almost certain that imaginative future studies will employ the new devices for the thermal, cardiac, and respiratory monitoring of living animals. Such records will give us much greater insight than we have at present.

I am led by this extremely subtle degree of vulnerability to elevations of temperature and the vastly greater tolerance for lowered ones to theorize that heat-avoidance mechanisms, along with structural devices for the same purpose, may have arisen long before evolution invented internal body heating and a consequent need for conserving energy from food. The heat protection of exaggerated scales, bony scutes, feathers, and fur may have been as indispensable to genetic stability, or moderation in mutation rates, as they are now for conserving and regulating the expenditure of metabolically generated warmth.

Without doubt, the study of what might be called biothermology will add to our fund of information and from time to time open totally new and unsuspected vistas into the life of plants and animals. It should greatly multiply the number of questions we must ask and then answer through insightful research.

Although it was once called "a useless waste of time and money," in retrospect the frustrating efforts to extrapolate and theorize from living reptiles the evolutionary progress of this great group of animals may well be the most important product of those days in the mesquite camp. The questions those efforts raised seem to be multiplying as fast as the gnats that once plagued me so. As more and more students and researchers attempt to find their answers, I am grateful for the curiosity that prompted me to ponder it all in the first place.

11: Wide Open Spaces

Scores of workers on desert adaptations have investigated the temperature and water privations of desert creatures. They have shown in exquisite detail and logic the way these animals cope with the problems of living in arid places. Such research workers as C.M. Bogert, Kurt Schmidt-Neilsen, George Bartholomew, William Dawson, Kenneth S. Norris, Charles Lowe, and later researchers have each in his own way presented information on the various means by which desert animals escape from or evade the full impact of their habitat.

As pointed out elsewhere in these chapters, all of the small nocturnal creatures have solved their special problems by an almost complete evasion of one of the desert's most important limiting factors, high temperature, by going underground during the hotter parts of the day or year. They have also met the challenge of water shortages in highly logical and individualistic ways. All of the burrowing animals, the geofodes, enter a very different world, which exists only a very short spacial distance from the actual desert environment itself. Though but inches away, its coolness and high humidity render evaporative cooling unnecessary and even inefficient. Water conservation in these subterranean retreats, supplemented by urine economy, is really quite simple.

With increasing familiarity with desert creatures I have become more and more aware of one of the most pronounced features of their arid environment: its open space. These animals became adapted to open spaces unobstructed by dense plant growth, and many even require them for their existence. Each of these desert dwellers is as fully dependent on this factor for survival as on other accommodations to what seems a very inhospitable place to live.

Until the last few decades most scientists and scholars had been conditioned by birth and long residence in areas where withstanding the winter's bitter cold is of major significance for living things. They had largely ignored or totally missed the meaning and impact of extremely high temperatures. By the same token, their native lands were heavily vegetated with forests, grasslands, or other dense covers of plant growth. Thus until recently they did not perceive many of the problems of survival that they would have had if they had grown up in super-hot summer deserts. Devoid of much vegetation, vast open spaces of rock, gravel, pebble-strewn "pavement," and drifting sand dunes are common features.

One of the most vivid illustrations of the importance of bare ground to crawling desert dwellers came to my attention some years ago in the Mojave Desert. Several kinds of foreign short grasses, particularly red brome grass, or *Bromus rubens,* had been introduced into certain areas in the high desert. They had managed to retain a hold and even flourish during the rare years when unusually high winter rainfall had by springtime clothed the slopes below the San Gabriel Mountains with an abundance of dense growth. In one of

Plate 9. The wide, flat body and short legs of the horned lizard were not "designed" for easy travel through patches of dense grass.

these especially generous spring seasons I had the good fortune to have the task of collecting fairly large numbers of the little desert horned lizard, *Phrynosoma platyrhinus,* for some experimental work. I returned to the desert to search in areas where previously these little stub-tailed lizards had been abundant and easily procurable. To my concern I discovered that they were now extremely rare and even threatened with local extinction, particularly where the brome grasses were several inches tall and thick. Quite clearly every horned lizard that emerged from its winter retreat into this new grassy world encountered a most formidable barrier in its search for food. The grass stems were so crowded together that these broad-bodied lizards were completely unable to move forward normally. To find food, and later to mate and produce young, the lizards would either have to develop leaping legs, or wings, or turn on "edge" and walk with two legs on one side or the other!

In a long and painstaking search for my supply of horned lizards it became increasingly apparent that starvation, because of inability to negotiate the newly hostile terrain, was staring the local population in the face. I found only one horned lizard alive, and it was in the last stages of malnutrition. In desperation this little fellow had somehow managed to bend a few blades of grass into a semi-horizontal position and, in a most uncharacteristic adventure, had crawled up onto the top of the bed of bent grass. Here it had become stranded and was able only to move its legs feebly in the air. It had no hope of either forward travel or even descent back to the ground.

The foresters, range management experts, or stockmen who persistently attempt to introduce new grasses or other vegetation into California's deserts and mountains are truly a threat to at least some species of our wildlife. If those attempts succeed, the foreign invaders will self-seed, spread, and take over extensive areas previously occupied by native vegetation. The prospect is slim, however, that many of these introduced forms will be as nutritious or nontoxic as those they replace. Unless the new growth or its fruits and seeds very closely simulate the endemic species, the animals that are specialized to feed on it will suffer.

Another creature obviously dependent on large open areas is the entrancingly specialized sidewinder. Just as fatal to it with its broadside locomotion as to the horned lizards would be the spread and dense growth of brome grasses. None but scientists and true desert aficionados, however, would probably mourn the snake's extinction! In many local areas it is now virtually absent because of the constant warfare waged against it by man and his pets. Fortunately, the Colorado Desert and much of the Mojave remain resistant to the further spread or denser growth of any introduced plant material. I am concerned, however, by the greatly accelerated traffic of off-road vehicles, particularly the en masse invasion of four-wheel drive vehicles, dune buggies, and motorbikes on so-called cross-country runs. Lined up but a few feet apart they charge across the desert plains leaving behind nothing but tire tracks and the appalling destruction of virtually every living thing or its den. This is a matter of too much open space!

Larger animals such as the jack "rabbit," or desert hare, may benefit from increased local supplies of nutritious grass or other low-growing vegetation. They seem to depend, nevertheless, on wide-open spaces where they can detect enemies at a distance and escape by fleetness of foot. A friend of mine had an experience that illustrates most interestingly this elimination of space and areas favorable to jack rabbits. He owned some thirty acres of carefully protected land high on a shoulder of a mountain overlooking the Mojave Desert. His view included magnificent stands of that arboreal lily, the Joshua tree, and numerous pinyon pines. A lover of nature, he had given protection to two or three pairs of jacks whose antics he would watch from the shade of his porch. These animals or their progeny had persisted year after year, furnishing amusement and delight to my friend, and he had come to regard this density of jack rabbit population as perfectly normal for that particular place.

Plate 10. The blossoms of the Joshua tree clearly demonstrate its relationship to the lily family (six petals and the reproductive parts in threes or sixes). A well-known symbiotic partnership exists between the tree and the yucca moth, which lays her eggs in the seed-producing part of the flower, pollinating it at the same time.

In time, however, the hazards of fire in the increasingly dense brush grew greater. Ultimately the inevitable happened. Fire swept completely around his house, clearing the adjacent slopes of all the scrub and even destroying the young pinyon pines that were encroaching lower into the desert. The landscape was devastated and apparently incapable of carrying life of any kind, including his beloved jacks. An abundance of winter and late spring rains stimulated a dense green sward comprised of species which my friend had never realized even existed prior to the burn. To his great delight, first one and then another jack rabbit returned to flourish, fatten, and reproduce on the newly provided food supply. The cleared brush had furnished open spaces in which they could detect predators and flee to safety.

So effective were both the replenishing of the larder and the enhancement of their security, that by the second year my friend saw twenty or more rabbits at one time in this small acreage. In the succeeding year he counted fifty or so in the course of a single day. Inevitably, because of their large numbers, food again became scarce, and his garden, shrubs, and trees bore the brunt of the jacks' efforts to stave off starvation. Every ornamental shrub and tree had to be surrounded with wire netting or perish under the attack of the multiplying jacks.

As the problem became more severe, my friend started shooting some of his erstwhile pals. This made but little impression on their total numbers. For once he welcomed the return of coyotes, foxes, and even an infrequent bobcat. Because of the attacks of predators, and, perhaps of more importance, the reappearance of brush with its hampering and inedible vegetation, the numbers of jack rabbits dwindled perceptibly. Within a few years the flush of life stimulated by the fire decreased, and his acreage returned to normal. Such episodes must have been frequent prior to the initiation of fire protection in chaparral and on semi-desert slopes just below the pinyon pine and juniper belts of the interior hills.

Man's increasing numbers, his meddling with nature, and his insistence on destroying all animals he considers less desirable—all have combined to reduce and even threaten with extinction many of our once-common creatures. Among these are the herds of bighorn sheep that in times past wandered through most of the desert ranges. The suppression of fire also may have reduced the total number of mule deer, condors, and millions of smaller creatures simply through the elimination of periodic burns, which once cleared away tall brush and stimulated bursts of renewed annual vegetation. Even coyotes, foxes, and bobcats have been forced to alter their way of life and to rely more on domesticated animals and less on the sudden multiplication of jack rabbits, such as that which occurred on my friend's property. Similar population fluctuations may have affected cottontail rabbits, kangaroo rats, and numerous small rodents resident in the desert or on its hilly edges, and thus their predators as well.

From the standpoint of taking pleasure in their mere presence, it is unfortunate that the jack rabbit, or black-tailed hare, has, for whatever reason, become almost a rarity within large areas of its former range. I can recall—in the days before the desert was so heavily frequented by man, cars, and guns— seeing anywhere from a half a dozen or more jacks at one time. Another friend of mine whose experiences date back to still earlier days tells of a trip to the Mojave Desert in the vicinity of what is now Hesperia, Victorville, and Barstow. Jack rabbits were so plentiful they resembled a flock of sheep through which he moved continuously all day long. He was rarely outside of an encircling mob of jacks, which gave way before him as he advanced and closed in behind as he moved on!

When he returned to the same area in the following year, he discovered to his surprise that there was scarcely a jack to be seen. By carefully searching over the ground he found numerous skeletons littering the desert floor. It was obvious that neither people nor predators were wholly responsible for this decimation of an enormous population of rabbits. Disease or starvation, or both, may have participated in the extraordinary destruction. Where rabbits had been superabundant they were now abnormally scarce. Since that observation, the jack rabbits in this area have returned to nearly, but not completely, normal numerical levels.

Little is known of the cycles of abundance through which creatures pass, but it seems probable that in some instances sheer numbers contribute to aberrant behavioral and metabolic conditions which in themselves can cause a collapse in the population. Many other factors, of course, contribute to these cycles. Jack rabbit populations never become large under normal conditions. The desert does not often provide the necessary forage to support a dense population. Furthermore, tularemia or other diseases pass from one animal to another most readily when the population is dense and either direct or indirect contact is most frequent. It appears likely that biological control in desert animals is exercised by food scarcity as well as by territorial necessity—the division of all suitable areas into living spaces each occupied by one male, with or without a harem, or a mated pair. The young on weaning must wander in search for food and a place to live. Mortality among the exiled young is always high.

Today the jack rabbit is most often seen around alfalfa fields and other irrigated areas where artificial supplies of water produce an unfailing source of vegetation. Under these conditions they may multiply until they become a serious pest for the rancher who must either erect expensive wire-netting fences or engage in almost nightly hunting by car headlight or spotlight, encouraging his friends to join in the sport. Unfortunately for the ranchers who eat them—and fortunately for the jack rabbits—the spreading knowledge of the prevalence of tularemia, so debilitating or even fatal to human beings, is acting as a partial protection for the jacks. We hope in time they will remain at fairly constant levels of abundance and be available for us and our children to watch and enjoy, nose in action, long legs loping, and the black-tipped ears in sprightly alert.

Part II:

Surviving Each Other

12: The Hunters and the Hunted

*T*o gain insight into the significance of predatory animals, one must take into consideration the all pervasive continuing flood of young that are, willy nilly, poured into this world—the millions of fish or frog eggs, insect larvae, and newborn mammals that keep arriving. There is slim chance for most, however, a hundred to one odds or a billion to one, in some instances, against any one animal's survival to adulthood. High reproductive rates are the only guarantee that enough of the young will remain alive until maturity and so maintain a breeding stock of adequate size.

On the other hand, countless eaters of other animals depend upon this prodigality and unconsciously even contribute to the welfare of their prey species. In an apparent paradox, if all the predators (in the broad sense, inclusive of parasites) were suddenly removed, total disaster from famine and attendant problems would overtake the prey animals. For their own collective good, to prevent excessive use of their food supply, most of the newly born or laid individuals must be eaten.

Despite acknowledgement that predators are of vast importance, both in population control and in moving essential nutrients through the complex interrelationships of innumerable food chains, most of us have heard, or probably made, highly emotional and vituperative remarks about bird-intent cats or mouse-motivated snakes. We leap to the rescue of the hapless prey, driving away the captor, which was simply stimulated by deeply ingrained instinct. We have heard similar diatribes expressed against "chicken" hawks, owls, "wild" cats, and other "varmints." Even frogs, when observed eating animals smaller than themselves, and fish, pouncing on smaller fish, get their share of unjustified criticism. Witnessing the demise of live and wriggling prey can be upsetting unless one has cultivated biological objectivity. But squeamishness is hardly an excuse for failing to understand that these episodes are but examples of an endless and fundamental food pattern in the living world.

How much sense or good judgment does all this misplaced sentiment represent? Is the classical view of nature study entirely true: that the only role of predators is to control numbers, thus preventing excess multiplication? Do predators contribute in other ways to benefit a population or a species? Aside from the high mortality rate among the young of vertebrate predators—for they too are beset by superfluous reproduction that condemns most of their offspring to die—the diseases and dangers to which they are subject act in concert to control overabundant fecundity. Starvation, parasite infestation, and subsequent death from weakness play a large part in the balance of nature among competing carnivores.

There are not enough fast-breeding herbivores to feed an equivalent number of their ecological partners. Nature is not crowded with vigilant predators. How many more sparrows and finches do you have around your home than flycatchers?

The emotional horror evoked by predators when seen in action is grossly unfair to these animals. All of them are irrevocably born to eat meat. With their morphological and chemical specializations most would quickly starve to death on any other diet. Their own freshly killed meat is a necessity for them since natural carrion is insufficient. They have no alternative except death by slow starvation if unable to obtain flesh, and nature does not provide them with a bloodless option. To understand the role of the predator in any given environment, we must be objective and abandon sentimentality for true knowledge and more rational attitudes and conclusions.

To explore further the vital role of the predator, I have chosen a number of examples for anecdotal discussion, including some representative fish, reptiles, and birds, which particularly interest me because of my involvement with body temperature research. Birds operate at the highest temperature level of all the vertebrates, and their nutritional needs are correspondingly demanding, whereas fish—with rare exceptions—are active at the lower ranges of the thermal spectrum. They and amphibians and reptiles operate no such internal furnaces as do birds and small mammals.

I first studied the predatory white sea bass (for some strange reason it is called a sea trout while young) on the pier of the Scripps Institute of Oceanography, at La Jolla, California. Curiously this fish really is neither bass nor trout. It is technically a drum, not the familiar rhythm instruments but a sciaenid fish. Some actually "drum" by regulating the passage of air through their swim bladders. Back in 1931 and 1932 this fish actually widened my biological horizons. I was studying ichthyology from the pier with a hook and line, a more sophisticated term for just plain fishing. I noticed that the best time to catch these predatory fish was when their usual victims were present in enormous numbers, often obscuring the sea bottom from view. Under these conditions a hook baited with a struggling little fish taken from the same enormous crowd of its fellow fishes almost always caught a young white sea bass even though it was in the midst of literally thousands of prey fish that were not attached to a dangerous steel hook! In fact, one of the ways by which I located a predator fish was to walk along the pier searching for what I can best describe as a giant "vacuole," a globular area from which the food fish had fled. In every such "vacuole" I looked for a vague form, but as hard as I tried I could not always detect it. Strangely enough, when there, it seemingly paid no attention to the scores of prey immediately around it within inches of its mouth and in plain sight. Yet the sea bass eagerly took my baited hook. Why?

What the Victorians called the "organ of curiosity" itched enough so that I tried to find the answer for myself, for no one seemed, at that early date, to have a good answer. Questions, thought-provoking questions, grew in number while I paced the pier. What was the difference between the bait fish and the rest of the school around the predator? Could it have been only the hook? I lowered several fishless hooks into the water, but none proved an attraction. How about the behavior of the bait? Being on a hook was obviously most awkward and uncomfortable, and this would cause abnormal movement. Additionally, because the fish had been out of water, the resulting partial anoxia could produce swimming patterns sufficiently different to attract attention. In contrast, the surrounding fish by acting normal would provide no identifiable target at all. Perhaps of more importance, aberrant behavior in schooling fish usually signals weakness, disease, or injury and thus an easier and surer chance of successful capture.

The eternal vigilance of natural selection has seen to it that normal and healthy animals are adept at escape. They are capable of making maximum use of their muscular and neural equipment to avoid being eaten before they can breed, exploiting their procreative ability for a sufficient number of breeding seasons to cope with a high death rate and replacement needs. They are the hardest to surprise and capture. In a hungry world, where energy to pursue and capture must be taken from accumulated food within the predator's body, only sick or crippled animals provide assurance that a minimal effort will be successful in replenishing this energy. Easy capture always has a high priority over attempting to catch an alert, fully endowed individual. The predator is not a sportsman playing games and taking trophies.

It looked to me as though I had found a predator that was very well oriented or adapted for the needed conservation of energy—the most return for the least effort. I tested my theory by tossing a number of both injured and oxygen-starved bait fish close to the vacuole. Not dead but obviously disabled, they gulped in water and made halfhearted attempts to swim. To my delight the dormant shape flicked with interest, flashed, and my bait was taken. Once again I knew that subtle satisfaction: my hunch was right.

Since those early experiments the ecological role of the predator as a necessary sanitizing agent has become well known. The capture and quick removal of abnormal individuals within a group of gregarious animals aid in the prevention of the spread of disease, either from illness or infected wounds that could introduce sepsis into scratches on their neighbors. Another plus is the removal from the breeding stock of individuals with obvious genetic impairments. In other words, with the defective phenotypes eliminated, they will not breed and multiply and thus burden their own kind. I believe that no exceptions have been found to the role of predation as a useful influence for the good of the group and successive generations, no matter how harsh it may be to the one removed. To our sentiments of sympathy, even this role of a predator seems brutal and emotionally hard to accept. It is but one example, however, of the fact that the group, and this includes not only the present, but innumerable future members, is far more important than the welfare or security of any single transient individual. This may seem like the antithesis of our present philosophy of the "sanctity of life" and the "dignity and rights of the individual"—and it is. As we are rapidly learning, sentiment, no matter how comforting, is no safe nor humane substitute for knowledge when dealing with immutable natural laws.

Nature cannot be otherwise. If the group is seriously periled by the reproduction of genetically damaged members, which could constitute a large portion of the species, selective attrition of the surplus born to each new generation is mandatory for the survival of that species. The totality, the entire assemblage, of each particular kind of organism would be jeopardized were it not for the constant surveillance of predators and their ability to detect impairments and other significant differences.

A question comes to mind at this point. Why should organisms be forever endangering their own welfare through bearing so many more than could possibly survive to reproductive maturity? In other words, why should they produce so many doomed to die of overcrowding, predators, deprivation, or disease? A number of factors are involved. Climates, past and present, are dynamically variable, and the effects of such changes on the supplies of food occupying the various steps of the pyramid of life are far-reaching. Extinction overtakes any species unable to adjust genetically to new environmental conditions or insufficiently prolific to produce a gene pool of necessary size. Breeding stock must always be sufficient to insure survival of the species, even though extensive natural disasters may take a heavy toll of contemporary and relatively ephemeral individuals.

In one sense, therefore, the extinct forms of life—as revealed to us by fossils—are those that failed to breed in the numbers needed to provide innate changes that could cope with some episode, or series of episodes, of heightened death rate. (There appears to be little evidence, however, of a sudden calamitous total kill throughout the entire range of a specific plant or animal.) Only by "excess" multiplication is there material for the operation of the important process of natural selection, with its lavish requirements, and the preservation of a few capably reproductive individuals. Only through the propagation of many unnecessary, and therefore "superfluous," expendable reproductive units can there be species plasticity and the cumulative changes inherent in evolution.

Moving along in our story of predation through the evolutionary series of animals, I pause at the amphibians—salamanders, frogs, and toads. Certain species of salamanders such as the marbled, or giant, salamander of central and northern California have rather keen perception of chemical (olfactory) clues to the presence of food. The larvae, which are completely aquatic, rapidly find places where fish have been cleaned at the edge of a brook. In general, most species of adult salamanders appear to be strongly cued to food by olfactory means, although under some circumstances they also use vision to detect the movement of both enemy and prey and their proximity to them.

That wonderful story of the jumping frog of Calaveras County is a most enjoyable example of the visual cuing of tail-less amphibians during their search for and capture of food. In this amusing tale pellets of buckshot were rolled within reach of a bullfrog, which rapidly grabbed and swallowed them. Obviously no chemical reception or sense of smell was employed in this display of reflex responses. The frog took the buckshot simply because it moved and was close enough and small enough to capture. The author, though no zoologist, must have been an excellent and observant naturalist. Mark Twain was well aware of this curious helpless response to movement and size, and he used his knowledge with telling effect.

Bullfrogs enthusiastically nab a piece of dangling flannel in which a hook is concealed, virtually capturing themselves. Neither color detection nor chemoreception is involved. It is wholly a matter of movement—the jiggling of the bait, its appropriate size for eating, and the involuntary reaction of the predator. For the most part bullfrogs and toads wait and grab at any passing object they can overpower and swallow. Its digestibility or edibility is a secondary matter. They fit a role filled by many opportunistic predators that have little or no ability to discriminate. This probably means that, unlike the sea bass, they are relatively ineffective feeders on disabled, diseased, and irregular food items. Because they are so casual in their feeding response to motion, their capacity to detect such aberration may have little value for themselves or, incidentally, for their prey species.

I noted such indiscriminate feeding when I was studying the stomach contents of more than a thousand toads. At the time I was working in a now non-existent section of the U.S. Bureau of Biological Survey, which was primarily involved with research on food habits of various species. These representative samples included many jumping amphibians that enjoyed a huge and varied diet containing an astonishingly large portion of dandelion floats and seeds, objects that drift close to the ground. Milkweed seeds and silk as well as tufts of cotton, wool, and blown fragments of paper were also on the menu. The amphibians reacted to these bits and pieces as though they were food items, and they were consumed, apparently, with equal gusto along with more nourishing fare.

Because of their large size, bullfrogs are sometimes capable of catching and eating newly hatched alligators. There was such a specimen preserved in the museum of Cornell University. They have also been observed to feed on incautious ducklings swimming too close to them on the edge of a pond. They eat a considerable number of crayfish as well.

The Colorado River toad is a touch-me-not animal protected by a dermotoxin. Captive specimens have demonstrated their ability to take young mice and even adults when the toad is large enough to overpower and eat them. In all these instances the movement of the prey is the precipitating factor in releasing the attack-and-swallow response pattern.

On the basis of the kinds of cues used in procuring food, reptiles can be roughly divided into those that rely mainly on eyesight—triggering of the feeding mechanism through movement and appropriate size—and those that employ both optical and chemical clues. Differentiating between the two groups is easy. Look at the tongue. If it is long and forked, as it is in the snakes and some lizards, one can assume they have an effective Jacobson's organ—a pair of elongate depressions in the center of the roof of the mouth—which appraises molecules captured and transmitted by the long, bifid (forked) tongue to this unusual chemoreceptor.

The visually cued lizards have a more "mammal-like" tongue. They show somewhat more discrimination in food than do the toads and frogs, an expectable advance over the less specialized amphibians. But the predominantly insectivorous kinds, nonetheless, respond strongly to any moving object small enough to appear edible. Most of them dash at such a moving target, but when it is at close range they detect that something is amiss and veer off. Others actually "leap before looking" and grab the supposed prey only to spit it out. Anyone can easily demonstrate this feeding behavior by using a trout rod, line, and artificial fly.

The layman tends to think of reptiles as rather unintelligent creatures that are incapable of gaining a conditioned reflex or learning, but this is not really true. I have demonstrated the learning ability of desert lizards by the use of bright green stink bugs that are unfamiliar to them. These insects live only in damper or coastal areas and have an extremely disagreeable odor, which supplements the protection of their concealing coloration. The unsuspecting lizards dash at the stink bugs, at first unaware of their obnoxious qualities. Some pick up and chew the little insects, but promptly drop them, giving every evidence of distaste or even considerable discomfort. Usually only one such experience is necessary. When I drop another such bug into the lizards' cage, they may dart toward it in response to motion, but, more experienced now, they usually "put on the brakes" and come to a skidding halt a few inches away. They may scrutinize the possible prey and then warily back off. This rapid learning and retention of conditioned avoidance reaction suggest a basis for the effectiveness of the bold advertising colors so common in bees and wasps, numerous butterflies, and bugs. Among the brilliantly colored insects are many obnoxiously tasting or smelling species, some with dangerous stings. Clearly even the visually cued lizards detect certain flavors and distinguish between acceptable and disagreeable food. Their lack of the bifid tongue does not wholly deprive them of chemoreception, which first might be inferred from the structure of their mouth and tongue.

Among the southwestern native lizards probably the whiptails, or "race runners," belonging to the genus *Cnemidophorus*, have the most snakelike bifid tongues. Their habit of projecting and withdrawing it with rapid motions, especially when they are searching across the soil, is apparently coordinated with this tool. I have seen them respond to some concealed tidbit of food, digging shallow little pits into the ground to extract insects or insect larvae. Though lacking a noticeably forked tongue, alligator lizards also are well able to find food by chemoreception. They can tell the difference between the occupied egg cocoons of the black widow spiders and those from which the young have hatched or in which they have died and dried up. Such a discriminatory diet enables these lizards to be especially effective enemies of black widow spiders.

I have been using the term "chemoreception," not for its scholarly impressiveness, but because ordinary words for the detection of chemical molecules in either air or water are usually inappropriate in some particular case. Olfaction means smelling, and gustation stands for tasting. We are able to distinguish between these two types of chemical detection; snakes and some lizards combine the two with their use of the long, divided tongue. By flickering their tongue in and out when alarmed or excited ("threatening" us by "exposing their fangs" is a common misinterpretation), snakes are picking up esters of airborne odor or vagrant molecules of chemical substances which most things give off. The tongue collects these molecules; then the tips are thrust up into the amazingly sensitive depressions in the roof of the mouth, the Jacobson's organ, where the actual chemical analysis or appraisal is made. Hence the term, chemoreception, which is what they are doing, irrespective of the function of taste buds or smell organs.

This use of the Jacobson's organ does not necessarily preclude sensing of odors in the nasal passages or on the tongue. In certain experiments with rattlesnakes implanted with elec-

Plate 11. The alligator lizard is a formidable control of black widow spider populations. Though they may look fearsome and will bite hard with tiny sharp teeth when captured, they should be encouraged around garages and outbuildings because of their feeding habits.

trocardiograph sensors, odors wafted into their cage were detected even if the tongue could not be used. When the tongue could be employed, the first odor alert appeared to reach them through the nostrils. Only then would they be stimulated to explore the air by protruding and withdrawing the tongue.

Most predators explore their environment in various ways. Many species of reptiles use the sensory equipment of the Jacobson's organ for investigating the lightless recesses of rodent shelter burrows and the underground haunts of other small animals. Rattlesnakes are especially well endowed with an infrared detecting organ. They and their relatives are all equipped with heat-sensitive facial pits, classifying them as pit vipers. While prowling they locate young, occasionally adult animals and, certainly, dead animals that have begun to decay but have not reached a toxic stage of decomposition.

Plate 12. This sidewinder is alert and curious. The loreal pit is directed forward for infra-red reception, and the tongue is out and spread to collect odor particles. The nostril above and forward of the loreal pit may or may not be a sensory adjunct.

In our laboratories we neatly killed one myth: all rattle-snakes feed only on living, active prey. We allowed dead animals to decompose for varying lengths of time at a given temperature and then gave them to our captive snakes. We found they preferred the slightly decayed individuals rather than those freshly killed. Their preference for slightly ripe dead animals may very well be due to the obvious fact that they have a stronger and more distinctive odor, making them easier to locate. In addition, they are less difficult to eat than live captives. They had not, however, reached a stage of decomposition injurious to the eater. Extremely "high" animals were usually rejected.

In all of these instances of predator food selection, detection, and preference, what has been written should not be interpreted as an all or none, a black-and-white statement. Every naturalist is aware of the existence of conspicuous differences between closely related species, individual differences within a species, and variations in the intensity of stimuli within an individual. These last are probably associated with variations in the intensity of hunger feeling.

Snakes find prey in several ways. Those that lie in wait while concealed, a trait rendered more effective by their beautifully matching coloration, usually feed by catching careless or inattentive prey. A number of these species also appear to crawl on occasion in search of food. This is particularly true of the sidewinder. Its many tracks on the desert floor suggest that it is both a hunter and a waiter. It is also an assiduous explorer of the burrows of kangaroo rats. Here in total darkness its facial or loreal pits sense particularly well. These snakes can discriminate between differences in temperature as small as one-tenth of a degree, Fahrenheit, as we learned in our laboratory by attaching an electrical connection to the trigeminal nerve and recording the results on an oscillograph. Other snakes such as the gopher snake, the red racers and their allies appear to do a great deal of their hunting by making a watchful traverse over their feeding grounds. At such times they definitely use their eyes as well as their chemo-receptive organs.

I was once resting in the shade of a grove of mixed sycamores and alders where Big Rock Creek opens out into the
desert north of Mt. San Antonio, or "Old Baldy." I was
motionless, and the twittering calls of nesting yellow war-
blers drew my attention to a nearby thicket whose under-
story was fairly open. To my surprise their calls alerted me
to a striped racer circling around a small densely foliaged
alder. Its head was raised some one-fourth of its total length
above the ground, obviously searching for food higher in
the tree. It paused and moved its head slowly from side to
side as it peered into the upper branches. Then it moved on,
stopped again, and continued searching for visual clues to
some object, presumably a nest, that would justify the effort
of climbing into the tree. As I discovered later, there was no
nest in the tree, nor were there any birds nearby. They were
flitting about well away from the snake's area of search. As
far as I could see, there was nothing attractive by odor or
sight in the tree itself to take the snake's attention. I can only
assume that the snake was using vision alone while alert to
the possibility of nests throughout the habitat in that season.

On another occasion I picked up a dead desert nighthawk
expecting to skin it later on in the day. By the time I reached
camp in an oasis of palm trees and cottonwoods the bird had
decomposed to the point where its feathers were loose and
it had an obnoxious odor. The day had been excessively hot.
Not being able to salvage the skin, I tossed the carcass some
15-20 feet away where it landed on the top of a small desert
bush and became caught in the twigs. About a half an hour
later, as I sat in the shade skinning some other birds, I saw
a red racer approaching my camp, screened from the bird
by intervening branches. It moved upward against a faint
breeze, actively exploring the air with its tongue and—because
of the elevation of its head—with its large round eyes as well.
As it stealthily crawled birdward, I was an immobile witness
to this intriguing spectacle. Never before or since have I had
the chance of seeing a wild snake approach what I knew to
be possible food. It curved over to the bush where the now
decaying bird was dangling. With reptilian efficiency of move-

ment it flexed its belly muscles over the twigs as it steadily mounted higher to the bird. With hardly a pause it began to swallow the reason for its chemoreceptive curiosity.

Both of these racers were using their eyes in their search, while the red racer was augmenting its hunting success by employing chemoreception, which the breeze and the presence of a decidedly smelly meal made possible for it. At that point I decided I should do far more reptile watching and less collecting!

The liers-in-wait for prey generally depend on vision, but from time to time they use other methods of detection. It is difficult for me to believe, however, that those that habitually crawl in search of food and capture it by a stealthy approach and a sudden strike would also resort to the equivalent amount of patient, watchful waiting. Crawlers are not likely

Plate 13. Careless littering and aimless target practice can have fatal results. Here a red racer was trapped by the sharp edges of the holes in the can and then exposed to the sun's heat.

to be waiters and vice versa, but there must be some over-lap in methods.

My present assumption is that aside from the highly spe-cialized feeders, such as the toothless African egg-eating snakes, most reptiles have a fair degree of flexibility in their food-getting behavior. There are a number of mammals, such as the termite-eaters, that have become such highly special-ized feeders that no other food can be used. I would assume a large amount of plasticity of behavior in most snakes and lizards and a degree of catholicity of taste regarding prey. Get-ting food is so difficult and chancy I expect that most hunters take what comes their way. We do know from the study of cer-tain birds that conditioning in the nest develops considerable degree of specialization, but with adverse changes in the envi-ronment possible, greater flexibility in diets is advantageous.

Raptorial, or predatory, birds occupy a good many ecolog-ical niches, as defined by their hunting habits. Among them all there is a fairly complete coverage of the various poten-tialities for food getting. Such variability lessens competi-tion and dependence on a single food source. Owls work at night and feed chiefly upon nocturnal animals or unwary day-active creatures that are panicked from their roost or shelter by the searching presence of a bird of prey. The size of the predator gives some indication of the size and power of its victim. The little midgets of the owl world, the elf and pigmy owls, feed on insects and other arthropods, supple-menting their diet by capturing small reptiles and birds. The great horned owl, by contrast, is capable of overpowering rabbits and even more remarkably, skunks. That skunks play a part in the dietary regimen of the horned owls is quite clear from the odor that many newly killed owls give off. At one time I was observing birds on a skunkless island in Puget Sound. I learned then that the horned owls foraged both on the mainland, where they were not infrequently sprayed by skunk odor, and on the islands for other types of prey. This is the only time an olfactory cue has given me insight into the extent of the territory of one of these owls.

Owls, being nocturnal, are seldom seen. For the most part

Plate 14. Territorial calling of the great horned owl is one of the memorable sounds of the desert night. Many of my students were badly frightened when they first heard its sonorous call.

what we learn about them is gathered from captive specimens, which may reveal only altered behavior. One of my
greatest pleasures in the field has been observing the various
hunting techniques of hawks, day-active raptors. Among
these one of the most superb and exciting species to watch
is the duck hawk. Back in the early 1930s I used to drop
down to the Santa Monica beach for a daily swim of a mile
or two depending on class schedules. During that delightful
distant time I often swam not far from a pair of duck hawks
occupying a ledge high on the cliff at the end of Santa Monica
Canyon. Between swims my favorite resting spot happened
to be almost immediately below them and from this vantage
point I watched them in operation.

My most entertaining and enlightening experiences came
when the early fall flocks of migrating sanderlings arrived.
These strongly gregarious birds would swing toward the beach
and settle in a mass to forage among the foam lines following
the retreating waves. Then the flock drifted up and down
as the water receded or advanced. When in flight their compact flocks are easily recognizable. They are the small shore
birds that in sudden marvelously responsive synchronized
swerves or long turns present either their light undersurfaces
as a mass of speckled white against the skyline or, then in
another turn, show their backs of tannish color equally well
outlined. In their maneuvering they flash first one and then
the other surface and thus are easily followed as they fly.

On a number of occasions one of the duck hawks took off
from its observation post high above the beach. The sanderlings immediately panicked, started to climb, and flew out
toward the open ocean. The duck hawk was soon after them,
chivying and herding them with leisurely wingbeats, first
in one direction and then another as the flock flew higher.
I noticed that as their flight continued, the shape of the flock
changed from approximately globular to pear-shaped. Then
it began to develop a stem-like end formed by two or three
wearying birds. Invariably one or more of these exhausted
sanderlings gave up and dove almost perpendicularly toward
the sea. This was the signal for which the duck hawk had

been waiting. It made its magnificent powered stoop toward one of the tired birds, and a puff of feathers signaled the victory for the one and death for the other. The hawk's tactics were so perfect they seemed to indicate an almost conscious wearing down of the flock to separate the weaklings that were easy to capture from the stronger individuals. We must rule out intelligent planning, of course, and instead credit the birds with a marvelously developed innate mechanism for assuring success with minimal waste of energy.

In those days I was able to follow duck hawks for many miles along the Coast Highway, which parallels the Pacific Ocean. In spring and autumn, rafts of migrating birds gathered in the open spaces between patches of kelp. Once I saw a duck hawk make numerous sham attacks on these aggregations of miscellaneous water birds, only to veer off and resume normal flight when all of the birds suddenly and simultaneously dove out of sight and disappeared. I had timed the speed of a duck hawk in normal flight (by varying the automobile speed so that the windwing continuously bracketed the bird, an excellent way of getting avian speed records). At coursing speed it maintained a ground average of 40 to 45 miles per hour, a noteworthy pace. The feints I was watching must have occurred at least a dozen times, but only in the last one did a resting bird's behavior become apparently different. This particular one appeared to be a cormorant, although at that distance I was unable to make certain of the species. Instead of diving to escape as did the others, the bird began flopping clumsily across the ocean surface toward the edge of the kelp. Of all the hundreds of birds spread beneath the duck hawk throughout its various sham stoops, this was the only one that did not synchronize its behavior with the rest of them. This was the bird the duck hawk chose in its final and successful downward power dive.

From these experiences and similar ones in Africa, now amply substantiated by those of other observers, I am quite convinced that some hunting predators rarely, if ever, seek out, pursue, and attack the most competent members of a prey species. To do so would be highly impractical in terms

of certainty of capture, the amount of energy that would necessarily be expended, and the relative value of the reward.
Personally, I believe that almost all hunting creatures are
amazingly specialized to detect and prey on the unobservant
and the distracted, the sick and the weak—the unfit.

13: Watching Eyes

Vision is far more than just the ability to see. In nature it must include what both predator and prey do to avoid being seen and how these devices interlock into patterns of nervous behavior that have only indirect connections with vision and the eye itself.

Many years ago I was tramping over the coastal hills on a quest for certain specimens. I paused on the edge of a small marsh and by chance glanced down at the ground near my foot. As if taking shape from the tangle of grass and twigs, a full-grown rabbit crouched motionless. Its eyes were open; only its barely twitching nostrils hinted at its fright. I was in full view and looming almost immediately above it, yet there it sat as immobile as though frozen stiff or stone dead. Purely by reflex I tried to pin it under my foot. My movement triggered its release mechanism, and the rabbit arched in a wild leap. As it spurted away, my foot missed its body but clamped down on its cottony tail. The momentum of the animal carried it forward leaving a neatly skinned two inches of furry white tuft on the ground. As I stooped to pick it up I pondered on the complexity of the vision-behavior pattern.

I remembered an incident from childhood. I had sought shade from the South African sun under a tree and was looking idly out into the light-dappled roadway. A small ring-necked dove was leaving a fretwork of foot prints behind it in the dust. Suddenly out of the corner of my eye I saw a cat stalking it from the grassy margin of the road. Like all cats engaged in such activity, it concealed its feet in a ground-hugging crouch and inched forward, almost imperceptibly diminishing the distance between the bird and itself. There were no overt strides to trigger the animal into flight, but its appearance startled the dove into "freezing." It stopped all motion, not even bobbing its head, and stood like a stuffed specimen in the center of the road while the cat crept toward it with only the tip of its tail, the remote part of its body, twitching spasmodically from time to time. Although I understood little about such episodes at that age, the excitement of the stalk, the hungry cat, and the frozen posture of the dove about to be converted into cat protein—all made for a tense and dramatic situation. It raised questions whose answers dawned on me only many years later. Never, however, has the selective advantage of tail twitching by stalking felids been accounted for.

As the distance between cat and bird grew shorter and still the dove made no attempt at escape, my small boy spirit trembled with excitement. My very human reaction mentally begged the bird to take off and save its life. For some reason I did not openly interfere. The part of me that was later to become a scientist was already curious about the outcome. I wanted to see what would happen "all by itself." At last, with hardly perceptible movements, the cat crouched and by a wiggling motion readied itself for the spring. Almost instantly, as though in response to that signal of intent, the bird sprang into the air. The cat jumped at the same moment but missed its prey by only a fraction of an inch.

Over the succeeding years I have witnessed several other examples of such seemingly maladjusted or stupid behavior, freezing in full view of the predator. We might even term it genetic folly—this demonstration of a widespread and apparently dangerous and valueless procedure. I think we can reason, however, that if natural selection works to perfect all animal behavior and insure the greatest survival, we can also assume that freezing in animals has some benefit. We can even give it a technical term, tonic immobility, and feel better but accomplish little. The new phrase provides no real explanation, but it keeps at bay the hint of hypnotism. Despite common beliefs, no nonhuman animal has the capacity to hypnotize other animals. It is true that under extreme fear certain animals become motionless, and only flee when circumstances release their set posture. But fear and hypnotism are unrelated. In fact, it is virtually impossible to hypnotize anyone when he or she is under the stress of great fear.

It is my experience that the only animals to freeze in the presence of danger are those whose greatest measure of security is by concealment through behavior and external coloration. On a statistical basis, interpreted in the light of natural selection, the best possible tactic for them to employ in the presence of a predator is to avoid attracting attention and to rely on probable invisibility. If never seen, they will never be captured by visually cued predators. Sooner or later, however, the accidents of existence will confront them with just such dilemmas as the foregoing examples represent; then flight becomes a matter of life and death. Those that fail to be triggered into flight by the awareness of danger are the ones that live the shortest lives and procreate the fewest times. Unless they die an early death, they will disseminate this behavioral malfunction to their offspring, among whom will be many who will suffer the same fates.

On numerous occasions I have experienced a strong inclination toward immobility in the presence of danger. With sudden and intense fear many people become motionless for a few fractions of a second until both source and nature of the threat are known. While hunting dangerous big game in South and East Africa I would stop without moving a muscle when I heard an unusual or unexpected sound in the bush. Only after this instant of immobility was I able to slowly turn my head in the direction of the noise and look for some indication of its source. This most often occurred after a day of exciting encounters with dangerous animals, and so I was unusually keyed to a high nervous pitch. I had the same reaction countless times during World War I while on guard duty at night. An unidentifiable sound around my dark post brought me to a halt, a period of listening, and even an olfactory testing of the air, all purely unconscious reflex responses to potential peril. Once I had identified a reason for my alarm, I followed with appropriate action.

I have often wondered if certain common mistakes in driving, such as slamming on the brake instead of accelerating when a car is bearing down from behind, or simply freezing to the steering wheel and doing nothing, may not be attributable to this resurrection of an old and almost atavistic instinct.

The fluttering of a parent bird around an assumed predator when nest or young are threatened is characteristic of a number of species. The "broken" wing or leg "act" is so realistic a behavior that almost anyone is tempted to follow the bird, even though he knows he will be led away from the nest and the parent will take off in perfect flight. One explanation suggests that fear cripples a bird's normal neuromuscular actions. Another proposes that the parent is consciously drawing an enemy from nest or young though endangering its own life. There seems to me to be less reason to ascribe the behavior to fear derangement or a deliberate attempt to mislead an adversary than to explain it as a form of tonic immobility. The functioning of instinctive behavior is so effective that we too easily attribute such behavior to intelligence.

When birds, and other animals, are panicked in behalf of their young or eggs, an automatic mechanism produces compulsive distress demonstrations as well as awkward retreat flight. As the danger diminishes with distance, the nerve and muscular impairment and other stresses caused by panic gradually subside. Suddenly acute anxiety ceases altogether, and the bird returns to normal behavior and later to its nest site.

The phenomena of tonic immobility may also be partly explained by the fact that the victim species are usually unable to see how close the predator is to them. Because of their need for acute peripheral vision—above, behind, and in front— the eyes of victim species are almost invariably placed prominently on each side of the head. This, unfortunately, is accompanied by a loss in their capacity for depth perception, or distance judging. In contrast, it appears, as far as I know, that the eyes of all visually cued predators either are mounted on the anterior, or face, of the head, enabling them to focus both eyes on an object and thus enhancing their ability to triangulate and in so doing judge distance, or their eyes must at least be so positioned as to allow rotation in a forward direction.

Figure 8. Great horned owls and bitterns have binocular fields of vision, and quail the monocular type. The diagrams indicate the range of view for each eye and where vision merges to give depth effect.

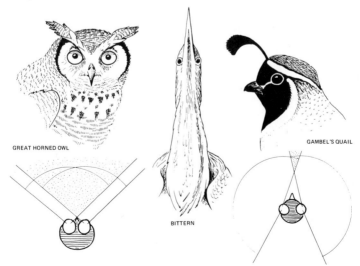

GREAT HORNED OWL

BITTERN

GAMBEL'S QUAIL

Judging from the positioning of their eyes, it seems of great importance to prey animals that they be able to see in all directions at once, even though that ability may deprive them of the sharpness or the acuity of stereoscopic vision. However, there may be a substitute for depth perception. The binocular vision in birds having well developed double fovea (areas of most acute vision) suggests this possibility. I have noticed in the field that many, though not all, of the animals with monocular vision also tend to bob their bodies and/or heads up and down with the eyes open, achieving the equivalent effect of binocular sight with depth perception. Others turn their heads rapidly from side to side as does the domestic chicken. Herons and a number of other birds have binocular vision directed along the tapered bill, which lies between the two eyes and thus obstructs part of their binocular field. When frightened or alerted by possible prey, these animals raise their heads to such a position that the beak points vertically, and the eyes look forward or down with lines of vision intersecting some distance away. In spite of this rather awkward stance, the animal probably enjoys excellent depth judgment.

Bitterns and little green herons when seen at close range have the most extraordinary appearance when they resort to this posture. They may look ridiculous to us, but it is of vital importance to them to have that apparently cross-eyed stare, as well as immobility, as they size up potential danger or possible prey. These little herons, furthermore, are more defenseless than the great blue and other large herons, and their attenuated head and neck, parallel to reeds, enhance concealment. The large species of heron, to my knowledge, do not ordinarily resort to such extreme head orientation. They are capable of vigorously defending themselves with their long sharp beaks and well muscled necks or, from their height, of detecting danger soon enough to take flight.

I saw a possible illustration of the value of binocular vision to predatory birds many years ago in Africa while collecting a pair of giant kingfishers. I needed both to complete a good scientific representation of the species. They lived near a shallow pool over which grew a tree they used for perching between diving forays for small fish in the sandy shoals below. As I picked up the birds I noticed that one had so repeatedly misjudged its plunging distance that its bill was frayed into a rounded, highly scratched tip. The other specimen had a perfect bill with no sign of repeated thrusting into the sandy bottom, though both fed in the same shallows and in the same way. I checked over the bird with the worn bill and discovered it was totally blind in one eye. I assumed that impaired sight also meant impaired fishing. The bird seemed to have hit the sand below the midwater target. It was sickly-looking, at any rate, perhaps because of malnutrition. If it was somewhat starved, the cause was either visual inefficiency or perhaps the malaise of persistent headaches! The jarring from repeated forceful contacts with the pool floor would rattle any fisherman, and until finally driven by intense hunger it was understandably reluctant to dive head first.

The tremendous ability of plunging birds to judge distance is to me, phenomenal. I witnessed a splendid example of this capacity once while sitting high on a ridge in the San Gabriel Mountains. Gazing down into a deep canyon some 500 feet below me, I watched a ground squirrel playing on the bare sand next to its burrow. I was suddenly aware of a roaring sound from above. It increased to a crescendo as a red-tailed hawk passed within a few feet of my head in an almost perpendicular dive down into and across to the bottom of the gorge. From its tremendous speed and the noise of its flight, I expected it to dash itself to pieces on the ground below. It aimed its course, however, directly at the ground squirrel. About a foot or so above the startled rodent, it extended its legs, grasped the squirrel, and with hardly a pause winged off down the sloping canyon. This was a magnificent demonstration of speed, power, and depth perception, and I was most impressed. In retrospect, probably any experienced slalom skier can judge distances equally as well and control his motions with the same degree of exactitude as the red-tailed hawk. We are not surprised at our own abilities, but we are sometimes unnecessarily overawed by the same capacities in animals we consider less endowed than ourselves.

How far one can go in the matter of substitutes for binocular vision is frankly speculation. Having given myself this latitude, I suggest the possibility that the pushups or head-bobbing or body-bobbing so common in lizards may serve several purposes. Such performances may increase depth perception when the position of the eye is shifted alternately upward and downward in a manner functionally similar to that of our eyeballs at close distance, superimposing two images from different head positions. Lizards go through such motions when excited—either in approaching territorial combat with their fellows, in courtship, or during jeopardy. When they are with other male members of their own species, the bobbing motions are often accompanied by gular, or throat, display, a flattening of the sides that exhibits bright colors, an impressive adjunct to their bluff. This display rarely occurs near dangerously close predators. It is possible that reaction to excitement because of danger from another male induces behavior closely similar to that elicited by a distant but feared predator. Thus display and bobbing may serve more than one use.

The only lizard that seems to have circumvented the compromise between need for peripheral vision for the detection of danger and binocular vision for precise measurements of distance is that pop-eyed oddity, the African chameleon. Its eyes protrude well beyond the margin of the head and are skin-covered except for the pupillary area. The chameleon can roll its eyes independently so that it can look forward with one eye and downward with the other, or back and forward, or simultaneously in a coordinated one-direction gaze. Each eye is completely independent of the other in this rotation. Thus, the chameleon can repeatedly view its entire surroundings, keeping an eye open, so to speak, for danger even while it is stalking its prey and is about to strike an insect with its potato-masher-shaped tongue. So far as I know, this extreme specialization of the tongue for capturing prey is, among reptiles, unique to this chameleon; its tongue may extend to better than half of its total body length and is very sensitive. The chameleon must need great precision in estimating distances while capturing food. When it is about to dart its tongue, both eyes rotate forward with the pupils aimed directly at the prey. While driving on freeways, I have long envied this ability for independent double vision. Though the human face would appear rather odd with chameleon eyes, think of all the advantages!

14: The Secret of
Success Is Blend

No one noticing the variegated and often brilliant coloring of wild creatures can avoid
wondering about the possible utility of such patterns and
hues. Before Darwin supplied the concept of natural selection
and evolution, animal coloration was anthropomorphically
explained as an obvious sexual attractant or as a God-given
ornament but otherwise as an inexplicable act of creation.

However, since Darwin, man has been freed to question
and explore for the causes of all natural phenomena, and
animal coloration has come to be one of the most commonly
employed examples of adaptation through natural selection

and of past and even contemporaneous evolution. We cite the beech moth blackening to match soot-darkened tree trunks in an industrialized England, along with other examples of current evolutionary history such as the growing resistance of scale and other insects to toxic sprays and of bacteria to antibiotics.

Because of such changes in the environment and the adaptive capabilities that make it possible to cope with these changes, the role of surface color is of great significance. The surface of an animal's body together with such integumentary structures as chitinous scales and keratinous feathers or hairs comprise the most extensive interface between the organism and its frequently hostile environment. This cuticular exterior makes detection, possession, and use of the potential nourishment inside difficult for the would-be user. Detection depends on acuity of vision, hearing, and smell—chemoreception—or a combination of all three. The skin and its covering, however, is a perceptible, and thus vulnerable, boundary between the animal's nutritious inner body and the hungry world.

Generation after generation, vast hordes of young are precipitated into limited habitats, and all of these infants are confronted with numerous problems of survival. Zoologists have the task of unraveling the equally numerous skeins of adaptation—including animal coloration—which millions of generations of every species have devised to surmount the heavy death toll.

Because of their sheer numbers, all organisms in their youthful stages experience a most ruthless weeding out. Once they achieve adulthood, survival through the entire period of reproductivity remains a major problem for the species. Natural selection continues to operate throughout adult life. There is no moratorium on its ever-present dangers to the individual and, certainly at any stage of the life cycle, escape from visual detection by enemies is a prime necessity.

If all of the visible wavelengths of light in the full spectrum of the rainbow—or of a prism that separates white light into its component parts—are completely absorbed, the result, in effect, is total nonreflectivity. The reflected visible light is reduced to a level where the human retina cannot send nerve messages to the brain. This absence of retinal response is what we call black. On the other hand, if all wavelengths of visible light are reflected equally and with no loss, we have the sensation of white light. This is the same light which, when broken up and differentially absorbed or reflected, gives us the full range of color. The clarity of any one part of the spectrum that is reflected to the eye will be governed by the amount, variety, and place of absorption of other wavelengths. Hues, or colors, are the product of absorption and reflection of different parts of the spectrum. Because no animal (except those with bioluminescence or phosphorescence) actually emits light, what we see as its color is purely a matter of reflection and absorption—the elementary physics of light.

Brightness of any object, or lack of it, is caused by the amount of absorption versus reflection of the total incident visible light. In living things this is most commonly modified through the medium of a black, or light-absorbing pigment known as melanin contained in cells, or melanophores. These cells appear to contract or expand, that is, they can cover greater or smaller areas in the skin of an organism, or they may be differentially arranged to form streaks or spots of black. The nutritional input, the breakdown of certain elements in food, and their use or elimination by the body that result in these skin colors involve a variety of metabolic activities. Of equal significance is the skin's relationship to the various environmental influences, appropriate body shape, and correlated nerve and muscle behavior.

Most of us have seen trees such as maples, aspens, or cottonwoods on a calm day when a puff of air may set one or two leaves into motion whereas the rest remain immobile. When this occurs, the moving leaf out of the thousands of leaves on the tree immediately draws our attention. In a very simple way, this illustrates the enormous importance of motion to our visual consciousness. Anything that moves among stationary objects gets our immediate attention, while the unmoving may, if small enough, almost completely escape our notice. An unmoving object is quite perceptible to our retina and brain. But compared with something that moves—just as with still versus moving pictures—a motionless object will be less likely to become a part of conscious perception. Probably most predators (and omnivores) have the same limitations as we have and are more visually stimulated by something that moves, particularly if this something is dangerous or edible. Therefore motion, which so quickly draws attention, can also undo or nullify almost any concealing coloration no matter how effective it might be for a motionless animal.

Plate 15. The Devil's Cactus Garden just below the eastern scarp of Mt. San Jacinto. Whitewater Wash lies between this wild "garden" and the lower slopes of the famed peak. It was on gravel wash beds such as this that I first noted the astonishing ability of many desert reptiles to blend with the color and patterning of the gravelly substrate.

When a rabbit jumps out from concealing undergrowth, my momentary pause has alarmed it; and it immediately reveals itself to me through its motion, otherwise I might have passed on and never seen it. My pause indicated to the rabbit—which had been watching me all the time—that I had possibly detected it and was about to attack. Though this required no real thought on the part of the rabbit, its ancestors' accumulated experience led to the survival of rabbits that did not rely on escaping through concealment alone. Inherited behavior patterns triggered the rabbit into adopting another way of remaining alive—running when necessary. Concealing coloration, along with the release-to-flight mechanism, is a double-pronged adaptation of important survival value.

The predator itself needs to be inconspicuous in order to be an effective hunter. To live successfully it must have not only the advantage of teeth, claws, agility, and strength, but—as no prey voluntarily submits itself as food for predators—it must also circumvent the keen eyesight of its intended prey and become as nearly invisible as possible. If the predator is one that lies patiently and waits for the arrival of food, it must also have the nervous control to remain motionless. If it stalks its prey, it must be inconspicuous until the last moment.

The color patterns of predators are essential to their efficiency and ultimate survival. To locate and capture prey they must move and risk revealing themselves, thus in part nullifying the value of camouflage coloration. Anyone looking at motion pictures of tigers or seeing them in their native haunts has probably been aware of not only the beauty of their stripes but also the difficulty of seeing them until they move into full view. When lions wish to conceal themselves, they are virtually invisible in their quite different type of habitat, now mainly the grasslands and savannas of Africa. Against that background they are, when motionless, extremely difficult to detect. Though many millions of people have had years of experience in outdoor life in North America's western mountains and wilderness areas, most of them have never seen a mountain lion even though in national parks and other protected places it is a comparatively common animal. It is quite possible that thousands of visitors to such parks and forested areas may have passed within a hundred yards or so—well within seeing distance—of scores of these supposedly rare creatures yet had failed to get a glimpse of them. Tigers roam in tall grass, canes, and other tangles of vegetation; leopards frequent thorny scrub or the edge of the forest; lions hunt in grassy savannas. They, like all predators, must conform to the need for concealment from their intended victims as well as from enemies.

The sharply marked black and white creatures, such as skunks, seem very conspicuous, and it is difficult to conceive of them as being effectively concealed. Skunks, however, are exclusively nocturnal and they possess a remarkable characteristic—gas defense. It may well be that rather than to conceal themselves they have greater need to advertise their identity and special means of defense against attack, injury, or death by predators. Skunks are comparatively slow, and they show little runaway panic when they are encountered at night or at dawn or dusk. They also apparently give warning of their nature by raising their white tails, stamping their feet, and moving their bodies to make themselves conspicuous. Their coloration, as we view it from our stance, is admirably designed to notify all predators that though they may be killed they will leave an indelible odor on the victor. However, from a mouse-eye-view (and mice are one of the skunk's chief foods), as the naturalist-artist Louis Fuertes used to point out in his lectures on concealing coloration, skunks are nicely concealed from the prey—white top side blending with the skyline and their black underside with the shadows beneath vegetation. It seems probable that skunks have a double-barreled reason for their remarkable coloration: advertisement against predators and concealment from their prey.

Having mentioned the skunk as an example of the usefulness of advertising a special type of weaponry with distinctive color, there are similar examples in the world of insects—wasps, stinkbugs, ladybird beetles, and numerous butterflies, among them. Seemingly helpless and toothsome, to insectivores, they advertise their identity by conspicuous colors and an attention-getting manner. They have retaliatory weapons, nevertheless. Several ladybird beetles emit repellent material from glands placed in various parts of their bodies. Other insects squirt or spit disagreeable substances such as formic acid on their adversaries. Very few hungry animals can stand the taste or smell of these creatures. A number of them are actually toxic with serious effects for their unwary predators. The most dramatic weapon of this nature is the sting. Many caterpillars, some of them tropical, have stinging hairs or spines which are capable of producing a most unpleasant irritation. Bees and wasps have stinging apparatuses, complete with venom glands, at the tip of the abdomen.

Many of these defenses, however, are useless in an immediate sense. The predator is only aware of bad taste or other disagreeable effects after it has attacked the victim. What advantage are such weapons if their possessors are injured or destroyed while in the process of using them? By flaunting possession of potent but delayed-action devices, they depend on the memory of unpleasant past encounters to protect them. (I return to an old theme: a few individuals must be sacrificed for the good of the species.) There are even other species which mimic those with such defenses even when they themselves do not have them. One learns to suspect repellant qualities of some kind in all brightly colored small creatures with no other types of defense. It appears to be universal that animal life has some means of protection, either for keeping out of sight or for penalizing any predator which ignores its victim's advertisement.

From the time of Darwin and his famous contemporary, Alfred Wallace, volumes have been written on the subject of concealing or adaptive coloration. Yet few of these volumes have dealt with coloration in the races of mankind. If, during much of our past history, we have needed concealment from possible predators as well as from the prey we have been seeking, should we not search for an explanation of racial color in the ecological role of early man? That is, why not from the standpoint of his success in getting food for himself and young while stalking prey and avoiding becoming food for other creatures?

Before pursuing an inquiry into the origins of human coloration, we need to delve further into the phenomenon of total reflectance—albedo, or the coefficient of reflection of visible light. We have seen that it is one of the very important properties of coloration that any object that reflects all wavelengths is white, whereas one that absorbs all wavelengths is black. Human vision depends on a system of nerve structures that extends from the retina of the eye to the brain, the retina responding to light stimulation and the brain interpreting the messages from the retina. An object reflecting no light is obviously invisible except against a visible background. If it reflects no incident light, then its seeming visibility comes exclusively from the contrast between the surrounding reflectance and its own lack of reflection. A black object shows only because its reflecting environment provides the necessary contrast. All black objects in an equally black environment merge invisibly just as do all white objects in a totally white environment. Black against white or white against black is very conspicuous indeed, and the degree of conspicuousness is determined by the relative degree of surface reflection, or lack of it. If the black or white object is a predator and it is, at times or during certain seasons, dependent for survival on successful hunting, then to be black against white or white against black would be a severe handicap, preventing success in hunting and the procurement of food for self and family.

On a dark, moonless night black objects are extremely difficult to see, in fact they are not actually seen unless they reflect what little light there may be. Conversely, in daytime a black object in surroundings that are highly reflective will become very conspicuous. Any black-skinned predator attempting to hunt in shadowless, sun-drenched fields would be so conspicuous that its pursuit of prey would be arduous and usually futile, as well as uncomfortably hot if such a predator lived in warm climates. These facts may explain the total absence of wholly black predators of any size whose bodies extend above the surrounding grass or brush. Such animals would stand out and would have far less chance of surviving either as individuals or as a species than would others more suitable for concealment in open savanna country. The only almost totally black, wholly predatory animal of any size is the occasional nocturnal melanistic leopard of forest, bush, and savanna. While bears are usually classified as predators and are often black or very dark brown, they are in reality not truly carnivores in the sense that they live exclusively on other vertebrates. Much of their protein food is gathered by turning over logs in the search for concealed insect grubs. Bears do not go out and hunt down healthy, large prey, which can all too easily escape through alertness, visual acuity, and speed. Anything but a very sick rabbit can readily avoid capture by bears. They are therefore chiefly omnivorous and are carrion eaters rather than active predators. Even so, most of the black-furred bears are denizens of dense woodlands or live at the margins of woodlands where intermingled sunlight and shade provide not only the greatest abundance of food but a measure of shadow as well.

Returning to the subject of man's skin color and more specifically to the black or dark skin of essentially tropical people, if we are to develop a workable hypothesis, we must go far back in time to when man was living at his simplest and with very crude weapons such as clubs and modified digging sticks. He was most truly and helplessly a part of nature in the african continent where he had his origins. From there with ever more sophisticated cultures he spread to other lands, some of which were vastly different from his original environment.

Assuming that the hominoid primates originated in the African tropics around 4,000,000 years ago (the date changes with each new fossil discovery), what environmental factors might have contributed to the coloration we see in the descendants of early man today? If, at critical times in the life of the species, man was definitely a predator, he needed concealment from his prey. If at that remote time he also had often been prey for some other predator, he would have had an overwhelming need for concealment, especially when he was concentrating on the hunt or he was weaponless while gathering firewood or going about other activity. The importance of concealment becomes doubly necessary if one is both predator and prey.

Ancient man's success was probably greatest in areas that provided the largest amounts of food and shelter. Such places are still found along forest margins or, alternatively, under groves of trees where there are patches of shade and sunlight, such as we still find scattered throughout Africa's savanna country.

To have been a successful hunter ancient man probably lingered in the trees at the margins of forest and savanna, taking advantage of the concealment within or under the tall, shade-casting vegetation as he crept to within the arm's-length distance of his prey demanded by his weapons. With nothing more effective than hand-held stones or clubs, this close approach was unavoidable, and to stalk prey successfully he would need to be carefully hidden. Under these circumstances the best concealment might have been a skin coloration resembling the leopard: light-and-dark spots rather than a solid black or white. Broken patterns of light and dark that best matched the scattering of light in marginal areas or under trees within the savanna proper should logically have been most suited. This raises the logical question: why has man not demonstrated in his genes this admirable spotted or striped protective coloration? Even at this late date why is it that we do not encounter occasional individuals that are piebald or spotted rather than uni-colored? We can only speculate as to why man was and is not so marked. Prey animals in the depth of the forest are almost universally dark and (except for the leopard, which is probably not often a prey animal) when adult they are rarely spotted. Presumably, if it moves any light spot in a very dark or heavily shaded area becomes a target for the eye, quickly attracting notice. Man, in his search for food, needed to move both in and out of forested areas, thus requiring a pattern of coloration not inappropriate for the shadow-dappled forest margins but affording the best concealment within the darker interior where he no doubt took shelter. A spotted skin would probably have served well while he hunted within or at the edges of the savanna, but it would have concealed him less effectively in the deeper forest where, resting or sleeping, he was more vulnerable to predation. It is of interest that forest-dwelling monkeys have dark brown or blackish faces except for the colobus monkey, a black-and-white tree-top denizen often posed against the bright sky.

It has been conventional to explain the black color of predominantly tropical people in terms of the physiological advantages of a black skin in heat regulation and in protection from ultraviolet wavelengths. Presumably black-skinned people may have survived in these warm climates better than those white-skinned. By vague and circular reasoning the notion has been expounded that black-skinned people live in the tropics and work in the tropics, therefore black skins *must* be advantageous in terms of heat. This is easily refuted. By absorbing so much of the white light, black-skinned people add to their total net (environmental and metabolic) heat load. Most tropical people assiduously avoid work during the midday hours. They work early and late or on cool, cloudy days, and this is also the time when hunting is most effective. "Only English people and fools work in the heat of the day."

When the argument in favor of heat protection is refuted, the next line of physiological defense is to assert that in some way the black-skinned—the people with heavy concentrations of melanin in the integumentary tissues—must have a selected advantage in avoiding erythema and skin damage that is sometimes followed by skin cancer and ultimately by death. Unfortunately for this argument, fatal skin cancers usually develop late in life—rarely during the reproductive years. Additionally, the primary defense of the human skin against too much ultraviolet light lies in its stratum corneum, a thin surface layer that, though transparent, reflects rather than transmits much of the impinging ultraviolet light. A stratum corneum, stimulated to additional thickness by exposure to sunlight, appears to be the primary defense against the shortwaves of light; at best, the pigmented area serves as a beneficial backup. It is true that dark-skinned people suffer less from skin cancer than do blonds or others with light skins. The most effective argument, however, against blackness as a protection from skin cancer is the fact that throughout the tropics most procreation occurs before age 30. That number of years is also the normal life span among primitive peoples generally. The supposed selection through death by skin cancer occurs at a more advanced age even among the much more sensitive fair-skinned people living in the tropics. A skin-cancer victim seldom dies until the late forties or, even more probably, in the fifties or sixties. Such a time in life is too late, of itself, to be a definitive factor in natural selection for skin pigmentation. Thus, if there is any reason for heavily pigmented skins to be concentrated in the tropics, with its predominantly tall trees and shady vegetation, then it would seem to be most reasonable to suppose that concealment may have been the definitive factor, and the skin's physiological advantages are only secondary in importance.

If we presume that man originated in tropical Africa and from there spread outward across the accessible world, we still have to explain the oddest skin color of all, that of "white" in the Nordic people of western Europe. The more easily understandable intermediate shades between black and white— namely reddish, yellowish, and brown—occur mostly in the Temperate Zone. To explain white skins, however, some factor other than concealment appears to be involved in the change of color of once-tropical people as they migrated from the center of human origin, Africa, to northern regions. White skins might be harder to see during times of snow, but not in the warmer part of the year when pale skins would be conspicuous. It is possible, of course, that the difficulty of securing animal food in winter may have been the decisive factor. However, this seems a trifle far-fetched. With new tools, hunting techniques, clothing, and ways of life, the ex-Africans might simply have been able to dispense with any particular skin color. In other words, there just was not any survival value in having pigmented skin.

Recently it has been proposed that another factor that may have played a decisive role is the need for the metabolically indispensable hormone, calciferol, and its dependence on the skin-penetrating ultraviolet light in the wavelengths of 290 to 320 millimicrons. This is necessary for the production of what was once called vitamin D, now reclassified as a hormone. W. F. Loomis (*Scientific American,* December, 1970) makes a strong case for the advantage in blondness in regions that are chronically or annually beset by low levels of sunshine. Conversely, he argues that heavily pigmented skins may be a protection against overproduction of this skin hormone in sunny areas.

In a thorough review, however, of the subject, Harold F. Blum (*Quarterly Review of Biology,* Vol. 36, 1961) pointed out that the thickness of the thin, outermost layer of the skin (the stratum corneum)—seen in the white scurfy lines left on a tanned skin by light scratching—constitutes an equally or more important regulating device than does the underlying pigment. Furthermore, the layer adaptatively thickens under exposure to light and thins in its absence. This characteristic is also found in black and dark-skinned people such as the Asiatics who also tan. Confusing the issue still further is the acquisition of adequate amounts of calciferol ("vitamin D") by the means of diet. In this respect rickets-suffering slum dwellers, who also constitute the most poverty-stricken segment of western society, are therefore the least able to afford foods rich in this antirachitic substance. Possibly the comparatively recent mandatory fortification of milk with calciferol accounts for the large size and strong bones of many of the present-day black basketball and football giants. Diet rather than ultraviolet light may be the responsible factor.

Dark or adaptatively darkening skin as a protection against sunburn (erythema), often attended by the much later onset of skin cancer, is also accompanied by the more significant simultaneous proliferation of the protective stratum corneum. Even the pigmentless albinos, whose skin cannot darken but whose cornified, or horny-tissued, layer of skin thickens on exposure to insolation, may not be prone to sunburn. One can only conclude that the details of this biological phenomenon, like so many others, are seldom conclusively explained by a simple all-or-none factor. This is the reason why Pieter

Dullemeijer of the University of Leyden, The Netherlands, has been so successfully employing a holistic (all of the angles) approach to his studies and teaching of vertebrate anatomy. With all factors in mind, I can only conclude that man, like all other organisms, is a working synergistic summation of the evolutionary acquisitions needed for existence and that perhaps concealment was one of the earliest necessities for survival. After all, most if not all animals except the warningly colored, benefit immeasurably from having the least possible visibility to their prey or their always lurking predators.

Another train of thought is evoked by the fact that people living in the excessively hot-and-cold climates of the Temperate Zone resorted to clothing of animal skins. By so doing they must have minimized their need for skin color concealment since they were borrowing the integument of other locally adapted creatures. Under these circumstances, a mutation leading to white skins could have survived despite their adverse skin coloring. With each advance in culture, whether of weapons, agriculture, food habits, or clothing, survival was enhanced possibly to the point where concealment was of little value.

We may never learn the true answers to the questions of the origin and evolution of man's skin color. But it is certain that we will have less chance of learning them if we concentrate wholly on what seems to be the fragile ground of physiological protection, even though this factor may have contributed to early man's original adaptability to tropical and other climates.

Gloger's rule holds true for virtually all other terrestrial animals. Where reflectivity in the environment is highest, as in cold or arid lands, animals tend to be lighter in color, whereas in the warm, humid lands that encourage forest growth they tend toward dark colors. Should we expect that man in his early stages should be so notable an exception to the general rules of pigmentation?

15: Discarded Tails and Blood-Spitting Eyes

*R*eflexive self-dismemberment, or autotomy, in lizards is a widely known phenomenon. Probably every youngster who has collected these little reptiles has discovered that in many species to catch them by the tail is tantamount to losing the important part, the body as a whole. The first experiences come as a shock, especially as the nerve and muscles in the detached tail continue to twitch violently as if in pain.

The strange mechanism for voluntary detachment is dramatically well developed in some species such as yucca and granite night lizards, geckos, and the skinks, with their gorgeously colored blue or pink tails. A touch on the body is enough to produce detachment of the tail if the animal is frightened enough. It wiggles strongly and attracts more attention than the body of the lizard, which in the meantime is either immobilized from fear or scuttling to cover. The writhing, almost bouncing tail tempts the would-be captor who pounces on it, letting the bigger mouthful, the self-amputated lizard, escape. At one time I owned a pet weasel that fed voraciously on lizards. It was repeatedly so misled by the writhing tail that it often allowed its prey to escape under a rock in the corner of the cage. The weasel never did catch on to the deception.

In general, movement is the primary trigger for attention and attack by visually cued predatory animals. Anything moving is noticed for capture, whereas a motionless object is often ignored. I have observed this escape device innumerable times. When I place my hand on a laboratory or field-captured lizard, it freezes to immobility but leaps to escape as soon as I lift my hand. Predators as well as human experimenters tend to hold on to a struggling animal and grip it tightly to prevent its flight to freedom. If it calms down and becomes motionless, we usually relax our hold. The animal takes advantage of this momentary relinquishment and immediately jumps away to shelter. I find it significant that the yucca night lizard's tail is more readily detached when the animal is living than when it is dead.

There is very little visible bleeding in a tail that has been voluntarily dismembered. Constriction of the blood vessels occurs simultaneously with autotomy. This prevents both a loss of blood and its tell-tale trail. Also, a lizard's tail does not break between the vertebral sections but within the vertebral bones. The groups of muscles, or myotomes, are not torn but come out in discrete sections. The broken ends can be temporarily fitted or mortised back into the cavities remaining when the tail is dropped off. Lizards, of course, do not use the neatness of this device to graft the disconnected member back onto the body. Instead, they grow new appendages whose appearance and scalation are quite different from the original tail.

This "mortise and tenon" appearance, however, has given rise to a widely held legend that after escape the lizard returns and reassembles the pieces of its caudal appendage and happily proceeds on its way. This story is told again and again in folklore, especially about the midwestern glass "snake," which is really an attenuated, limbless lizard. Its tail is so large and long that it is often thought to be a part of the body. After danger has passed the glass "snake" supposedly returns, reassembles the discarded parts, grafts them onto its body, and continues about its business, unaffected by the disaster. The legend does not take into consideration what might happen if a piece were removed by the predator, leaving the victim minus an essential connecting segment.

Many years ago I debunked the legend and promptly received numerous letters saying that I was all wrong. The glass "snake" did return and reassemble itself, my critics insisted. One person said that he had even experimented

Figure 9. Muscle bundles readily come apart during autotomy, and this diagram illustrates the mortar-and-tenon "fit." The regenerated tail almost always looks somewhat different from the original. In many lizards the new scales are usually smaller.

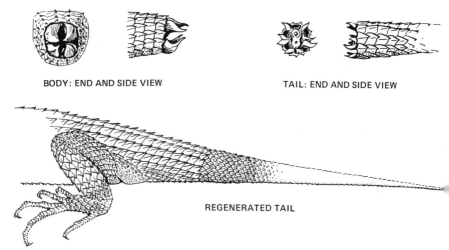

MUSCLE BUNDLES AT TIME OF BREAK

BODY: END AND SIDE VIEW   TAIL: END AND SIDE VIEW

REGENERATED TAIL

with such a reptile that had been torn into five segments. He collected all the parts and placed them in a box. Now came the proof. He returned the next day and found the box open and the lizard gone! That other explanations might have made more sense did not occur to him.

Curiosity led me to experiment very casually on one of a pair of desert iguanas I saw wandering along a sandy slope one day much interested in each other. They were also picking up morsels of food as they walked leisurely past my canal-side shack about 25 yards away. Well within good shooting range with a .22 rifle, I aimed for a spot about two-thirds of the distance back from the lizard's body and amputated the tip of its tail. Since the iguanas were on a slope, the disconnected tail tip started rolling downward, wiggling as it went. At once the dispossessed owner darted in pursuit, picked it up, mouthed it, and dropped it, only to chase it again until both lizard and tail piece reached the bottom of the bank. The lizard appeared confused by what it was mouthing, but it did not eat it. Cannibalism is rare in this predominately herbivorous lizard. After finally discarding the piece of its own body, it walked up the bank and joined what I presumed was its mate, apparently entirely undisturbed by the event. Obviously any pain messages from tail to brain were at such a low level they did not divert the deprived owner from inspecting the tail fragment as a potential morsel of food.

The regenerated tail differs from the original in scale pattern, and the new vertebrae are cartilaginous rather than bony. If autotomy is practiced again, it will not be through the newly grown segment but through the region anterior to the former breaking point. In rare instances where the break has not been complete the lizards may develop two tails.

The horned lizards of the Southwest do not self-amputate their stubby tails, but some species have one of the most bizarre defense mechanisms of any vertebrate. They discharge a fine spray of blood from a point in the lower eyelid. Apparently they obtain partial immunity at least from some kinds of enemies by this behavior. For years I had assumed that the blood-squirting "horny toads" were mere legends, as I had collected many horned lizards without witnessing such behavior. I was becoming convinced that even reports in scientific literature must be erroneous interpretations of some other activity. One sunny morning in our local hills, however, changed my point-of-view. I was out scouting a possible collecting area when I noticed a dog barking at something on the ground. My curiosity aroused, I investigated and discovered it was pretending an attack on a horned lizard. The dog was bouncing around it, charging in to bark and then retreating. The lizard remained motionless as I walked toward it and reached down to pick it up. When I touched it I realized that my shirt sleeve was stippled with red droplets. Examining its head, I discovered that the region around the eye was suffused with blood.

A noisy pouncing dog will induce one reaction and a careful hand another. Subsequently I frightened a number of horned lizards into squirting blood, but I was no rival of a lively dog. It was far more successful than me in evoking this peculiar response. The dog was still around after I had been sprayed, ill at ease and evidently nervous and excited. I called to it and patted its head as it approached me. For some reason (again, triggered by curiosity?) I slipped my bloody finger into its mouth. To my surprise it gave every evidence of extreme distaste. Shaking its head and still dripping moisture from excess salivation, it retreated from me. Son-of-a-gun, I muttered to myself. Is the blood so distasteful to a potential predator that, if squirted, it would not bite or injure the lizard? I immediately moistened my finger in the blood from the eye socket and tasted it, but I could sense nothing objectionable.

When roughly handled, the coastal horned lizards sometimes suffuse their head region with a thin film of non-bloody moisture, probably from some ocular gland. When I returned to my laboratory that afternoon I smelled the head of one I had captured; there was a slightly acrid, metallic odor, quite different from the rest of the body. Was it possible that this special secretion could have repulsive qualities? Following up these observations, I introduced horned lizards to a white rat and to a cat. To my surprise I found that neither showed any aversion whatsoever. In fact, the white rat not only feasted on the body of the reptile but evidently relished the head! I found no dogs, however, that did not evidence extreme dislike of the odor of a horned lizard's head. Cats indicated little or no repulsion. Checking further at the San Diego Zoo, I learned that certain members of the dog family—coyotes and foxes—were also repelled by the odor. It is clear to me that some species in the dog group react with considerable distaste to horned lizards. Blood and whatever fluid causing this discomfort are mixed and discharged in a fine spray, giving the lizard protection from one type of enemy at least.

These experiences were so experimentally tempting that I and one of my fellow staff members, Gretchen Burleson, made histological investigations of the region around the eye of the horned lizard. Apparently there is a weak spot in the lower eyelid. When blood pressure in the head rises markedly, this may rupture and discharge blood mixed with fluid from the Harderian and tear glands. The mixture is certainly efficient in repelling certain predators and illustrates a not uncommon fact of nature: any device for self-preservation provides protection only from a part of the threatening environment, seldom, if ever, from all enemies.

Rattlesnakes, however, possess an admirable protective device that serves as a safeguard from most predators, with, I believe, the exception of bobcats (western lynx). Once on rounding a bend of a highway I surprised a two-thirds grown bobcat. It had a freshly killed rattlesnake in its mouth and was carrying it away into the roadside brush. A former student of mine, Dr. Willis Pequegnat, also came upon a bobcat that had killed a rattlesnake. He leaped out of the car to investigate. The snake's tracks revealed that it had crawled out onto the road to sun itself. There it had been surprised by the bobcat, which apparently sprang from a high bank onto the ground beside the snake and killed it. In consuming its prey it had eaten first the head—poison glands, fangs, and all! Taken aback by its visitor, it dropped the body and fled for cover.

Skunks are probably safe from attack by most predators, but great horned owls have been known to utilize them for food. The flat little relative of the skate, known as the sting-ray, has a weapon in its tail that causes excruciating agony in a human being. Certain sharks, however, apparently feed by preference on these creatures. Many of the stings end up embedded in the cartilage of shark jaws, with no evidence of inflammation or pain.

Returning to the horned lizard, its eyelid blood is released by an intriguing vascular device, Bowman's swell mechanism—a control valve in the internal jugular vein that under special stress restricts the return of blood, thus increasing blood pressure within the head of the lizard. When the reptile is threatened the valve is activated, blood pressure mounts, the eyes bulge, and the weak spot in the eyelid ruptures, causing the discharge of blood. A similar vascular-pressure control device has been observed in the fringe-toed sand lizard, *Uma notata*, by Dr. Robert C. Stebbins while he was searching for mechanisms that protect the eye from damage by sand entry. According to this former student of mine, now one of the foremost herpetologists of the United States, some fine dust does penetrate through the outer defenses of the sand lizard's eyelid, but from time to time the swell mechanism comes into play. The accumulated dust is rolled up by a mucus-like secretion. Bulging of the eye and swelling of the third eyelid sinus at the corner of the eye exposes the packaged dust so that a delicate flick of a hind toe removes the debris. I have no doubt that other sand-dwelling lizards are capable of the same contrivance.

Although the eyes of reptiles, particularly of snakes, are generally regarded with superstitious horror, they are fully as interesting and, in their way, as beautiful as those of other animals. There are no mystical qualities about reptilian eyes and their "glassy stare." They are like those of other animals and designed for coordination with the environment—perception of food, predators, and obstacles in their path—and for more obscure functions such as activating circadian rhythms—biological clocks or innate rhythms based roughly on the 24-hour day. Above all, the eyes must be protected from damage and the consequent impairment of the animal's ability to survive.

As they evolved from lizards, snakes abandoned movable eyelids as such. Instead, they universally possess "spectacles," made from the same keratinous material as the scales of the body. Beautifully transparent, a complete close-fitting scale covers the outer surface of the eye, a "contact lens," if you will, sealed around the edges to prevent the entrance of dust. It is sufficiently strong and elastic to give ample protection against mechanical damage to the eye. These spectacles are renewed each time that the rest of the cornified (keratinous) covering of the skin is shed. The transparent envelop of the cornified material sloughed off by snakes always contains this eye sheathing under normal conditions, and one can examine it at leisure.

I have experimented with an interesting photographic technique by floating out the thin, transparent covering of the head and body onto a piece of optical-quality glass. After allowing the whole cornified layer to dry until it adhered tightly to the glass, I used it as a negative through which I projected light onto photographic enlarging paper. To my delight, the simple process made high-fidelity photographic copies of the head's scalation for permanent taxonomic records (identification of reptile species requires use of the head scalation). Sometimes I had to manipulate things a bit to get maximum rendition of all the scales, but this required very little alteration of the contours as I spread the diaphanous material onto the slide.

The eyelids of the fringe-toed sand lizard are arranged in a scalloped pattern, and the mechanisms for closure against dust are truly superb. One should examine the eyes carefully to appreciate fully the beauty of the devices for protection against dust entry and other injury. The use of Bowman's swell device in protruding the eyeball, and thus exposing the small pellet of dust, is merely a secondary defense against sand, another bullet left in the gun, as it were. Additionally, the position of the eye with respect to what we might call the "eyebrow" and the color of the iris and tissues around the

Plate 16. The valvular sand-swimming fringe on the toes of the fringe-toed sand lizard fold out and spread on the pushing stroke of the foot.

Plate 17. Tracks of the fringe-toed lizard, *Uma inorata*. The direction in which it was running is indicated by the tail marks that underscore each of the upper row of contacts by the hind foot. At high speeds these animals run on their hind feet.

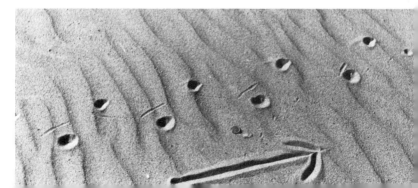

Plate 18. The encircled white spot is the pineal or third eye of an adult western fence lizard, *Sceloporus occidentalis*. (photograph from *The Third Eye*, Richard M. Eakin, University of California Press, 1973. Credit: Eakin and Blaker)

eye afford protection against the excessive glare of light and its reflection from the open, sandy, light-colored desert soils.

Until rather recently few comments have been made regarding the presence of a "third eye" on the top of the head of the fringe-toed sand lizard. This third, or parietal, eye is such a conspicuous feature that its careful study should not have been so long overlooked by herpetologists searching for evolutionary, physiological, and other relict or active functions. If you have the chance, take a hand lens and look at the top of the head of one of these creatures in the parietal area back between the eyes and in the center of the dorsal part of the head. You will see a beautiful iris-like yellow circle with a black center that resembles the pupil of "seeing" eyes. This third eye has been commented upon extensively as a unique feature of a very primitive reptile, the *Sphenodon*, or tuatara, its Maori name, a living relic from the age of the dinosaurs. Actually, the third eye in this reptile almost disappears as the animal approaches adulthood, whereas in the fringe-toed sand lizard it remains conspicuous, far more so than at any stage in *Sphenodon*. Under a hand lens with even reasonably low magnification it gives all the appearance of a normal eye with iris and pupil. As in the snakes, the surface of this vestigial organ is protected by a spectacle-like corneal covering.

In none of the examples of a third eye in terrestrial reptiles is there any mechanism for true vision. It does not see objects in the environment as do regular eyes. For this reason it was thought to be a nonfunctional vestige of a useful third eye known to have been present in earlier ancestors such as the dinosaurs. If it is completely nonfunctional, it is remarkable that such a structure has been retained over so many eons of time. More logically, one could assume that if vision is not available through this eye some other useful feature is present, retained under the aegis of natural selection. Cave salamanders and fish, having had no chance to use their eyes over a period of time far shorter than that through which the third eye has survived, became blind simply because of some non-selective direction of evolution. Therefore, this long-retained supplemental structure should have some functional value for its possessor. It appears to be involved in the control of total light assimilation by the animal.

The third eye has long been under investigation, chiefly by Stebbins and his co-workers at the University of California, Berkeley, and he has kindly supplied information on his work. The parietal eye, he found, apparently helps regulate daily and seasonal exposure to sunlight. It aids adjustment of the reproductive cycle and accompanying activities of the cold-blooded animals that have them to climatic fluctuations. These animals are more at the mercy of thermal changes than are the warm-bloods. The most recent work has demonstrated the third eye to be functional as its removal causes disturbances of daily activity cycles and reproduction. (For those interested in pursuing the matter further, I suggest reading an article by Dr. Stebbins and R. and N. Cohen in 1973 *Copeia,* number 4.)

In any event, presence of this third eye has always brought forth enthusiastic speculation among my students who see it for the first time. It occurs not only in the fringe-toed sand lizard, but in the small but common fence and side-blotched lizards, as well as other iguanids and species of certain other families of lizards. Since the response of some animals to higher- or lower-than-normal temperatures appears to be regulated through the central nervous system—more specifically, the brain—it seems inevitable that completed investigations will establish beyond further argument that the third eye is definitely functional.

The more thoroughly we investigate any seemingly adaptive features whose uses are still obscure, the more certain we are to find that there are explanations for their existence. For a long time there was skepticism about the utility of incompletely understood bodily structures, but this seems to be waning as through holistic study we become better informed about the multitudinous interrelationships of structures functioning within an animal and about the variations in the environment to which an animal must become adapted if it is to survive.

16: Dividing Up the Habitat

*A*ll animals fit into one or another of the multitudinous types of environment. These habitats are broken up into still smaller sections into which the more precisely specialized creatures have found their way and to which they are committed for their exclusive way of life. Some are more flexible than others and, at times, may wander through highly diversified terrain, whereas others are extremely limited and are incapable of surviving, much less of multiplying, in environments to which they are not specifically adapted.

Amphibia must have access to water and to shelters with

high relative humidities or they will desiccate and die. Toads, for instance, may venture out into desert conditions for short periods of time. Then they must withdraw to water or to deep underground, cool, damp retreats in order to recoup any water losses. The amphibia are so obligated since some or all of their breathing is carried on through the skin. Some salamanders, for example, have no lungs at all. The exchange of gases necessary for metabolic processes can occur only through a thin film of water. When amphibians are exposed to dry air, evaporation from the skin surface is rapid. Body temperatures are lowered and metabolism slowed, which may be advantageous in certain circumstances. Skin moisture, however, must be maintained, and as that further accelerates the total loss of body fluids, it is an unsatisfactory compromise at best.

Ordinarily we think of birds with their capabilities for flight as being relatively independent of their environment. This is not wholly true, and the misleading aspect of this oversimplification is particularly well illustrated where the upper edges of the desert merge into the moister environments of higher altitudes. The restriction of birds to special habitats is exemplified by two species of birds common in southern California—the scrub, or California, jay, *Aphelocoma,* and the crested, or blue-fronted (Steller's) jay, *Cyanocitta.* The scrub jay (which, like many other western jays, is miscalled a blue jay) seems most unwilling to move from the chaparral into the closely adjacent coniferous forest. Similarly, the crested jay remains in the cone-bearing forest and ventures with reluctance into scrub or chaparral. The difference in preferences is so well developed that I often camped at the edge of the yellow pine forest to watch the scrub jays working below in the chaparral while the crested jays foraged around me in the pines. Only rarely did I see either species in the wrong environment.

Since the crow family has many self-reliant birds that roam freely in many habitats, the fixity with which these two jays cling to their respective environments never fails to puzzle me. So far as I know, the food requirements of the two are rather similar, but there are probably specific differences that would show up over a long period of observation rather than be manifest in minutes or even a few hours. Separated by only a hundred yards or so, the shady places under both brush and pine should have much the same ambient temperatures, and this is also probably true of the sunny exposures of both environments. I doubt then that food or temperature are the definitive factors that prevent any but brief excursions of either species out of their preferred habitats. Both of these birds are powerful fliers over short distances, and it seems improbable that their confinement to special conditions can be attributed to flight requirements alone. If none of these more obvious necessities is involved, what does determine the suitability of each to its particular environment? All factors probably combine to produce this specialization, but an additional question comes to mind. Are coloration differences, so pronounced especially when specimens of these two species are compared "in the hand," of significance? The crested jay is predominantly dark in color, and the blues are richer than those of the scrub jay. The chaparral-dwelling bird, on the other hand, is composed of pastel shades of gray and blue. In general, its hue more or less approximates what would be expected from Gloger's Rule—darker colors in birds liv-

Figure 10. A humid environment favors damp skin, which is indispensable for the salamander's respiration. The exchange of gases in this process takes place through the skin's moist surface.

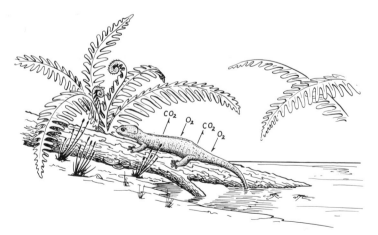

ing in more humid areas and, in reverse, a lightening of hues in a species whose varieties occur in progressively drier habitats. However, as noted above, there is no particular difference in the relative humidity or precipitation along the closely adjacent margins of chaparral and pine forest. Here the two plant communities may actually parallel each other no more than a few feet or yards apart. They often intermingle in the transitional area where pine and scrub join hands, as it were.

However, Gloger's Rule, dealing specifically with differences in the humidity of the environment, may not be nearly so important as the average difference in the amount of reflected light and shade under conifers as compared with that under the short shrubs of chaparral. The dark greens, browns, and deep shadows of dense forests of pine, even if somewhat scattered, give more suitable concealment to the darker-toned crested jay than they would to the softer hues of the scrub jay. Though the difference may be slight, over long periods of time the bird's vulnerability to avian predators, through mismatching with an environment, may produce an innate preference of each species for a particular background. No conscious choice is involved, only a simple instinctive aversion of one for the other's habitat.

In southern California the rubber boa is largely confined to the wetter parts of the Transition Zone, whose typical vegetation includes yellow pine, big-cone spruce, and deciduous oaks. This is an unusually variable environment with its summer drought and winter snows for an animal whose centers of population, considering the whole group, are in the genuinely temperate, or constant climates—the tropics and subtropics.* The precise parts that temperature and humidity play in the distribution of the boa could prove very interesting. The necessary studies have not been made as yet, perhaps because of the difficulty in capturing and maintaining sufficient numbers of this uncommon and secretive montane snake.

---

*Calling hot-and-cold climates of the mid-latitudes "temperate" is highly inaccurate and misleading.

The common name of this boa is doubtless due to its rubbery, brownish-black dorsal surface, and in some instances it is almost latex-rubber yellow on the underside. It is also called the two-headed snake because most adult individuals have equally blunt tails and heads that are not easily distinguishable by the usual brief glance that people take at a snake before they depart in flight. Interestingly enough, adults of both the rosy boa and the rubber boa start life with slender, tapering tails. By adulthood they usually have stubby caudal ends. The reasons for this change are not known. It may be genetic or it possibly might stem from the dangers of their environment. The prey on which they feed consists largely of rodents, many of which are quite capable of inflicting serious bites. I am inclined to believe that the shape of the tail is predominantly determined by some genetic trait resulting in the tail's slower growth, which may or may not have survival value. Altogether these two members of the boa family, three if one includes the desert form of the rosy boa, constitute fascinating examples of the northerly extension of what is conventionally thought of, and rightly so, as a tropical-subtropical reptile group. Such examples are not as rare as commonly believed. The North American deserts have been the site for the coexistence of a number of unlikely species, organisms whose antecedents developed in quite diverse environments ranging from the Temperate Zone to the Tropics.

Rubber boas are difficult to keep in captivity for any great length of time. Some amateurs have come to the conclusion that they do not feed on rodents. In one instance a newly captured individual from the Mt. Pinus area (near Frazier Park just west of the famed Ridge Route in southern California) regurgitated three very young mice when it was captured. It appears that small or young mice are consumed by these little (mostly less than two feet long) reptiles and are part of their natural diet. If, while captive, they are provided with the proper environmental conditions—a dark burrow to which to retreat and humidity and coolness to their taste— they might be induced to feed and thrive as pets.

Rosy boas, on the other hand, are usually easy to feed and

will take young mice, even full-grown mice, with gusto. They also do well on birds of a size they can swallow with ease. In one experiment devised to study feeding habits, a live sparrow was released within the boa's cage. We were amazed to discover that these sluggish animals are remarkably agile and even capable of capturing a passing bird in mid-flight, a feat that would be difficult for any species of snake. They also feed on bats with considerable relish, and these as well they captured in flight, at least within the confines of their cage. Capture of either birds or bats in flight out in the open might be more difficult. Having observed their tree-climbing abilities on occasion, I have little doubt that they also feed on fledgling birds. They may even capture mature birds while they are in flight defending their nests from the reptilian predator.

During many years of teaching elementary students about California's wildlife I always made a special effort to remove their fear of reptiles. I learned that the rosy boa proved the most interesting and evoked the least distaste. It was most useful while indoctrinating students into their first handling of a snake, the primary and most difficult step in eliminating the fears most of us have during our youthful years. I have never known a rosy boa to attempt to bite its captors. Its usually slow movement, its attractive color, the presence of vestigial limbs near the base of the tail in the males, and other traits of this gentle creature—all make an exceptionally good subject for introductory studies. It may surprise many prospective and present teachers that a large amount of time in natural science courses can be profitably spent on reptiles, especially the useful but fear-inspiring snakes. The fact remains, however, that of all terrestrial vertebrate animals, snakes and lizards are actually the least repulsive to the touch, and *touch* is the first step toward losing fear of an animal. Salamanders, toads, and frogs have damp, clammy, cold skins, which may also be slimy or covered with a viscous secretion that is highly toxic to the eyes or mucus membranes.

Mammals and birds may be more attractive to the beginner, but both these creatures may actually carry diseases. No reptiles, however, transmit rabies. As for birds, their feather-scales may cause violent allergies. It is not only the danger of disease from wild-caught animals that makes them somewhat impractical for teaching confidence in nature; such animals are likely to bite, their movements are fast, and they usually struggle to get away when handled. On the other hand, the harmless, gentle-tempered reptiles harbor no known contagious diseases, insofar as man is concerned, which makes them safe and desirable as teaching exhibits. The little aquatic terrapins may, however, void excrement containing *Salmonella*.

There is one disagreeable trait of the rosy boa that is not known by many people, even those who have kept them captive for years on end. I would probably never have discovered this trait had I not been conducting experiments in the low-temperature tolerance of these creatures. When they are chilled almost to immobility and then frightened or irritated, they may discharge an anal secretion. It emits one of the most repulsive smells I have ever encountered in any animal—not acrid and repellent in the sense that a skunk's or weasel's anal secretions may be, but utterly nauseating. Because it is never used by any rosy boas except under this unusual condition and then only rarely, I can make no adequate guess as to how it may serve them in nature. Aside from this rare disagreeableness, I find that this well-mannered, attractive snake is an excellent demonstration of a good-neighbor-in-the-wild, inviting children to share and appreciate its home and fellow creatures.

17: Adaptation, the Mechanics of Survival

*T*hroughout this volume the word adaptation has been repeated almost to monotony. This is necessary, for only through adaptations and resulting special characteristics do all living things become fit to live in any given place and time. Many adaptations are apparent to anyone on an outdoor excursion in southern California: the superb engineering of avian anatomy for flight, the characteristics of leaves of plants adapted to dry habitats, reptilian behavior in response to heat and cold. Obscure inner details, of equal importance, can be detected only with the use of microscopes and other instruments. Still more fundamental are the structure, chemistry, and functioning of the hereditary mechanisms that give stability to every species of living things. It also provides genetic accidents, or mutations, because of which the offspring differ significantly in one or several ways from the "normal" individuals of the species. While most of these variants are doomed to die before passing on their defects, they are the very materials out of which evolutionary progress and adaptations develop.

Unfortunately, in any small volume, it is possible to touch upon but a few of all the adaptations—the fitness-to-fit devices—in worlds of enchanting specialization and differences. Much research has been done on the major environments of the earth, but we are still quite ignorant about numerous smaller habitats, particularly those whose soils and soil moisture patterns differ markedly from the surrounding terrain. I have in mind the vernal, or springtime, pools common in many places in the San Joaquin Valley. Most animal life in these transient ponds—wet in winter and spring, dry in summer—is small to the point of being microscopic. Even to the unaided eye there are many things of interest such as the tadpoles of local frogs and toads and hosts of specialized arthropods, crustaceans, and hexapods. How do they survive the long, hot, dry summers? Are they descendants of far more widespread populations of the valley when it was cooler and damper than it is now?

An equally diverting collection of fauna and flora flourishes in torrential mountain streams. These creatures must be adapted to resist in some way the violence of floods when boulders are torn loose to pound and smash down the stream beds. Changes also must take place in the living things inhabiting these rivers when they flow onto the lowlands, settling to quiet water with far less oxygen and greater turbidity. The riparian habitat changes even more radically when the streams enter tidal areas where they become brackish in hightide and fresh at lowtide.

To concentrate on adaptations alone is to deal with a bewildering amount of detail that can, if one is not careful, become a way of thinking in which we rarely get glimpses of the total, the whole machinery of life. We do gain fleeting bits of insight, ephemeral revelations of at least parts of the magnificent but in many ways simple machinery that has operated through eons of time. Important as they are, these glimpses are often evanescent despite their underlying beauty and value. What seems most difficult of all is to see in one "glance" the present and, in perspective, the long past leading to the present. Sometimes I am granted the almost priceless gift of a vivid mental picture extending back to the once lifeless seas that rolled with swelling waves against the shifting protocontinents. Through accident and inputs of solar energy (perhaps as lightning) into these sterile waters came the first spark or perhaps sparks of life that down through the ages have become ever more modified through evolution into the myriad forms of living things existing today.

Figure 11. Flowering succession in a vernal pool in the south end of the San Joaquin Valley. As the pool gradually dries up various species of plants die and give way to those adapted to the changing conditions.

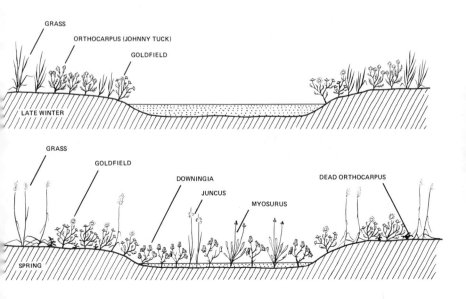

Probably the single most important feature of life is that it reproduces itself in a multitude of self-created replications of parental forms. They collect necessary chemical elements from the environment and then procreate in endless numbers, producing similar aggregations of chemical elements. (Recycling waste has many primal antecedents!) It is impossible to overemphasize the importance of organismic multiplication, this capacity to procreate in a potentially extravagant, plethoric, and always expanding number of food-consuming individuals. And it is subtle, not easily perceived by those of us who are enchanted and diverted by each evolutionary adaptation. Most of the time we fail to realize the immense consequence of this one profoundly significant aspect of life.

Take a coast live oak tree as an example. We may notice the acorns dropping to the ground to be fed upon by many other creatures whose lives depend on this crop of mast. To complete our view of the tree as an entity within a natural community, we must keep in mind not only the oak's supply of food for other organisms but the possible production of other oaks from the few surviving acorns left by their users, the scrub jays and acorn woodpeckers. It is but one representative of thousands of live oaks that grow over the hills and valleys of coastal California and is a member of a species that has existed for numberless generations, each tree producing its annual crop of hundreds of potential offspring. The multiplicative dynamics of this one example, extending far back in time, result in what we see today, and they will continue far into the future in successive generations of other oak trees.

What might be more difficult to imagine is the fact that if the oak's reproductive effort were wholly successful, if no other creatures gained advantage by eating the acorns, and all acorns survived to germinate and mature, the terrestrial world, climate permitting, long since would have consisted only of oaks crowded so closely together that there would be little space for branches. Under such conditions the trees eventually would kill each other to the last one, unless there were some that differed from others—growing faster, taller, shading out, and killing the competing seedlings so that some of the new type could live to produce other generations.

Every mature acorn could produce an oak, but by far the majority of acorns are destined to provide food for a host of animals ranging from insects to birds and mammals, an illustration of the interdependence of life. This is true of the reproductive products of all organisms, even including man. Most birth products are destined to support life of other species rather than perpetuate their own.

Diversity between the progeny of the young oaks—those growing taller, more robustly, and thus able to crowd out the others—depends upon the mechanics of biological inheritance. They are so structured as to allow innovative differences whose chances increase in proportion to reproductive number.

The tremendous capacity for reproduction, inherent in every living thing, has permitted the web of life to enlarge and become complex. It has permitted diversification in all forms of life and enabled them to occupy every available, livable site on the surface of the earth. The seemingly spendthrift outpouring of reproductive products, generation after generation, continues to flood endlessly until the species for a reason or a complex of reasons becomes extinct. Most probably, I believe, extinction occurs because of the failure of the reproductive potential to cope with a changing environment. Because there is no real excess and no real wastage, semantic accuracy requires a new term for this prodigality. Until a better word is found perhaps *biokrene* from the Greek roots, *bio* (life) and *krene* (flowing well), will suffice. To me it conveys some of the magnificence of the ceaseless flow of life and the significance of death. No form of life can reduce or increase its procreation without denying life to some interrelated organism. The living world is wholly bound together and is dependent on the circulation of nutrition created by the events of life and death, the grandiose, endlessly repeated sequence of birth and the ultimate return to basic molecules. The biokrene, or "flowing well of life," is the substance of life and death, and it is indispensable for both individual survival and species evolution by means of natural selection. To intervene in its normal operation insures disaster, particularly for the future of mankind. A future chapter will discuss this in more detail.

Of equal importance to sheer number of offspring in the fight for species survival is the ability of living things to adapt, to attain special fitness for their inconstant biological and physical environments. An obvious prerequisite for the flow of life was genetically based change, which allowed variants to invade and occupy the infinite variety of weakly held and unoccupied niches in water and on land and also allowed the evolution of defenses against predator pressure. How did all the necessary millions of adjustments come about—all of the myriads of changes that lie between the first blobs of assembled molecules drifting in the open seas and their billions of succeeding modified forms?

Self-reproduction or replication was an absolute necessity in perpetuating the original spark of life. No living thing escapes death, and replacement by replication has been as essential as life itself. It is the one assurance that so rare an event as the creation of the first living thing was not a one-time phenomenon. Furthermore, the production of only one replica could scarcely assure survival in an environment that has proved clearly hostile to large numbers of successful episodes of original appearance of life. Though it is impossible to prove, replication must have followed replication in rapid succession.

The pattern of reproductive doubling, attended by a potential for an ultimate infinitude of duplicates, has characterized all subsequent life. What living organisms exist today were preceded by numberless generations extending back to the original molecules of protoplasmic life. All are samples of survival from countless intervening generations of replicas and *near replicas* extending backward through time in an immutable pattern of doubling and redoubling numbers with each passing generation. No living species survives if its breeding stock reproduces only enough individuals to replace the parent stock, for it would be reduced by successive attrition of an ever-dwindling, diminishing, and then finally vanishing type. But continued multiplication of boundless, unvarying duplicates would lead either to the exhaustion of the material necessities for the maintenance of life processes or to limits imposed by the pressure of finite space.

Perfect replication prevents change; only imperfect replicas permit change in form and function and can introduce flexibility into what otherwise would be an inflexible repetition of totally similar living things. They would be doomed to self-destruction for lack of the variability needed for adjustment to new conditions of the physical and biological environment. Rigidity, no matter how perfect the organism may be for any one time or place, is nihilistic, and living things do change, as their diversity testifies.

Differences among progeny enable them to occupy slightly different and perhaps less desirable places. They lead to the invasion of previously unexplored and thus unoccupied environments. This is precisely how harsh deserts, the frigid Arctic and Antarctic seas, the inhospitable world of timberline became colonized. Reproductive superfluity, the biokrene, is necessary for perpetuation of the original stock, but the capacity of individuals to modify in readiness to survive in or to occupy new areas has been as important to the persistence of life as has the capacity to reproduce in extravagant numbers.

To a degree there is individual flexibility, but, so far as is known, no newly acquired, non-genetic individual traits that may assist in survival have been inherited and so passed on to progeny. Evidence for the inheritance of bodily acquired characteristics has been sought since the problems of evolution first arose, but major, non-cyclical changes in environments are not predictable nor can they be recognized in advance of need. Thus it was necessary that all replicating individuals from time to time produce the necessary accidental genetic innovations—mutations—that would fit them to novel conditions intolerable to the original stock.

Most progeny differing substantially from the parents have far less chance of survival than do the conventional offspring.

For the most part these deviations from the standard and time-tested genetic patterns are useless and even harmful to the new generations and thus the species. Fortunately, the differing individual carries the seeds of its own early elimination. Though most mutations are either worthless or render the individual more susceptible to harm, some rare innovations may increase the chances for survival. In a lavishly multiplying and thus competitive world those who are best endowed persist.

Darwin and Alfred Wallace were the first to perceive the importance of huge numbers of new lines, the high degree of mortality that reduced these numbers to comparatively few survivors, and the place of divergent individuals in the process of evolution. Malthus introduced us to a world where reproduction is so lavish that only ruthless natural selection can ensure survival.

It is because of this richness of reproductive number that there is a continual supply of individuals having useful mutations. These deviants flow like water, to use an analogy, seeking their level—places suited to their endowments—and escaping the ancient bondage by the ability to creep into numerous adjacent, newly hospitable habitats. There, if they survive they will breed; and because the deviation is inherent in their genetic makeup, they are able to pass on to their offspring the advantageous trait.

Although all living things in this unconscious proliferation of progeny attempt to occupy the world, all are kept in bounds by environmental adversity or utilization by another species. Only man, and then only in recent decades, has temporarily achieved an overwhelming upset in the balance between productivity and the forces of death that eventually harvest most of those born to any species. Mankind has new techniques for ensuring that most of his progeny will reach reproductive age and beyond to old age, its attendant organic diseases, and death.

We thoughtlessly speak of this as a victory over the forces of nature; our present survival rates are almost unbelievable when contrasted with those of several hundred years ago.

Good health and increased longevity are testimonials to the accomplishment of science. *But,* and this is a most important "but," nature's chains of interdependencies have existed for billions of years and have operated on principles that cannot be judged as having been defeated by the testimony of some two centuries out of all time.

18: Mesquite—A Vignette of Desert Survival

*F*or thousands of years mesquite trees, in sprawling, thorny, thicket-like groves, have dotted the desert slopes and plains. Where favorable habitats occur, various species are spread throughout much of the Colorado and Mojave deserts. Mesquite clusters also are scattered through much of the Southwest, as far east as Arkansas and Louisiana, southward into Mexico and beyond, intermingling with tropical and subtropical vegetation.

Clumps of mesquite often occupy some most unlikely looking places, appearing as islets of brilliant green surrounded
by bleached desert with its scanty vegetation and sparse shade.
It often mingles with arrowweed and other riparian desert
growth wherever water reaches the surface in seeps or flowing
streamlets. Wherever they occur they become oases throng-
ing with specially adapted life of all kinds. In southwestern deserts that have adequate summer precipitation, they
form short, dense forests, which have been given the name
of bosques. The thick boles crowd together, and the feathery
foliage droops gracefully over bough and limb. From a distance they seem, and often are, hospitable places, but only
by attempting to penetrate the denser groves is one aware
of their spiny resistance.

There is some popular confusion about the various kinds
of mesquite. In distinguishing them I refer to an old friend,
A Manual of Southwestern Desert Trees and Shrubs by Lyman
Benson and Robert Darrow, University of Arizona, 1945. All
of the mesquites of the southwestern deserts have conspicuous, creamy-yellow spikes. They have fewer stamens than
related genera such as *Acacia* and *Calliandra,* and the spines
are straight rather than curved, distinguishing them from
another related genus, *Mimosa. Prosopis juliflora* is the "patri-
arch," the original mesquite of Mexico and Central and South
America. Three of its varieties, *velutina, torreyana,* and *gland-
ulosa,* occur in the Southwest. They are known as velvet,
western honey, and honey mesquites. The first variety is
found in but one location in California, near San Diego, but
it is widespread in southern Arizona and occurs in limited
distribution in western New Mexico and western Texas, near
El Paso. The second variety is *the* mesquite of California. It is
found throughout both deserts, in the southern end of the
San Joaquin Valley, and in several places west of the desert
proper. It also extends into southern Nevada and Arizona,
where, oddly enough, it never seems to co-exist with *velutina.*
It becomes common again in southern New Mexico and in
Texas along the Rio Grande drainage as far east as Corpus
Christi. Both continue south into Mexico. The third variety

is at home on the southern plains and prairie from New Mexico to Louisiana and northeastern Mexico.

A fourth variety, *pubescens,* is screw bean, at times referred to as screw bean mesquite. Its tightly coiled pods differ from the relatively straight or slightly curved pods of the other three varieties. It also occurs in both California deserts and in the San Joaquin Valley, and it extends to Texas and into Mexico. Catclaw, *Acacia greggii,* is often included in a general discussion of mesquite and mesquite-like shrubs. The flower clusters are cylindrical rather than round, which is also true for the mesquites, but the prickles, like those of rose bushes, are curved, hence the name. Unlike the true mesquites, it is not winter deciduous, and it appears to be able to withstand drier sites than its cousins of the bosques. Another of the desert mimosas is also called catclaw, but it does not occur in California.

I have long been mystified about mesquite seedlings. Knowing that in the rainless summers of California older plants must be rooted in permanent moisture, I assume that younger plants, or seedlings, must have access to plentiful subsurface moisture as well. I suspect that the rootlets of sprouting seeds must get their start in the rare years of frequent, fairly heavy rain. Immediately on germination, they plunge downward in pursuit of the gradually retreating moisture until they reach sources of dependable wetness that can tide them over the season of prolonged drought. In the eastern Sonoran and Chihuahuan deserts of Arizona, New Mexico, and Texas, summer rainfall is of great climatological significance. It provides moisture during the months of high temperature, and it adds to the average annual amounts, which are higher than that of California's Colorado Desert. Under these conditions, mesquite thickets are not confined to wash bottoms, river courses, and seepage or streamlet flows. They flourish in such locations, of course, but one can find them scattered about in drier areas, making use of precipitation from passing storms.

On the northern side of the Coachella Valley I have known the roots to thrust at least a hundred feet below the soil surface to reach permanently available moisture. On one occasion where grading for a farm had exposed the surface of the land to wind erosion, I saw a large mesquite perched on a stilt-like framework of roots. One root extended almost horizontally about 180 feet away from the tree and then turned sharply downward in search of the water table. In the 180 feet of horizontal growth, the root diminished in size to about a fourth of its original dimension. If the downward turning portion of the root is assumed to have penetrated an additional 100 feet or so, it appears that the total length of a root in pursuit of water may have extended much beyond 250 feet. This is a phenomenal length, but in its way it matches the other accomplishments of this remarkable tree.

Once past the original hazards of germination and the race for dampness and water, young mesquite trees become established, assured of necessary moisture unless people drill wells and pull the ground water out from beneath their roots, which unfortunately has happened in many places around and east of Palm Springs. Their growth is slow, but many of the trees in older groves have had time to reach a girth of five feet or more. When they reach this impressive size, the massive weight of branch and trunk sends them sprawling outward until they lean with crooked elbows on the ground, resting there as they spread outward once again.

Mesquite trees lose their leaves in winter, and for months their stark branches etch intricate patterns against the sky. At that time of year the twin thorns that grow at each node on the twig can easily be seen. By late March or early April, their seemingly almost lifeless branches send out a tender flush of vivid green. In the heat of the spring sun the new leaves rapidly unfold and are soon followed by the golden pendent tassels. Bees hum as they gather the delectable nectar for making the honey from which the common name of two of the varieties has been derived.

As the blossoms begin to fade, the foliage grows in density and soon casts a heavy shade below the branches, furnishing shelter from the desert sun as the days warm up with the advance of spring. Cool places are hard to come by in any desert during the warmer months, and providing this delightful screen is one of the most valuable attributes of these leafy trees. Even as early as May the unshaded surface of the ground may reach a deadly temperature for various animals. The superheated desert soil is only relieved by tiny patches of dwarf-like growths of burroweed and other desert shrubs or the filmy shade of the sparse-foliaged creosote bush. The blossoms themselves are followed by a crop of slender beans. When the pods ripen, they turn to a pale yellow or straw color. The beans are sour-sweet, full of sugar, and they have a high protein content as well.

Long before the Spaniards arrived, long before Palm Springs was even thought of, the Indians sought sanctuary in and near mesquite groves. The signs of their occupancy are still numerous: shards from clay pots, rings of stone that encircled ancient campfires, and charred wood and bones. They gathered mesquite beans which they valued highly for their nutritious characteristics as well as their pleasant flavor. Game was plentiful, as numerous animals were attracted to the thickets in search of food and shelter. The trees also provided firewood for cooking, keeping the Indians warm during the frosty nights of winter, and for baking their primitive pottery. The Indians used the branches in constructing lean-to shelters and made tool handles from the hard, tough wood.

The Indian was at the apex of a pyramid of feeding relationships involving trees and a host of animals of various kinds. Rodents congregate and thrive in food- and shelter-rich mesquite patches. Pack rats and various mice are common residents, and even the ground-dwelling cottontails take to the leaning trunk and limb, climbing six feet or more above the ground to nibble on the shoots of succulent green twigs.

Jack rabbits, those leggy denizens of the open plains, occasionally take refuge in mesquite. This appears a most unlikely bit of behavior, but I witnessed just such an episode one moon-bright desert evening in my heat research camp. A chorus of coyotes in pursuit of prey caught my attention. As the chase bore down in my direction, I wondered if the victim would escape. The moon was out, and I glimpsed both pursuers and pursued as they headed toward me. Most fortunately for me, the jack rabbit, though rapidly losing ground, ran straight toward my camp. Then it plunged into a thicket of shoots growing from stumps of cut mesquite along one edge of my campsite. I was on one side of the thicket, and the coyotes rushed in on the other. In bewilderment at being confronted on both sides, the jack paused, turned, and instantly two coyotes pounced. There was a short agonized scream by the jack rabbit, and that was all. The coyotes silently left with their prey, and the desert returned to its peaceful quiet.

Wherever herbivores find vegetation to convert into animal protein, the protein-hungry predators gather. Diamondback rattlesnakes, spotted night snakes, gopher snakes, king snakes, and red racers prowl ceaselessly when temperatures permit. The first three hunt chiefly at night and others by day, or dawn and dusk, harrying the rodents around the clock. Coyotes, kit foxes, and gray foxes are co-hunters with the reptiles, and the western lynx or bobcat also investigates these thickets in search of food. The latter is a successful predator of snakes and habitually kills and eats even rattlesnakes, thus placing it on the level of a third-order consumer in the classic schematics of the food pyramid. (Herbivores are first-order consumers, predators that prey on them are second-order consumers, and predators that prey on these predators are third-order consumers.) When nocturnal owls and diurnal hawks eat reptiles, as some do, they rank as third-order consumers. With the possibility of all these creatures about me day and night, whenever I camped in a mesquite thicket I always felt that I was in the heart of a unique drama of life and death.

As I hiked through these clumps of water-enriched vegetation, I noticed conspicuous growths of another kind of green perched high on limbs and branches. When dead, remains of this particular plant often form tangles of almost black brittle twigs around a knob-like center. Such clusters of vegetation are parasites on mesquite trees, freeloaders on the water and minerals brought up by their host from deep underground. They are desert mistletoe, another fascinating member of the mesquite grove community.

From late fall to mid-spring I seldom failed to come across mistletoe in full bloom. Then its fragrance permeated the air and attracted swarms of insects to its nectaries. Later it would be loaded with small, pearly-pink fruit—food for many birds and a number of rodents. Of all the creatures that feed on the fruit, the silky flycatcher, or phainopepla, alone depends on it in a complex way of life.

Though it eats insects, one of its local staples is mistletoe berry. In turn, the mistletoe depends on this and other fruit-eating birds for propagation. Such a relationship is termed

Plate 19. Tracks showing the incipient sidewinding of a spotted night snake and a shovel-nosed snake while they were crawling on a super-hot substrate. The track in the upper left-hand corner shows a trace of normal sinuous progression.

mutualism, in which both members are dependent upon each other for a life necessity. In this case, the phainopepla eats the berries and when sated roosts on the highest dead twigs of the mesquite thicket. There, while watching for insects on the wing, the bird digests the outer nutritious coat of the berries. The seeds pass on through the bird's body and are dropped at random. They are waxy-white in color and as sticky as Scotch tape, and as they drop down through the trees, many strike twigs where they adhere tightly.

Shortly after the seed becomes attached to a twig, a dark red radicle, or rootlet, penetrates the bark. In response, a healthy mesquite twig opens a minute orifice in its bark immediately beneath the seed. A clear gum that dries and hardens rapidly is exuded from the tiny opening. It pushes the sprouting seed upward, away from the vulnerable bark, but the seed continues to send its rootlet toward its only hope of life, the vital tissue under the bark. More exudate material forms and pushes the seed still farther away. A race develops between the growing column of hardening gum and the rootlet reaching for the food and water conduits of the host plant. Usually the twig and its exuded gum are victorious; the seedlet is perched lifeless, exhausted of its initial nourishment. Only a few succeed in reaching into the bark and attaching themselves to the host mesquite. Lack of success, however, ensures that the hosts are not unduly overburdened with parasites which would eventually kill the tree and themselves. The birds that feed on the berries, as well as mammals that use seeds from the pods of the host plant, share the larder with a large array of other animals that gather around mesquite as a source of moisture, food, and shelter. If it should die, they would be deprived of a major supportive factor in their lives.

The phainopepla contributes heavily to the loss of mistletoe seed and influences the balance between host and parasite. Beneath perch-site twigs, compact clumps of seeds collect. Piled together by the thousands, their sticky coats adhere to each other to form masses often as large as a football. And each of these seeds is dead, lost to posterity as a progenitor of a new plant. This additional device to prevent overpopulation of the parasite is accidental. The phainopepla's habit of returning to its favorite perch on high, dead twigs serves to concentrate the seeds in one place.

Even dead mesquite trees or their dead branches support many types of desert life. Wood-boring beetles lay eggs, and their larvae tunnel through the dead wood until it is reduced to a crumbling powder. I could always tell when these beetles were at work. I would sit quietly, particularly on a warm spring day, and listen for the curious clicks they produce either as they gnaw with their heavy mandibles or stir within the burrows. Unconsumed wood that falls to the ground is taken over by termites. They encase every piece of dead wood in a tube of clay within which they work until they have

Figure 12. Mistletoe seeds attempt to invade mesquite trees by sending rootlets into the bark. The mesquite retaliates by discharging gum, which accumulates, pushing the seed and its penetrating rootlet away from the bark.

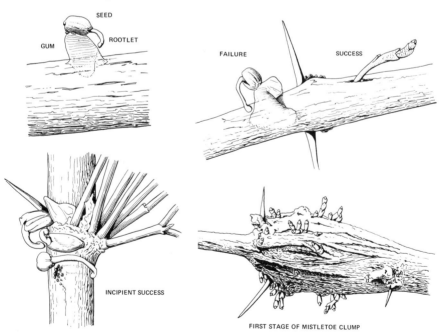

reduced the twig to almost nothing. The next stage in decomposition is taken over by fungi that flourish whenever rain falls. Between fungi and bacterial action, the wood is ultimately reduced to a nutritious molecular dust. Its elements can then recycle through another series of organisms.

A mesquite grove is a place of never-ending fascination. The interrelationship of living things, the drama of their life and death, the extraordinary beauty of the plant as it progresses through the seasons, and the behavior of the tree itself—all enrich one's experiences. On exceedingly hot days the leaves collapse their surfaces against each other and hang pendent, shedding light and conserving moisture, thus minimizing the danger of desiccation and overheating. The size of leaf and the choice of site are additional factors ensuring life in an arid land. Where the mesquite exists it is as completely used as the proverbial pig of the Chicago packing plants of which all was used but the squeal. But the mesquite tree does the pig one better: even its shade is used.

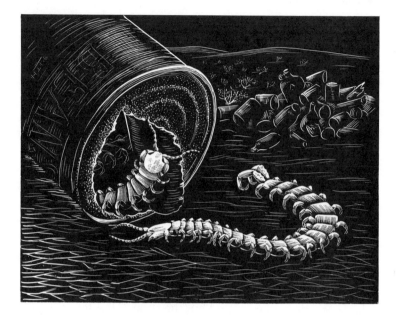

19: The Desert's Brushy Edges

*C*ucamonga, Ontario, and San Antonio peaks tower above the eastern end of the San Gabriel Valley near Pomona. Of the three, San Antonio, familiarly known as Old Baldy, is the largest and highest. For me, at least, Ontario Peak with its vertical, cliff-like slopes, virgin seclusion, and sharp, pointed summit was more inviting for exploration. Some decades ago it was said that this peak had never been ascended from its southward-facing slope. This was, of course, a challenge to any youth. Its sheer beauty and the rumor of inaccessibility from the south had attracted friends of mine. After some weeks of periodic exam-

ination of this very steep and difficult face, it was agreed that
when the time was right we would take a weekend and
explore the possibility of ascending it.

We packed our knapsacks one morning long before sunrise, and the three of us set out from our camp near the then
small village of Upland. We followed the path that led through
the brush downward into Cucamonga Canyon with its tumbling trout-filled creek. Then we clambered up the canyon to
the knife-ridge we presumed would offer the best approach
to the mountain itself. Unfortunately the weekend we had
chosen was also one of enshrouding fog. Though we could
make our way along the path with little difficulty and ascend
the canyon without much trouble, when we arrived at what
we thought to be the takeoff for the climb we discovered that
our views were totally obscured by the clinging mist. We
had to guess which of the many ridges reaching downward
would provide the best route for our initial climb. It soon
became apparent that the one we chose was not the one we
had planned on. We found ourselves inching along astride
a cleaver-sharp ridge down which the dislodged pebbles
plunged with a lingering rattle. Then there was an interval
of silence and finally the strike of falling objects. We knew
then that just out of sight below the fog there were almost continuous precipitous drops to the bottom of the gorge below.
Looking up and along the fog-mantled ridge we could see
nothing except the closest shrubs, and we continued crawling forward until at last the broadening shoulder of the prom-
ontory led us into the security of flatter ground.

For an hour or so we squirmed through the chaparral,
sometimes on our hands and knees, sometimes semi-erect,
but always slowly and most painstakingly. We needed no
admonition to be cautious. We must have crept with considerable silence despite the unavoidable contact with the
stiff-twigged but damp brush. For the first time in my life I had
a close view of a mule deer in magnificent action. I was leading the group on hands and knees, forcing my way through
dense masses of manzanita, when I thrust my head into an
opening of some 20 yards of bare ground. Out of the fog as

though by an act of magical creation emerged a huge ant-
lered buck, alarmed by the sound but unaware of the direction from which it came. It trotted past within yards of me,
appearing and disappearing with equal suddenness. I was
so close that I could see the play of muscles in the great shoul-
ders and haunch and note every detail of muzzle, eyes, ears,
and antlers.

As the sun lifted so did the fog. Now we could select an
easier, more brush-free route as we ascended higher on the
mountain slope. Occasional cloudlets of fog obscured our
view, and once as we emerged into the clear, rocks clattered
just out of sight to our right. A number of large animals must
have become alarmed and sought shelter higher on the slope.
With deer in mind we assumed that we had startled a herd,
but after checking tracks and droppings it was obvious we
had disturbed a flock of mountain sheep! Apparently they
had been resting in the open, awaiting the sun's warmth that
had been interrupted by passing clouds. A patch of little wild
onions had been pressed to the earth, and their slender leaves
were still springing upward where the sheep had just de-
parted. We never saw the animals themselves, but it was an
exciting discovery. Even at that time no one apparently knew
of the existence of this flock of sheep so close to civilization.

We continued to climb by a zig-zag route. At one almost
impassable place we noticed a pile of rocks and we paused
in astonishment. We were not the first visitors. Others had
been there before. As no reports had been made of their exploration, we had believed until that moment that we were
the first to leave bootprints in this wilderness. In considerable disappointment we removed a flat rock from the top of
the pile to discover that someone had left a note. Rather for-
lornly it remarked that he had made it this far from the canyon bottom, but that he had become lost, out of water, and,
if anyone was looking for him, he was headed for Ice House
Canyon, our own destination. The note was dated two years
earlier and, since no one had been reported missing as far
as we knew, we assumed he had been able to reach civilization without too much difficulty.

As for ourselves, we now needed far more water than we had brought in our small canteens. We had expected, in our enthusiastic innocence, to encounter springs and streams along the way. The climb continued to be arduous, and we had been greatly slowed by mistakes in routing and the baffling tangles of chaparral. By late in the afternoon we were extremely thirsty and still miles away from any known trails. To conserve body moisture we moved more slowly, rested frequently, and as a result were caught at dusk on the shoulder between Ontario Peak and the lower ridges leading down to Ice House Canyon and the resorts on Mt. Baldy. Despite the gathering darkness, we made several attempts to descend directly into the canyon below. Unfortunately, each attempt ended above a vertical rock face. Twice we set talus slopes in motion and once had to roll to the safety of a pine tree that, fortunately for us, was growing in the right place. After these mishaps, we were forced to follow a deer trail that led in the general direction we were going.

About nine o'clock that night we paused to assess our situation in what was turning out to be a very foolish enterprise. In the dim starlight the chaparral seemed to extend from where we stood well into the canyon, indicating the absence of cliffs. We worked our way downward, now careless with thirst, to where we thought water might be. Stumbling over unseen obstacles, we pushed through the brush to the canyon floor. The small creek was dry. We attempted to go on, but the going was even worse. After one of us had stepped into space and fallen several feet to a rocky gully we decided the danger was too great. Chewing on dry and swollen tongues, we stopped and cleared a large area of its flammable debris, made a very small fire, and, in the sharp cold of the night and canyon bottom, huddled close to the flames, dozing and waking as we waited for the moon to rise or dawn to break.

During the darkest hours some animal continually circled us out of sight but within easy hearing. From the sounds the creature was obviously large, and we concluded, thrills now adding to chills, that we were being inspected by a mountain lion. These animals are by nature curious, and though they never attack, such close proximity is exciting. Exhausted and dehydrated though we were, we tried to see beyond the shadows and catch a glimpse of this experience trophy. After the moon rose, we tramped out and buried the fire and pushed ahead through the ceanothus. Just before dawn we heard the first whisper of the sweetest music to thirsty ears, a running stream. All of us were so parched we found it difficult to speak. Our saliva was thick and gluey, and our lips were dry and blackened by accumulated dust. Oddly enough, even this purest mountain water tasted bitter and unpleasant until we had absorbed enough moisture to stimulate the flow of saliva.

This hike had another reward. As I sat apart from the others, recuperating from thirst and fatigue, a mole emerged from under the thick leaf-mold at the edge of the stream, crawled to a small pool nearby, walked down into it, and with no hesitation or any sign of concern or discomfort made its way across the bottom. It did not swim, but crept along and came up on the far side to again dig into the leaf-mold and disappear. I sat bemused with surprise at this unheard of and unreported behavior, but not so startled that I did not notice the silvery coating of air that clung to its fur throughout the entire traverse across the pool floor. I have no doubt that such behavior is common to moles, but for me it was most unexpected.

The rest of the hike—which eventually totaled some 45 miles in a day and a half—was uneventful. We had to remove scores of ceanothus spines that had penetrated our arms and legs. They left no infections or soreness, but were painful to pull out. From this mountain climb and that ghastly night-long struggle to escape brushy cliffs and reach water, I learned something about myself. Leisurely strolls through the countryside with attention to the fine details of nature study are well worth the time spent, but in retrospect the intense pleasure of wilderness experiences seems to be commensurate with the amount of effort and even discomfort involved!

Many birds and mammals reside in the canyons such as

those we explored on that memorable hike, but the birds, chiefly diurnal, are more readily seen. Fishing along the tumbling torrent of a mountain stream is sheer delight. Canyon wrens send their peals of silvery notes echoing against the walls of cliff and gorge. I never weary of their song, and to me their singing is as truly a part of their realm of canyon and streamside as the topography itself. Often the water ousel flashed past my trout fly as I explored the streams of the San Gabriel Mountains after release from army duty in World War I. I would see the dusky little bird darting around the bend of the stream or disappearing up or down canyon, engaging in its search for food. Its nest is a beautiful affair under the spray of a waterfall or cascade. In its pursuit of food, it unhesitatingly walks down a slanting rock into the water's turbulence and forages around on the bottom of the rocky stream bed for aquatic insects.

Along the larger creeks, where the streams debouch out among the foothills, the rattling calls of gray-blue kingfishers intensified my pleasure, as did the damp fragrance of humus and the perfumed diffusions from many species of plants. In the canyon bottoms the heavy odor of the western bay or laurel is as characteristic as the smell of sage on the drier hills. The distinctive fragrance (though some would call it stink) of the bay tree was so attractive to me that in my earlier and inexperienced years I never passed a tree without grasping a handful of leaves, crushing them, and breathing in their spicy odor. It was an embarrassingly long time before I associated the violent headaches that attended some of my fishing trips with possible overindulgence in this habit. Later on I read that the Indians sometimes used a mass of crushed bay leaves over face and nostrils to induce a sort of anesthesia when setting broken legs and treating other injuries. Judging by my own reaction to much lesser dosages, I would assume that whether or not it resulted in anesthesia, the distraction of a very severe headache could readily camouflage the pain of having a bone set.

For most fishermen and hikers, one of the minor plant nuisances in coastal and mountain areas is poison oak, a close

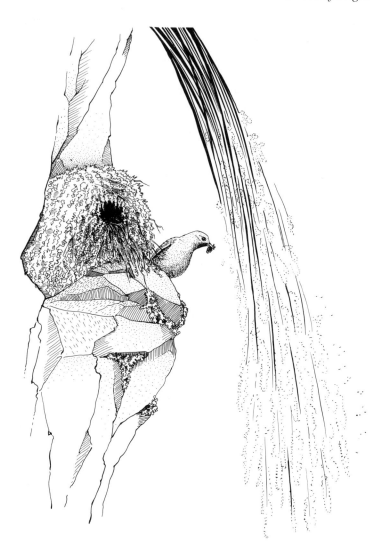

Figure 13. The water ousel characteristically makes a nest of moss, attaching it to a rock that is very often behind a waterfall or small cascade. One of its more unusual habits is that of feeding while walking underwater on rocks or the stream floor.

relative of and very similar to eastern poison ivy. This plant with its resinous secretion is a serious obstacle to off-the-trail fishing and hunting. I have found that a widely recommended preventive preparation is the application of a homemade salve of 10 percent sodium perborate in a base of vanishing cream with some 2 percent potassium periodate. This should be applied before going into the field. Its effective protection time is about four hours. Then it should be washed off and renewed. At the end of a day in the field, removing the vanishing cream with strong soap and hot water should be sufficient. Those who still suffer should consult a dermatologist. Possibly immunization may serve best and permit full, unworried enjoyment of leaving the beaten track.

A word of warning to those who think they may get poison oak from wind-blown toxins. Several instances of this kind have come to my attention. On questioning, however, I have discovered that in each case the persons were accompanied by dogs they had allowed to run free in the brush and which they had petted after returning from their romps through poison oak. Wandering cats can be as dangerous. Though convinced that their troubles are airborne, people really get the dermatitis with all its itching misery from dog or cat fur and its load of accidentally acquired resins.

20: Nothing but
Noisy Tree Frogs

Spreading development, flood control measures, water impoundment, and channelization—confining streams to concrete-lined slots—are rapidly depriving much of our wildlife, particularly that of riparian biotic communities, of their homes. Man simply cannot multiply without spreading over the land and inevitably dispossessing practically all of its previous occupants.

The little tree frog is just one example of the thousands of species of animals that are being evicted by so-called progress, another name for simply making room for more of one species. Following the long period of California's summer drought, the first good rains of any normal year bring the tree frogs out in great numbers. All through the dry months the mature survivors from the preceding breeding season and multitudes of newly bred are precariously sheltering wherever damp and cool hideaways can be found—in abandoned gopher holes, down at the bottom of deep cracks in adobe soils, and under boulders. Most of those in the vicinity of our garden take refuge in the scattered patches of lawn and irrigated fields adjacent to our home. In this respect they profit by man's presence, making them one of the few wild animals that could possibly owe us anything.

Wet spells in winter and spring are marvelous for these green, tan, and brown—very rarely, almost golden-hued— acrobat-musicians of our soft spring nights. Until recent years multitudes of mud puddles, rainwater ponds, or quiet pools in seasonally ephemeral streams provided ample trysting sites for amphibians. With vanishing cienagas (spring-fed marshes) and other shriveling wet places, there are fewer and fewer breeding sites with each passing year.

During one summer that was cooler and foggier than usual, many newly transformed toadlets worked their way up to my hilltop home in search of life-saving moisture and dark retreats. Every pile of rotting hay, flattened cardboard carton, or stack of boards harbored one to several fingertip-big mites of leaping life. Some of the toadlets may have even followed upward along a trail marked by the feel or smell of cool, damp air flowing down from my watered lawn toward their gradually drying birthplaces. Whatever brought them to the hilltop, they became most welcome aids in keeping the smaller spiders and bugs down to tolerable numbers.

Later in the summer there were many indications that too few had wisely chosen sanctuary from the heat and desiccating air. Elfin mummies appeared mysteriously in our driveway and on the weedless patches of dry dirt. Even so, a number remained safe throughout the dry, but fortunately foggy months of late autumn and early winter. An almost unrelieved drought, however, lay on the land. Dead weeds like tangles of stiffened string grew dustier and dustier, and brown leaves, crackling to the touch, dropped to scrape along street and driveway in the winds that gusted down the canyons leading to the sea.

I am always somewhat uneasy late in the drought season, and the little creaking, dry-weather calls of the tree frogs hearten me, reminding that the winter rains shall soon be with us. They sustained me through that long fall, assuring me of the remarkable persistence of life. Once more we would enjoy the special nocturnal music of the first days of wet weather in arid California. And so at last, the promise of rain was fulfilled. The storms, as if by some cosmic legerdemain, took slow shape; the drenching showers drifted in gauzy sheets across the face of the mountains in back of our home. The harsh, dry cold of winter drought was tempered by moisture. From every fair-sized puddle and rain-collecting hollow came the triumphant mating calls. Spring itself could not be far away.

These songs of the *Hyla* (tree) frogs may well be among the most well known of animal sounds. Whenever gloom, the danger of the dark, or just the mystery of a quiet night appears on television or in motion pictures, these are the sounds they record as mood-matching accompaniment. Only rarely do these media of public information and amusement realize that they are using not crickets but frogs as symbols of night and suspense. As that grand old naturalist, Loye Holmes Miller, has said, "These frogs are California's harbingers of clean air and new washed earth, the reclothing of California in her green and gold vestments." Not as the film world would have them, omens of gloom or conveyors of the fearfulness of nighttime, but the prognosticators of a new and fertile biological cycle.

So once more, in the sheer sensory delight of our most balmy evenings, from every sheltered corner of our garden came the musical pipings of my beloved *Hyla regilla*. For the most part they were clarion calls to mating areas, sharp, clear, and far-carrying. Only a few belatedly slow frogs croaked their ratchety, dry-weather sounds, and soon they would repair to puddles far down the slopes of our hill. With yet different voices and overwhelming libido they crowded into favorite puddles, insuring another chorus when spring returned again.

But now it is too late to hope that these precious sounds will persist and give me pleasure indefinitely. The pond below our house has been drained and filled for a housing development. Already new dwellings for a multitude of new human beings cover the old tree frog mating grounds. Gone are the woodlands and the green-clad grazing fields that followed the oaks and chaparral. Gone too are the field crops and the lemon, walnut, and avocado groves, moneymakers for their owners and sources of gastronomic pleasures and healthful vitamins for their users.

And gone as well are the deeply satisfying choruses of *Hyla*, now forlorn and isolated nocturnal reminders from our more gracious past. No one has killed them out. They have been plowed out of home and shelter by ruthless shearing blades or deprived of wet places wherein to sing and mate. But *Hyla* is only a lowly cold-blooded creature. He had no game laws for his protection, but even if he had them they would have been of no avail against the relentlessly rising tide of humanity. The fate of the little tree frog is symbolic of far greater changes that man is imposing on his environment.

Water shortages now and again are the result of local drought, but soon the problem will be widespread and chronic, another of the symptoms that reflect our excess numbers. We actually do not suffer so much from the "shortages" of resources as we do from the "longages" of consumers. Already throughout most of California it is absolutely essential for the survival of our expanding population of consumers that every water course be treated as a valuable, controllable, exploitable resource. Most of the larger streams have been or are being dammed to impound the floodwaters that come in such seeming abundance during the winter rains. Behind the dams, water backs up for miles along the river beds, destroying natural vegetation and the wildlife dependent upon former riparian habitats. Fish can live in these man-made lakes, but their constantly changing elevation, the rise and fall with winter plenty and summer scarcity, thwarts the development of shoreline life that depends on a fairly constant supply of moisture. As a result, for much of the year the borders of the reservoirs are bare of vegetation and of the animal life that must rely on a lush green cover of plants for food and shelter.

One would suppose that these lakes provide ample food and resting places for migrating wildfowl, the ducks, geese, and their aquatic neighbors. Such bodies of water, however, have few shallows, and their margins change constantly. Thus the food supply is limited, and only a few species, and of these only a comparatively small number of individuals, can rest and feed during their long journey. Places to escape from the bombardment to which these birds are subjected during the hunting season are much needed.

Our verbal support of conservation of wildfowl is a mockery. On one hand we cut down on the limits of birds to be taken, shorten the length of seasons during which they can be shot, and sign international treaties for their preservation. On the other hand, bowing to the pressure of land-hungry speculators, we utterly wipe out the most essential of all their needs: a place for them to feed, breed, rest, and replenish their energies during migrations.

From the marshy "pothole" country of the north-central states, such as Wisconsin and Minnesota, where once numerous water-filled depressions excavated by the continental glaciers of the Pleistocene harbored millions of birds, to the shores of the Gulf of Mexico, population pressure for farmland has led to the drastic destruction of water bird habitat. Ponds, pools, shallow lakes, and marshes have been drained, converted from duck sanctuaries to farm plots in the rich muck soils that have accumulated for eons. Wherever wetland has been drained and put under cultivation, including the San Joaquin-Sacramento river delta, the Everglades of Florida, the submerged lands of Louisiana, and westward to the eastern edges of Texas, the rich organic soils so profitable for farming oxidize rapidly on exposure to air. They deteriorate, year by year, actually shrinking in depth. Ultimately

these richest of all soils will become artificial beds for plant-
ing, with heavy fertilization and irrigation a costly concomitant of their cultivation, producing crops that will require
higher prices than would those from virgin, rich topsoils.

Elsewhere throughout the drier regions of our land, not
only must floodwater be impounded for summer use, but
now this valuable essential to all life, human and nonhuman, must be channeled into waterproof canals for transportation to the evermore distant farmlands and towns with
their water-dependent industries. At one time most irrigation systems resembled those of the Imperial Valley, where
water was confined to dirt-banked and dirt-bottomed channels from which it overflowed, seeped, and occasionally even
escaped in a rush of flood where a pocket gopher or, more
rarely, a beaver burrowed through the bank. The pressure
of water rapidly widened the gap in the soft soil, inundating
adjacent low-lying areas and farms. Large amounts of seepage constantly escaped, and the rich damp soil bordering
the man-made, dirt-lined water courses nurtured reeds and
rushes, willows and even larger trees. They produced a can-
opy of shade that cooled the water and protected it from the
hammering sun. Under these conditions wildlife, minute and
large, flourished, adding interest and beauty to the often
monotonous farmlands—vast, flat stretches devoted to a few
prime crops.

When at last it was recognized that truly huge amounts of
water were absorbed by such "useless" vegetation and made
unavailable to man, it "became necessary" to eliminate these
water-requiring plants. First they were cut down; then plant
poisons were developed. The sprayed poisons killed the
streamside vegetation known collectively as phreatophytes.
Under the rain of poison poured down from planes or hand-
held pumps, such plants gradually vanished along the water
courses. Without their life support, all the forms of animal
life also dwindled. The chief effect was starvation and extermination of insects and, in turn, all the creatures that feed
upon insects. These one-time easily reached sanctuaries for
living things, havens of recreation for people and rich envi-

ronments for field trips for naturalists, have practically disappeared. Remaining natural oases have become extremely
valuable, many of them now, fortunately, nuclei of nature
reserves and parks where wildlife is encouraged.

A certain amount of sardonic humor can be garnered from
following the history of just one species of duck and its fate
in the San Joaquin Valley. At one time large numbers of the
extraordinarily beautiful wood duck flourished here. One of
our most handsome wildfowl species, these ducks must nest
in trees. They get their sustenance from marshes or cool,
sheltered pools where water and shoreline plants grow in
great profusion and provide food, especially for the ducklings. With the known decline of the wood duck population
under the impact of too much hunting, the ducks were ultimately given complete protection. Nevertheless, their numbers continued to fluctuate, and a steady downward trend
developed over the years. Despite increasing numbers of water conservation projects such as impounding and channel-
ing, the demand for this resource continued to exceed the
supply that reached the end of the ditch lines. The phreatophytes were cut and poisoned. But with the destruction of
riparian vegetation, the nesting places and feeding grounds
of these beautiful and harmless birds, one of the living jewels
to which America fell heir, continued to diminish. Although
the Department of Agriculture and its cohorts of farmers were
busily engaged in destroying the very things upon which the
birds depended, the state Fish and Game Department nobly
came to the rescue with a suggestion that every interested
person build nesting boxes for the wood duck, sparing them
the extermination that would inevitably follow the destruction of their nesting trees! That their feeding places were also
disappearing seems not to have occurred to the wise heads
in the department. After all, who were they to get involved
in a five-way fuss among the Federal Department of Agriculture; hydrological experts of many persuasions, including those callous destroyers of nature, the Army Corps of
Engineers and the Bureau of Reclamation; the farmers; the
Fish and Game Department itself; and the ill-fated wood duck?

I have chosen the wood duck as just one example of what is happening to hundreds of species (thousands, if one includes the insects) of amphibians, aquatic mammals, numerous rodents, birds, and multitudes of unseen creatures that squirm and wriggle underground. By their activity and decaying bulk, these latter creatures add cost-free richness to the soil, *if* it is allowed to lie fallow. By constantly farming it and preventing it from regaining naturally its fertility and usefulness, we deny these indispensable creatures a home and a chance to join the human species in a quest for a permanently livable and tolerable natural environment. I am very concerned that the exploding populations of the world and their ever-increasing demands for food will force us to overuse and abuse the most precious resource of all, the land upon which we all depend.

At one time it was taken almost for granted that the salt marshes of coastal California were relatively immune to human activity. Vast stretches of low-growing plants capable of living in what is really a chemical desert occupy soils far too saline for cultivation. Along each estuary on the low-lying coast thousands of acres lay for centuries, untouched and seemingly untouchable. The margins of the marshes were covered with mixtures of salt grasses and *Salicornia,* or pickleweed, so called because of its fleshy stems that look like rows of tiny pickles strung together and its habit of storing water against periods of drought and high salinity. Even these soggy, mud-drowned acres were gradually encroached upon by land-hungry people who built drainage ditches to carry off excess water and raised the land into ridges of less salty soil where crops of celery, beans, and other vegetables could be grown successfully. As these workable though marginal lands dried out and as methods were developed for their cultivation, still further encroachment occurred. Additional land was reclaimed, though at higher cost; yet it still yielded valuable produce. Fresh water from irrigation systems was used to flood the soil, leaching out the salts and converting the land to an important, though more or less ephemeral resource.

Recent infringements upon the salt marshes include the building of vast housing tracts. More and more of these low-lying embayments of the sea have not only been built upon, despite their susceptibility to earthquakes and floods, but marinas are steadily making inroads into the increasingly scarce salt marshes. This is particularly true in southern California, where natural harbors are scarce and boat-owning populations reflect urban prosperity.

In my early years of teaching at the University of California at Los Angeles the salt marsh habitat of nearby Playa Del Rey fascinated me. I used it for wildlife photography and as a demonstration area for many field trips in biology. Back in the late 1920s and early 1930s, beautiful marsh hawks flew low over the marshlands, hurrying back and forth in search of their prey. Though rare, the slaty-blue adult birds were always present and, in season, one could glimpse the less colorful immature hawks. They nested here, found forage, circled for miles across the islands of pickleweed, and hunted over the scattered patches of tules and cattails. Their nests were hard to find and harder yet to photograph, but in the hours spent tramping across the marsh and around the fresher water areas I was continuously fascinated by the wealth of biological surprises. Teal nested here, tucking their down-filled nests in the shelter of plants where they were, for me, most difficult to find. Gopher snakes also wandered through the water-logged terrain in search of food, including duck eggs. Once a large gopher snake had crawled into a fluffy down and twig nest. Prior to my arrival, it had consumed three of the ten eggs that had been laid there. I captured the snake and took it back to my lab where by gentle squeezing I worked the eggs upwards into its mouth. Then I carefully extruded them onto a bed of sand. I wanted to see if the embryos had survived being swallowed. Apparently they had been without oxygen for too long a time and were no longer viable.

After winter storms flooded the flat reaches of pickleweed, large pools of relatively fresh water, swarming with insect and crustacean life, lingered long after the rains. In these warm prolific waters black-necked stilts and avocets foraged assiduously. The stilts built their nests on top of the crushed pickleweeds, scarcely above floodwater stage. These nests, so precariously close to flooding, were difficult to find, and the eggs were beautifully camouflaged to blend in with the pickleweed. Only the distressed chattering of the stilts, loath to leave the nesting area, indicated that we were reaching the vicinity of their cherished progeny. Then we could locate and photograph the eggs.

We constructed a blind near one of these nests and took a series of pictures that covered from early incubation through to almost the moment of hatching. On the last day of these photographic efforts, we examined the nest. Though the chicks had just hatched, they were already capable of great mobility. As I approached they ran to the shelter of the adjacent pickleweed. Their protective coloration made them almost impossible to find, recover, and return to the nest so that we could complete our picture taking. We had hoped to draw the parents near by returning the young to the nest

Plate 20. I used the salt marshes not far from campus for field trips and outdoor study. We often saw avocets, black-necked stilts (such as this one), and other shore birds, particularly in nesting season when they would attempt to lure us away from the nest by distress demonstrations.

and hence to obtain a picture combining nest site, young, and adults. Though this is possible with altricial birds—those whose young remain in the nest for a period of time and are fed by the parents—the young of precocial types such as our stilts depart almost immediately upon hatching. Such a "shot" as that described above would be, even though somewhat artificial, of great interest. I couldn't possibly estimate the amount of aggregate yardage we covered in chasing those babies through the marsh. Exhausted, we finally gave up the project. Nature's deeply engrained habits were too much for us.

All of this natural beauty and interest so close to busy Los Angeles is gone, vanquished by the impact of man's rapidly multiplying numbers. It is difficult indeed to still find un-touched coastal habitats except where military or naval forces have reserved to their exclusive use some of the remaining natural areas. Although it may distress many people to know that such agencies are responsible for the preservation of a number of outstanding natural areas, we must give credit to the assiduous guard of the military for the results of their indirect, if not purposeful, conservation. I only wish that some of the other agencies of the federal government could have proved so effective in the stewardship of our wildland heritage.

21: Birds in Black-and-White

*F*ew birds are equal to the California condor. Only the wandering albatross and the Andean condor consistently outdo our famous native in wingspan, though individual records have been established for other species such as the marabou stork, certain swans, and the European white pelican. The heaviest flightless bird is the ostrich, while the Kori bustard of south and central Africa has been recorded as weighing the most of the birds able to fly. The largest eagle, incidentally, is the harpy eagle of South America, but it is considerably smaller than the great vultures, which include both condors.

Plate 21. The California condor in its rugged native terrain. Plentiful thermals support its glides on motionless wings. (With permission from the Santa Barbara Museum of Natural History, Dr. Dennis Power, Director. Photographer: Bob Werling)

Combining both weight and wingspread, most references mention the two condors as the largest flying birds now in existence. Size and its soaring ability are certainly noteworthy features of California's enormous vulture, but its numbers are diminishing, and the threats to the remaining nucleus are increasing every year. Regrettably we may never have the chance to complete studies of their physiology or for long enjoy the rare aesthetic thrill they afford us. At one time the California condor occupied an area extending from Oregon down into the peninsula of Lower California. Now it is confined to mountain ranges behind the city of Santa Barbara, including parts of the Santa Inez Range and the high mountains at the headwaters of Sespe Creek in Ventura County. Occasional individuals wander out as far as Kern and Los Angeles counties over the Liebre Mountains near the town of Gorman on the Ridge Route. Sightings of this giant bird have been reported from the Tehachapi Mountains, and there is a questionable observation from the southern Sierra Nevada. Essentially, however, the birds are almost exclusively confined to the Los Padres National Forest, where they still nest and rear young.

Laws are supposed to protect them from molestation and shooting, and their nesting areas are protected from intruders who might inadvertently disturb them and cause loss of young or eggs to be abandoned. Under various guises, however, dangers threaten even this remote National Forest sanctuary of the few remaining birds, the last of their kind on earth. The menaces range from dam building to invasion by trail bikes and highways, some of which are being built to provide transportation for fire-fighting equipment in remote areas. The latter projects may serve some useful purpose in terms of the protection of the watershed and even supposedly in saving the condors from destruction by wild fires sweeping through the mountains. Condors can fly, however, and they have survived fire for thousands of years, and I know of no instance of their being burned.

There are those who believe that this impressive bird is on its way to extinction irrespective of what man may do on its behalf, though it did well enough when man left it and its mountain habitat alone. The supposed causes for its dwindling numbers, a diminution that seems to have accelerated of late, are sometimes ascribed to senescence of the stock; to occasional shootings, which are still possibly numerous enough to result in a steady attrition of numbers; to lack of sufficient quantity or quality of food, a concept which at present is only partially proven; and to other unknown factors including the inability of the birds to adjust to long-term climatic or other changes. Though much effort has been made in the last few years to get an accurate count of their number, it is very difficult to estimate the total. Approximations have ranged from a high of 70 to a low of 30. More reasonable guesses place their number at some intermediate level. The ruggedness and inaccessibility of the terrain are the major reasons for the impreciseness of the surveys.

Paradoxically, the suppression of forest fires may very well be another factor militating against condor survival. Now that tanker planes can drop fire suppressants even in the most difficult country, fire fighting has become far more effective and mechanized. Even small winter fires, which might burn locally and be self-limiting, are quenched. Despite these modern aids, several widespread and fast-traveling holocausts fueled by fireless years have burned into portions of the sanctuary, but not throughout the entire range.

The concept that fire containment is, in the long run, of very questionable benefit to the condor is based on the fact that for thousands of years before the advent of white men, Indian tribesmen regularly set fire to the native vegetation, inadvertently or deliberately. They most probably wished not only to destroy hiding places for enemies but to replace old plant growth with new green shoots that increased the area's carrying capacity for wildlife, making hunting, which for the Indians meant survival, far more effective and less arduous. Hunters and food-gatherers the world around habitually use fire to promote the pursuit of game, encourage the growth of more palatable food, and to make the procurement of animal protein more efficient.

Certainly uncontrolled fires sweeping over the brush-covered mountains of California have never been a substantial danger for the condor. During the millenia prior to fire control by modern man the condors flourished in far larger numbers than at present. I personally believe that after the rainy season, frequent fire promotes runoff and that brooks and rivers of earlier times were periodically enlarged, swollen with the runoff from denuded slopes and flushed of obstructing debris. Dr. Harold Biswell and now many others have studied experimental burns and have noted that even today, after fire has "ravaged" the wrinkled landscapes of California, flow from springs commences within two or three weeks after brush burning, even before the start of fall rains. Thus, it appears probable that in the days before fire regulation, numerous springs now dry or buried in tall plant growth were conveniently scattered throughout the condor habitat. Here the birds could alight and drink unhampered by overgrowth of chaparral, which would impede their landings and departures and make them susceptible to attack by predators.

The point has been made that the quantity of food alone is not the limiting factor in condor survival. It seems to me that because of fire control the condor suffers from both the absence of easily obtainable food, including small animals, and the extreme difficulty of landing and takeoff in tall brush. It is rather a clumsy bird when grounded, and dense cover may have forced it to a present diet that is not at all representative of the kind upon which it subsisted in the past. Recent students of condor activity apparently have had no opportunity—because of fire suppression and rigorous preservation regulations—to determine if small-boned ground squirrels and rabbits might not be an essential part of the diet for condors, particularly the young, rather than the bulk carrion flesh of deer, sheep, and cattle, all with large, indigestible bones from which calcium carbonate is less easily procured than from those of smaller animals.

Heavily gorged with food, condors on level ground are slow and cumbrous in takeoff and thus possibly are endangered by predators also attracted to a mass of food. Furthermore, it occurs to me that condors would be able to carry a larger load of food for their offspring if they attempted takeoff from a mountainside than they would while beginning flight from level ground. The birds could run for a few steps down a steep slope, particularly if it was bare or lightly brushed, before becoming airborne in rising thermals.

I had long heard of the majesty of a condor in flight, but it was many years before I enjoyed a first-hand experience. That encounter was accidental. It resulted from one of those rare gatherings of enormous numbers of ravens—usually content to live in pairs or solitarily—soaring, diving, and calling to each other below the slopes of Mt. Pinos above Cuddy Valley. These large black birds were gathered in hundreds, if not thousands. They were making use of the rising currents of air between two ridges to engage in their aerobatics. I was so enchanted that I immediately left the car, walked over to the shade, and lay on my back for a comfortable view of the avian circus, focusing my binoculars on a spot of the sky. Within seconds a dark shape soared into sight, much higher than the ravens. It glided into my circle of vision and majestically crossed the valley. I rested entranced, reminded of nothing so much as a battleship moving among a squadron of speeding destroyers. I quickly noted the badge of the condor—the long-distance identification mark that differentiates it from its equally gifted relative, the turkey vulture, or a soaring golden eagle. It is the conspicuous patch of white on the underside of the wing between the wrist and the body. I could see it clearly as I was viewing it from below.

My next experience with a condor was also unplanned. I had a wonderful close-up glimpse of the bird as it passed almost at my level beyond a group of pines growing on the side of the same Mt. Pinos—a favorite condor lookout site to this day. I was on a deer hunt (this was some 40 years ago; I have long lost any enjoyment in needless killing of wildlife). Standing on the brink of the little valley with another hunter as we paused to compare notes, I froze in surprise as a large bird soared into view so close that we could hear the whistle of its wings. Instantly my chance acquaintance threw up his rifle and took aim. I had just enough time to flip up his barrel, causing him to miss the bird. Naturally he was irate, but after I explained the penalties for shooting a condor, he calmed down. I often wonder how frequently such chance encounters end disastrously—and, of course, unreported—for these rare birds.

For size and mastery of soaring flight, the turkey vulture ranks only slightly below its larger relative. To me, however, the most improbable candidate for impressiveness of flight is the clumsy-looking white pelican of the western states. These birds are locally abundant around Pyramid Lake, Nevada, and at times on the Salton Sea and other large inland bodies of water. In their annual migration between fishing and breeding grounds, the huge wheeling masses of flashing white equal the spectacular glides of the condor. For me they are more attractive than the scientifically interesting but somberly clothed turkey vulture. I have seen hundreds of pelicans streaming across the desert in the vicinity of Palmdale. They formed a long line in which upward and downward bulges, like the lines of a business graph, revealed rising and falling air currents. The birds carefully matched the effects of gravity against wind currents and lift from their aerodynamic structures, and most of the time their wings were motionless. They seemed to be sustained only by their forward movement. At one point, only a few miles away, the forefront of this long line of birds encountered a strong vertical thermal current that lifted them rapidly in a circular soaring pattern higher and higher. At the bottom the late arrivals still poured into the base of this convenient aerial elevator. Within minutes the entire flock had risen several thousand feet. Even with the aid of eight-power glasses they became mere scintillating specks in the sky. At this point the lead birds again took off in a straight line, heading in the direction of Owens Valley.

Despite their ungainly appearance, chiefly because of their enormous bills, these are truly beautiful birds, and I find them well worth watching. They are adept at the game of cooperative fishing. I have observed on occasion a hundred or so pelicans arranged in a semi-circle or long line driving small fish toward the shallows. They converge in stately fashion upon the herded victims only suddenly to lose their dignity as they gobble up the bewildered fish. One tends to overemphasize their pontifical look—from the position of the bill and gular pouch against the neck—but they are really neither solemn nor pious, nor ridiculous gluttons. They are simply another species of our enchanting avifauna, and, in fancy, a beautiful reminder in silhouette of the remote times of the pterodactyls, the flying reptiles of the Mesozoic Era.

To return to California's condor, it is unfortunate that so little is known of the details of its behavior and physiological characteristics, especially since its low numbers rule out studies—even those that might endanger just one of them. Any scientific collecting is out of the question, and it appears that even too prolonged or close observation of their nesting sites discourages them from normal breeding. In recent years, however, there have been several research projects focused on condor behavior, and a number of monographs are now available. No doubt in time we will learn far more about this intriguing bird.

Both the turkey vulture and the condor spend almost no energy on propulsion while in flight. Ligamentous supports assume much of the burden, and they rarely move their wings unless they absolutely have to. This conservation of energy is of great benefit because they depend for their food upon already dead animals, which they must locate and to which they have ready access and from which there is a good escape route. Chapman, in *My Tropical Air Castle*, Chapman, Frank, Appleton Co., 1929, has speculated that the vultures he observed in Panama can survive up to a week or more with no food and yet suffer little damage or strain. Their magnificent soaring capabilities allow them to fly with slight effort. Because of similar habits, probably both condors and turkey vultures as adults require only occasional meals to maintain them in healthy working condition.

There have been years of debate by experts about the way the turkey vulture discovers its food. Logically, in view of the kind of food upon which it feeds, it has been proposed that, unlike most birds, this particular scavenger has a highly effective sense of smell. Eyesight, this argument goes, might be of little help or secondary importance in locating food sources; though from my observation of old-world vultures, I conclude that at least they rely heavily on keen sight. Chapman and others, including Dr. Kenneth Stager, curator of ornithology at the Los Angeles County Museum of Natural History, have undertaken a number of tests in which the decaying body of an animal was concealed by various means, and the turkey vultures were watched until they located the corpse. From his experiments and description of them, Chapman presented the earliest convincing arguments in behalf of food detection through olfaction rather than through vision. The diehards, most of them familiar with the old-world vultures, countered by saying that birds, with what they believed to be such amazing sight, would certainly have been able to see the carrion flies and beetles arriving at or departing from the carcass. Supposedly it was such clues that led the vultures to their food supply. For my part, despite the probable acuity of vision in the turkey vulture, it is hard to believe that they can locate their prey by detecting the flight of such small objects as flies. To ponder further, if a fly can trace odors why not a bird whose life also depends on locating decomposing protein? Another great naturalist, Joseph Grinnell, observed these birds soaring on the wind currents in back of a cliff, out of sight of its base where a decomposing sea lion carcass had washed up on shore. He noticed that although the food supply was invisible the vultures appeared to detect the odor, following it down to the base of the cliff in search of a meal.

While attempting to discover whether or not rattlesnakes would be attracted to the odor of rotting meat and thus find dead rodents, I placed a dozen or so dead and partly decayed white rats, wrapped in neutral-colored paper, along the roadway of Mulholland Drive in the hills above Los Angeles. Though I spent many hours waiting for a rattlesnake to discover the bait, I saw none at all. Again and again, however, turkey vultures soaring along in the updraft above the ridge faltered in their flight, swung about to repeat the traverse through the odor-carrying air, and followed the air current to land within a few feet of one of the well concealed rat carcasses. Their vision is not poor, for after landing the apparently mystified birds peered under bushes and examined the roadway for the source of the smell. Clearly, however, they had located the food from a distance by olfaction alone.

Turkey vultures and, presumably, condors may conserve energy, especially during the night, by another device. It involves a drop in body temperature, a kind of brief nocturnal "hibernation," and consequently a drop in metabolic rates. Unfortunately we have few data on which to proceed, but perhaps someone may be persuaded to carry on the necessary investigations. Reports have been made about the early morning sunning behavior of both turkey vultures and condors. They expose their backs and elevate their dorsal feathers, being warmed by the direct rays of the sun on the skin and its blood supply. On cold mornings both of these avian species usually bask for awhile in the sun before takeoff. It is possible that, instead of just waiting for sufficiently strong thermal currents to develop, they are unable because of night-chilled muscles and nerves to produce the requisite speed of wing motion. If so, they would not be able to propel themselves on takeoff or while airborne or to control their direction with sufficient promptitude, accuracy, and efficiency. A tentative exploration of these possibilities was accidentally terminated before adequate data could be obtained, but it seems safe to suggest that these birds may tolerate environmental temperatures as low as 29° F. or even lower during the night. Because, however, of their slowed metabolic rate when cold, they must rely on external heating to supplement internal heat generation.

One of my most interesting experiences on the Mojave Desert was highly suggestive of this phenomenon of energy conservation. I had reached my camp late at night along with my class. Quite unknowingly we had selected a spot near Paiute Butte that had also been chosen by several hundred turkey vultures for their nighttime roosting place while migrating to the Imperial Valley or points south, perhaps even as far as the high plains around the Amazon Basin. Whatever their ultimate destination, we inadvertently camped in their midst. On awakening shortly before sunrise, we discovered them all around us, on the bottom slopes of the butte and among the rocks below the hillock itself. As we moved around camp, the birds gave way before us, clumsily hopping with outspread wings, others stumbling along the ground. As they neared the butte they leaped to the tops of the scattered boulders but made no attempt at real flight. Their wing motions were clumsy and ineffective, apparently incapable of lifting the birds from the ground. As the sun rose the birds basked in the warmth. They soon showed signs of greater agility and began to make short casting flights from one pile of rock to another. Only when the air temperatures were considerably warmer did they eventually take off in true flight.

The discernment through some sense or another of developing thermals on which the birds can soar is apparently a reality, but it is difficult to understand. That morning the birds we were watching took off in an obviously direct route for possible flight-sustaining thermals. If the air currents did not attain adequate velocity, the birds turned and went to others. Within a short time successfully spiraling fellow birds were clear evidence of satisfactory updrafts. Not long after, the several hundred turkey vultures began to ascend in three major thermals. We estimated that probably 1,500 to 1,800 birds rose in these great columns of air, all within a square mile of air space. From the comments of the students, they shared my sense of awe at this magnificent demonstration of aerodynamic adaptation and success.

22: True-or-False

Nature folklore is inextricably entangled with human history and intrinsically involved with religious beliefs. Sir Arthur Fraser's *The Golden Bough* and *African Genesis* by Robert Ardrey discuss the subject in great degree and with fascinating detail. *The Natural History of Nonsense* by Bergen Evans has excellent accounts of the nature folklore of our own land as well as its origins in other countries.

Legends are of great importance in ethnological studies since they are retained within cultural structures for unnumbered generations, suffering comparatively little modification. They afford valuable insight into "primitive" thinking on all cultural levels. We may consider ourselves highly "civilized," but we still react in gut-instinctive ways when we believe we are being threatened by some aspect of the natural world around us. We have now, however, a vast body of information derived from the study of natural science and its critical analysis that should help emancipate us from many baseless fears of the out-of-doors and so contribute to our enjoyment of a world often quite apart from that in which we spend our daily lives. A study of folklore reveals the sources of many superstitions. We are accustomed to think that other people's beliefs are superstitions, but that ours are not. This is particularly true of religious faiths differing widely from our own, *e.g.,* the animism of tribal Africa as contrasted with Christianity. The adherents of other faiths, in all fairness, are equally entitled to describe our tenaciously held beliefs as superstitious and fallacious.

Possibly this brief discussion of folklore may support additional efforts to be tolerant and understanding of other people's views. Wherever encountered, the folklore of each race or culture demonstrates the human need to explain the unknown and to accept the products of imagination as substitutes for unknowable facts. All cultures share a failing based on the need to feel superior to others—the pleasure of indulging in the investigation of human gullibility. It is quite probable that a number of erroneous notions about the living world have been perpetrated merely by the storyteller's delight in putting something over on somebody. He really knows better, but what a remarkable tale, especially if he is the hero! The wide open mouths and eyes of his listeners are ample compensation for the stretched "truth," usually made wholly believable by the firm statement, "I saw it myself!" No argument with eyewitness accounts, even though those "eyewitnesses" lived many years ago and in distant places.

For some as yet unproven reason, superstitions pertaining to reptiles, particularly to the snakes, excel in drama and number almost all other bits of folklore combined. The Adam and Eve story has little to do with it, for other cultures indulge in the same fears. According to Lawrence M. Klauber's *Rattlesnakes,* University of California Press, most of the legends about snakes came to him from hunters and trappers who spent much of their time out-of-doors and knew the terrain and its wild inhabitants with a thoroughness, but fallibility, found in few others. Sheepmen, cattlemen, and even fishermen who encounter an occasional snake along the streams add to the accumulation of lore. India also is a source of a vast number of most interesting legends, and tales of snakes on the African continent compete with those of South America, famous for such giant reptiles as the anaconda.

In their attempt to promote sales, the popular press and popular literature have been among the chief offenders in perpetuating misinformation and building grossly exaggerated accounts that have little resemblance to the truth. I had a personal experience with some of the distortions commonly found in newspapers some years ago. While in my mesquite camp on a research project, I was using some very valuable scientific equipment with no other protection for it than the walls of my tent—fine shelter from the weather but no guard at all against theft. In the neighborhood were large numbers of migrant workers among whom word of my peculiar interest spread rapidly. Since small boys are so excellent in collecting specimens, I paid a reward to the youngsters in the worker camps for finding rare and interesting animals. Soon I was visited daily by the boys and their parents who wandered about my camp and inspected the instruments and other objects lying about with such apparent carelessness. I had no reason to suspect dishonesty, but it is always possible that among large numbers of people there are a few lightfingered individuals. I had to reduce the number of visitors, especially those who came while I was away from camp. Relying on bush telegraph, I dropped strong hints about the dangers lurking in the region about my camp and the viciousness of the snakes housed in the cages I had built. One was a specimen of the locally abundant western diamondback rattlesnake, a species greatly feared by everyone, and justifiably so. Within days, attendance dropped as the tales became more and more embroidered as they spread among my curious neighbors.

A number of the caged rattlers were females, and I had the vague hope that by keeping captive females at the time of year when breeding activity was at a peak, wild uncaught males might be attracted to the vicinity, making my observation of them a little easier. It took little ingenuity to foresee the result of my spreading among my visitors the story that these female reptiles gave off special odors (we now call pheromones) during the mating season that were highly attractive to male snakes. While in search of possible partners, the males, though baffled by the cages, might be eager enough to hide themselves temporarily in the bushes surrounding my camp and emerge at any time! My collectors heeded the word with such extreme caution they would stop several hundred feet away from my impromptu laboratory and hail me. Now I was forced to walk to them to purchase specimens rather than having them come conveniently into camp. My initial purpose was served, however, and I could spend whole days away from camp, when caught by a storm, for instance, with no fear that intruders would make free with some of my valuables. There were no tracks, incidentally, of men *or* snakes in the rain-smoothed sand!

Not long afterwards, a public relations employee of a famous institution asked me if I was not concerned about losing valuable material belonging to the university. I told him the above story, stating that I had no fear whatsoever, for I was protected by services far better than those of any watchdog, an unfortunate choice of words as I soon discovered to my astonishment. A few weeks later I received a clipping from Buenos Aires, Argentina. According to this "account" I had trained two rattlesnakes to act as watchdogs in my home. On returning one evening to my residence, the story went, I opened the door to hear the sound of terrific rattling by my snakes. They had chased a burglar to the second floor and cornered him there. Meanwhile, they were sounding the alarm so that I might call the police! Such deliberate distortion of fact no doubt accounts for much false folklore. It also raises the question of how much of our really important news stories reaches us ungarbled.

Plate 22. The sidewinder has vertically eliptical pupils that are adapted for night vision. Above the eyes are the protruding scales, which give it the common name of horned rattlesnake. The "hypodermic needle" fang has the hole for venom injection at the anterior end of the groove.

One of the most widespread stories about rattlesnakes has been so frequently repeated that it has become formalized in content. It concerns the species, *Crotalus cerates,* or sidewinder. It always happens to a friend or a friend of a friend, never to the narrator. I shall dub it the Boot and Fang Legend. I have had the story told me by Arizona cowboys and California prospectors, Texans (in whose state the sidewinder does not occur), and various other "but I know it is true" raconteurs. The tales of the events often extend the limits of this little horned rattler far beyond its natural range. The San Joaquin Valley has been invaded several times, to add zest to the stories. The first time I encountered this legend was in the Imperial Valley some decades ago when the frontier hamlets were settling down to more law-abiding ways of life. At that time a few people were still toting guns, old bad-man style, but shootouts were steadily dwindling in number. Craving vicarious excitement, the old-timers told and retold this

tale which supposedly happened at headgate Number 5 on
the high-line canal, along part of which I once "rode ditch."

The story went that the foreman on the ranch, or the tender at the irrigation watergate, in this instance, was called on
to supervise an emergency night job. He was struck by a sidewinder whose fang penetrated the leather of his boot and injected venom into the man's foot. After his arrival home, his
wife attempted to stop the poisoning process, but within a
few days the poor man died, leaving his unfortunate widow to
carry on as best she could the tasks that formerly had been his.
Three months later (the story gains in credibility by such precise details as this) a newcomer to the area ingratiated himself with the worthy widow and helped her with her work.
She, in turn, was grateful for his services and loaned him her
deceased husband's boots. Within a few days the Good Sa-
maritan dropped dead, and the widow was forced to continue on as before. Three or four months later the episode
was repeated again and then again. More often than not the
victim made out his will and insurance in behalf of the hard-
working but kindly widow. When she had conspicuously
amassed some capital, and lost several successive menfolk,
the sheriff was finally compelled to probe the noble little
woman's sad plight. On investigation he found the fatal sidewinder fang, still protruding from the inside of the leather
of the boot. Each successive man had died from rattlesnake
poisoning inflicted by the embedded tooth when he tried to
fill the original owner's shoes.

In actuality, snakes considerably larger than the sidewinder
are totally incapable of driving their fangs through the leather
of hiking boots. One local naturalist by the name of Walker,
of Indian Wells, Coachella Valley, collected desert diamond-
backs—large, robust, and highly dangerous—by tracking
them to their shelter under brush where they had crawled
after a night of wandering in search of food. As they started
to depart, he, somewhat inconsiderately, stepped on their
tails. Immediately the snakes recoiled and struck at his boots.
He pressed their heads down with a stick, a common step
in the process of subduing the creatures. By using specially

made tongs, he picked them up and dropped them into a garbage can, his receptacle for live reptiles. He wore knee-high boots, which he improved by adding an extension over the kneecap. I once watched him catch six big, active, and savagely striking desert diamondbacks during one morning's tracking. Despite his habitual collecting tactics and many vigorous strikes on his boot, he never suffered a single fang penetration. He did, however, admit to some concern lest a fang go through the boot eyelet or the softer leather of the underlying "bellows." Ultimately he died from a bite on the hand.

It is difficult for me to imagine how the story of the generous widow gained currency, although I can understand its spread throughout the Southwest, notorious for gory fables anyway. An even more frequently repeated tale, one that for a long time cropped up in newspapers every two or three years, is about the young couple who visited a remote area. In wandering away from camp, the wife encountered a huge rattlesnake. Despite her terror, she killed it and, in triumph, dragged it back to show her husband. Unfortunately, he returned late in the evening and couldn't view his wife's trophy until the next morning. They went out to see the carcass of the snake only to be attacked by its mate which had been lying in wait to wreak revenge on the killer of its beloved. At this point the details vary somewhat, but at least one of them escapes the attack and lives to tell the tale to a newspaperman.

As to the sexual behavior of rattlesnakes, they do not mate for life, but only for as long as it takes to accomplish the mating act. One part of the story, however, may have roots in fact. If a dead female snake, ready for mating, was dragged, it could leave a trail of feminine enticement (pheromones) from the site of the kill to where it was dropped. It is possible that male rattlesnakes, which travel extensively during the mating season in search of olfactory clues to the whereabouts of a receptive female, might encounter such a trail, follow it to the carcass, and then in frustration or mystification coil up to await more enthusiasm than that of a potential but very dead mate. The young couple could have stumbled upon a thwarted lover and have been spared by its subsequent immediate flight. But, of course, that would have made a most unsatisfactory ending, so attack it had to be.

Stories of unprovoked aggression by rattlesnakes, their savagery, and the danger from aggravating one to attack are based on fragile facts. Far from being vicious antagonists, rattlesnakes are among the most timid of all creatures when they are in the presence of anything larger than a victim they can swallow whole. Oddly enough, another bit of rather contradictory folklore makes them chivalrous to babies—they invariably refuse to bite them!

A salesman of live rattlesnakes, known as Joe by some and the peddler of "Little Samson's Herbal Remedy for Rattlesnake Bites" by others, was well aware of and employed one behavioral characteristic of his reptilian merchandise. When a small mammal, in this case a "lab" rat, dashes directly toward a hungry rattlesnake, alert and waiting for prey, the snake will usually lower its head and remain defensive and immobile in the face of such a head-on direct charge. Joe had observed this reaction, and while in my office on one occasion, after his sales talk had failed, he commented that he could "charm" and thus capture the most excitable black diamondback. When this brave statement was questioned by one of my students, he placed a large nervous diamondback in a cage. It coiled in the usual erect-head, loop-and-a-half-high posture of striking. Without hesitation Joe moved his spread hand directly and quickly at the snake's face. It lowered its head as though in submission and hid it under a coil. Joe grasped it by the neck, lifted it from the cage, and placed it back in the sack from which he had taken it. Unwisely I made the comment that he had probably manhandled and intimidated this particular snake; a wild one would be a different matter. Joe suddenly stepped to the cage where I kept my own rattlesnakes and opened it. A particularly "savage" diamondback reared menacingly. Joe calmly repeated the performance, to my chagrin.

A moment or two later the realization of something I had noted but not analyzed dawned on me. Rattlesnakes have fragile cranial structures and would seldom survive if charged and bitten by animals of even comparatively small size. The helter-skelter dashes of tame rats often so intimidate freshly captive snakes that they become poor feeders, even after years of successful food procurement in the wild. They usually recover from this initial fear if conditions are right and the white rat runs diagonally past them, perhaps suggesting flight. If thus stimulated to strike, they envenom the rat with one instantaneous blow and then waiting until the rat dies, they usually begin immediate ingestion. After one or two encouraging experiences of this kind, they usually become ready feeders in captivity.

One experience certainly taught me that the rats may not always be the victims. One of our staff had placed three or four white rats into an unheated cage containing two large, pugnacious, and irritable desert diamondbacks. When he checked on the cage the next morning, the snakes were quietly coiled in a corner. To his astonishment, one of the rats was perched on top of a snake and busily gnawing at the last rat-

Figure 14. A captive rattlesnake has been intimidated by a laboratory white rat, which was then able to sit on the coiled reptile and eat the rattles of its tail. Rattlesnakes are not always the victor; they may be victims in certain circumstances.

tle of its tail which was bleeding, chewed to the quick. The rats were lively and obviously "unstruck," but the cold-bodied snakes were completely intimidated by their small adversaries. Based on these observations and other subsequent discoveries, I have no doubt that warm-blooded predators profit from finding cool and lethargic victims.

Actually, rattlesnakes have a number of enemies that prey on them successfully. One is the California king snake, a brown- or black-and-white, ringed species common in coastal California. They feed on lizards, mice, small birds, and other small prey, but their feeding on rattlesnakes has become part of western folklore. The tales assume that king snakes are the inveterate enemies of all rattlesnakes; they will attack and consume any they encounter. In point of fact, some king snakes do hunt rattlers, but others never do, at least in the laboratory. Many of the specimens I have collected over the years have shown no interest whatsoever in rattlesnakes of any size. They appear to either avoid them or show aversion. Those that have fed on rattlesnakes, however, have done so repeatedly, as though they were a common article of diet. In several instances the attacking king snake was fended off by a convulsive reflex, a sharp downward blow with a loop of the body that hit the aggressor across the head with dizzying violence. The slapping blow could be heard the length of the laboratory. The king snake withdrew to spend the rest of its days in captivity in one corner of the cage, while the rattler occupied the opposite corner. Neither snake trespassed on the other's territory, and both seemed content to leave well enough alone. In a note to me, Dr. Robert Stebbins states that in their demonstrations of this behavior in zoology classes at the University of California, Berkeley, they have seldom seen a "directed" body blow. Obviously, more observations are needed.

Even the odor of snake-eating snakes evokes this convulsive slapping reaction. One a number of occasions I have followed the suggestion of C. M. Bogert and rubbed a cloth over the dorsal side of a king snake and then presented the cloth (on a stick) to the rattler. Once its tongue has carried the odor

Plates 23 and 24. The leopard lizard has taken on a fearsome enemy, the king snake. In this instance, the aggressor has turned into frightened victim, a reptilian David-and-Goliath story!

to the Jacobson's organ, the characteristic defense behavior ensues. At first the head is hidden under its coils, then, when touched, it delivers a body thrust or blow or, in some instances, resorts to avoidance movement. Dr. Bogert of the American Museum of Natural History discovered that the odor of *any* snake-eating snake, regardless of what part of the world it comes from, produces this reaction in rattlesnakes. There must be some common body chemical that identifies reptilian enemies to rattlesnakes and perhaps to other victims.

From time to time an "epidemic" of rattlesnake encounters in the suburbs hits the press. Self-styled "herpetologists" at once see the chance to make some easy money and advertise their ability to guarantee that they will rid an area of all rattlesnakes for a year, an impossible claim. One such "expert" reportedly made hundreds of dollars from a solicitation in a small canyon community. He wisely waited until the period of the greatest snake activity—March, April, and May—had passed. Then he announced that he would capture

all the rattlers he could find and, furthermore, liberate king snakes, which would continue the task after his departure. He crawled into the chaparral amid much dramatic preparation. Finally he emerged with one of the frightening creatures in hand and which he proudly displayed to his gratified customers. He did not know that he had a careful observer in his audience. From the way it was described to me, the fearless captor was holding a specimen that could only have come from Texas or the East Coast! In true western style, he had "salted" his mine. The king snakes might have remained for a few days cruising in the vicinity, but soon they would have left in search of their home territory, having done nothing more than temporarily discommode some of the infrequent local rattlesnakes.

Are rattlesnakes really dangerous? In one sense, yes, they are. Their venom can be lethal though not all of those bitten actually die. The venom causes extreme pain and destruction of tissue. Rattlers may be locally abundant. I have tallied sidewinder populations as high as two to four an acre. Most accidental exposure can be expected among hikers in the grass-covered inland valleys and coastal hills. Of benefit to both the snake and the hiker is the reptile's characteristic behavior when something swiftly and directly approaches it. It drops its head and remains immobile, beautifully concealed through protective coloration. No doubt many a wanderer in the hills has passed close to several rattlesnakes in the course of a day's outing without ever seeing them—eliminating much wear and tear on the nerves of the hiker and the fragile body of the snake alike. Of the few that unnecessarily revealed their whereabouts by threatening and rattling, most probably died at a younger age and had fewer progeny than the discreet and timid members of the species.

Taking the long step from reptiles to mammals, we find another storehouse of folksy myths. Anyone familiar with country lore "knows" that if one picks up a skunk by the tail, it is "unable to spray" its scent. It is true that skunks appear to be somewhat reluctant to use their chemical weapon even in battle and that they will fight against one another with tooth and claw alone before resorting to the last-ditch defense. A friend who once kept dozens of wild skunks around his home by feeding them nightly has described their pugnacious territorial behavior. Only when the bully gets its victim down and does not back off when the proper tokens of defeat are given does the victim resort to its ultimate weapon, a spray of mercaptan, which drenches its opponent as well as itself in the process. This final desperate maneuver ends the battle instantly; both participants retreat to roll on the ground and rub their faces in the vegetation and dirt.

Most of the time people can gently handle skunks with impunity so great is the reluctance to spray. The sight of dogs, however, usually triggers them to this defense. One of my students caught a skunk, believed he had successfully deodorized it, and was surprised and delighted at the birth of young skunklets. He brought his prized pet into our large lecture hall and displayed both mother and offspring before a class of more than two hundred students. She raised her tail in maternal warning when she thought her young were being tampered with, but this and the usual demonstration of petulance by stamping her feet and rising onto her front legs were as far as she went. It was amusing and fun, and we thought no more about it. Later that week this same skunk, and in the same cage, was set down beside a car while the packing of camp gear was in progress. A dog bounded up to investigate the skunk and her young. To our surprise she sprayed liberally. The dog fled, but the odor lingered for days and blew into nearby classrooms on the ground floor. Until then we had no idea that the operation had been unsuccessful.

Picking a skunk up by the tail is actually more a matter of luck. While I was attending Cornell University a skunk fell into the deep window well of the Faculty Club on the campus. An instructor friend of mine decided that he would capture the animal for a pet and that this was as good a time as any to demonstrate the safety of the tail-holding technique. D. J., as we called him, lay down on his stomach and reached full length into the deeply recessed window well. He grabbed her by the tail and while triumphantly holding her aloft was heavily sprayed. Much of the odor drifted back into the ventilating system of the Faculty Club, widely advertising his predicament.

The world around, bats have been endowed repeatedly in folklore with many interesting though false capabilities, none of them really as intriguing as those that are true. Their ability in echo-location, or sonar, is a remarkable feature of the animal world. One of the most common legends about bats blames them with harboring bedbugs. They are said to transmit the insects from the attic of one dwelling to that of another, yet uncontaminated, home. From their new locale the bedbugs spread to the quarters of the human occupants. Careful investigation has disproved this notion, but bats are known to harbor flat-bodied wingless flies that faintly resemble the bugs and scurry over the bat's body, diving into the fur where they hide and search for food. It is possible that this bat-fly relationship is a form of symbiosis known as mutualism, in which the bat may benefit by the fly's removal of potentially harmful parasites, and the wingless fly is given transport as well as food by its bat companion. So far as man is concerned, the flies merely tickle him slightly. They actually are innocuous little creatures.

Bats, birds, and other insectivorous animals contribute to a tolerable balance in the number of insects that plague man. Though the vampire and fruit-eating bats of the tropics can and do prove troublesome, the many species of temperate regions are, by and large, harmless or even beneficial. It is very unfortunate that these fascinating little beasts should sometimes suffer from rabies and, unlike most creatures, recover from the disease but for a time remain carriers. There is no reason to fear bats in general, though another legend has them commonly becoming entangled in women's hair. Theoretically there may be rare instances of bats flying into some fluffy hairdo. The fine, curly strands could conceivably absorb the echo-locating sounds emitted by the bat. If no echoes returned from this absorptive cushion, the area would sound empty—a void—into which the bat might fly. Bats are insectivores and should be uninterested in the investigation of any woman's hair. On the other hand, any bat that seems overly familiar and flies about one in an unusual manner could be the victim of mental derangement because of rabies. One therefore should be cautious about any bats that appear to be sick, weakened, or flying in an uncoordinated way.

Another group of wildlife legends centers about the porcupine and its supposed ability to discharge or shoot quills at its enemies. The quills are actually much enlarged hairs made rigid by their pithy centers. The hairs are tipped with velvety-feeling, but barbed, sharp points, which serve as effective defensive devices. Many more normal hairs protrude beyond the quills. The adventurous naturalist can reach down, get a grip on these tough but harmless hairs, and lift the animal off its feet. Those who do so should beware of the flapping tail, however, which the porcupine lashes from one side to the other, driving spines into arms and legs with lightning-like strokes. It is this flick of the tail and the embedding of the still-affixed spines that are pulled out of the animal as the victim retreats that give rise to the legend. Some of the stories about porcupines flicking their quills into tent walls several feet away are possibly true, but the propelling force comes from the energy of the flick and not from any volitionary act on the part of the animal.

That toads have something to do with warts is an idea of great antiquity. I am quite sure that it must go back to primitive medicine. As the skin of all true toads is dotted with wart-like excrescences—extremely interesting and rather complicated mucus and venom-producing glands—one can understand the thinking behind the admonition never to touch or handle a toad because of the danger of infection-producing warts. The notion may even antedate the homeopathic doctrine that like cures like; in this case, like causes like. Possibly witch doctors of ancient tribes observed children playing with toads and drew the seemingly logical conclusion that bumpy growths resulted from handling warty animals.

Amphibians are notably lacking in protective devices. Few have sharp teeth; they are seldom sharp-clawed, cannot run fast, are small in size, are relatively powerless, and have thin, delicate skins. Their tender covering is necessary because toads, even the more terrestrial, do most of their breathing through it. The skin not only must be well supplied with ample blood but also moist enough to facilitate the exchange of gases. Amphibians are not totally defenseless, however. Some toads and frogs are able leapers and jump either away from the pursuer or into the nearest water or far enough to break their trail of scent. Many have poison glands located in the skin.

Three excellent examples of amphibians armed with toxins secreted from specialized skin glands occur in California: the common toad of coastal areas, *Bufo boreas,* and two related subspecies; *Scaphiopus hammondii,* or the spadefoot "toad," a toad-like amphibian now practically extinct in the Los Angeles basin; and the Colorado River toad, *Bufo alvarius,* a giant among the tail-less amphibians. The common toad is often attacked by inexperienced dogs. If the poison is swallowed, they may suffer serious systemic disturbances or merely salivate heavily. Though the spadefoot has no conspicuous glands on its skin, when it is roughly handled it exudes an extremely irritating mucus, especially annoying around the eyes and mouth. The Colorado River toad has fairly conspicuous glands over its head and body. Many dogs and cats have died as a result of ingesting the highly toxic venom secreted by these glands. A number of years ago a scientific journal reported that this toad's venom was volatile. Inhalation of its fumes could cause the death of pet animals and even illness in humans. One incident was described in full. A toad had escaped into a standpipe of an irrigation system. A collie and a fox terrier pursued it, but it escaped to well beyond the reach of the highly excited animals. In their attempts to get at it, however, they stuck their heads into the irrigation pipe and barked violently for several moments. Then they retreated a few steps and collapsed, showing signs of paralysis. The owner, in search of the cause of his dogs' illness, peered down into the standpipe. As soon as his eyes were adjusted to the dim light, he saw a Colorado River toad, a warty greenish lump with yellow eyes. Shortly after, he himself began to feel some discomfort.

This was a most intriguing story, and I made plans to con-

Figure 15. The paratoid gland of a Colorado River toad is ejecting poison under the pressure of a finger during an experiment in my laboratory. Ejections of this venom may account for the death of dogs living in the vicinity of this species' home.

duct some experiments. After I captured a specimen, I placed it in a glass aquarium, divided in the middle by a piece of doubled wire netting a half-inch apart. The toad was on one side of the netting and a white rat on the other. Then I fixed a piece of glass very tightly across the top of the aquarium and watched to see what would happen. The toad retreated to one corner, while the rat explored every inch of his temporary jail. Realizing that a perfectly calm toad might not give off any of its supposedly volatile toxin, I prodded the amphibian with a stick, causing it to react by bending its head downward at a sharp angle. Suddenly I noticed a drop of whitish substance ejected from the glands that were strongly pressed by this odd posture. A fleck of venom, a possible source of the supposedly volatile emanations that I needed for the experiment, adhered to the wire netting an inch or so away. I waited and waited for the rat to show distress. Finally it became so damp from moisture condensation, I removed it from the cage. It promptly groomed itself and resumed eating the meal I had provided for it.

Now either the venom was not sufficiently volatile or the rat was immune, a most improbable assumption. I concluded that though the man's observations of his dogs' behavior had been correct, his interpretation was not. Several years passed before I had another specimen of the toad. This time two of my students volunteered to see if the supposed ejection of venom that I was certain I had witnessed could actually occur. They made several experiments and found that under even moderately firm pressure the glands discharged droplets of venom for a short distance. Then they compressed a large head gland by hand, squeezing it firmly, and measured the distance reached by the most distant drop of venom. It was approximately 12 to 15 feet!

Now it was easy to see what really must have happened. As the dogs barked, the scared toad put pressure on the gland and ejected drops of poison that entered the dogs' open mouths. We never did succeed in upsetting our captive toad sufficiently to make it discharge spontaneously for more than an inch or two, but I have little doubt that under extreme distress it could send a drop into the inhaled air stream of an excited dog.

One brilliantly colored little toad from South America, *Dendrobates tinctorius,* is used as Indian arrow poison. The venom is so toxic that the men who extract it take great precautions to avoid its reaching a scratch or wound on their hands. Another toad, the large tree toad, *Hyla vasta,* of Santo Domingo, secretes a caustic substance capable of blistering the hands of those who handle it.

Some rather careful studies conducted in Europe indicate two general types of amphibian poison. One, a milky venom secreted by glandular, or warty, surface structures, is toxic to the stomach, eyes, mouth, and other mucus membranes. The other is a more generalized mucoid toxin that breaks down red blood cells when injected and produces symptoms very much like those from certain snake bites. It affects the heart and acts in a manner somewhat similar to digitalis. Both types are very effective against *some* enemies, but probably for others are nothing more than a delightful flavoring!

Effective defenses against certain but not all predators are fairly common in the animal world. The exceptions can be explained on the logical basis that there is no supply of food, regardless of how well it is defended, that some specialist predator does not discover and exploit. Many, if not most, adversaries, however, are repelled, and the prey animals survive a tolerable load of predator pressure. If they had no defenses, the total number of their enemies would be overwhelming.

Though much nature folklore is innocuous, some can actually be dangerous. The common tarantula provides an example of danger accruing from a legend rather than from the animal itself. These huge spiders are most commonly seen from August to November. Not infrequently their wanderings take them across high-speed lanes of traffic, and inevitably they cause excited concern or fear. They are reputed to be highly aggressive, very venomous, and able to leap from 10 to 20 feet. Intimidated by their size, hairy coat, long legs, and enormous reddish and black venom injecting fangs, most people keep their distance if they have courage to watch them at all.

I was once the fortunate observer of a series of tests involving their dangerous attributes conducted by Dr. William Berg. He had a number of native California tarantulas captive in his laboratory. After using various small animals as experimental subjects, he decided that the ultimate and really valuable test would be on a human being. He invited me to be a witness and assistant. I was to hold a stopwatch while he induced the spider to bite him and then described the symptoms as they developed, if they did. After a great deal of teasing and rough treatment, the large spider, whose legs reach across one's palm, was harassed into biting. It implanted its fangs deeply into the skin at the base of his middle finger and injected enough venom so that a milky fluid mixed with blood oozed out of the puncture marks even before the fangs were withdrawn.

I heard a muffled "ouch!" as the fangs went home. Now I began to watch the volunteer victim closely. A red wheal developed around the site of the bite, and a whitish areola formed in the center. The pain began to subside soon after the wound was inflicted, and Dr. Berg was insistent in saying that he really was feeling very little discomfort, totally unlike his experience with black widow spiders. Although there was some sign of venom activity, his hand scarcely swelled at all. After a couple of hours of sitting around watching for more dire symptoms and talking idly, we abandoned the session. We concluded that despite their possession and use of venom, tarantulas are not dangerous to people. The purpose of the venom is to kill small prey.

In numerous attempts I was never able to induce a tarantula to jump or leap upon my hand or upon its prey. When disturbed, they elevate their bodies almost to the full extent of their long hairy legs and raise the first pair in a "threatening" attitude. I never found them aggressive, and when confronted by a larger or possibly dangerous animal, they resort to bluffing rather than attack. They do have rather unusual

weapons, however, which can be annoying but seldom if
ever harmful or dangerous. These are the long hairs with
which the body is clothed. I discovered the potency of these
hairs purely by accident one time when a pet tarantula fell
into its drinking water and nearly drowned in the small petri dish. I quickly carried the spider to an outlet of our compressed air system and blew a steady stream of air over its
surface to dry it and to help restore respiration in the curious
"book" lungs, peculiar to this group of arthropods. As I gradually dried and resuscitated it, I began to feel a faint itching
or prickling sensation around the cuff of my shirt. Within the
next few hours this dermal irritation spread up to my shoul-
ders and parts of my chest and back. It intensified, and the
site of each irritant was reddened. Both arms became covered
with a rash that was extremely annoying. After I removed
my shirt I looked inside its sleeves. Large numbers of tarantula hairs had lodged there; they had been blown off the spider's body and up into my shirt. The irritation disappeared
in a few days and left no permanent effects. But I thoroughly
discourage anyone from playing too roughly with their hairy
pets. (I do have a number of friends who own pet tarantulas,
including the artist of·this book who is also the husband of
my collaborator.)

How can such an innocuous animal become dangerous
through its false reputation alone? The point was well illustrated on a highway in the San Joaquin Valley. The car just
ahead of me swerved violently from its side of the highway
clear across to the opposite lane and then swung back in an
equally abrupt but successful attempt to avoid a head-on col-
lision with an on-coming car. I stepped on my brakes and
watched the errant car return to its own side of the highway,
missing the approaching vehicle by the proverbial coat of
paint. It stopped, and the driver, his wife and three children
emerged, all plainly "shook." I stopped my own car and got
out to discover the cause for this wildly erratic behavior. The
man shouted at me to stand back, there was a tarantula in the
road! Didn't I see him dodge it so that it would not leap into
the car where it could have killed his family? Sure enough,

in the middle of our side of the highway was a light brown tarantula serenely walking along.

Angry as hell at this dimwitted performance—his driving could have killed the lot of us—*I* put on a performance. Ignoring the screamed warnings, I ambled up to the spider, touched it lightly on its stern, and let it walk up onto my hand. My audience was dumbfounded. They nervously peeked at it, all the time certain that it was going to leap on us. In the case of the tarantula, as with so many other animals, its reputation is far worse than its bite.

23: Epilogue: The Promethean Myth

*S*urprising insights can often be gleaned from even the most primitive myths. In a discussion of early Greek mythology, George Boas and A. O. Lovejoy* reflected on mankind's most ancient views regarding its status in the world:

> The elements in Greek mythology which are most significant are two—the legends of the Golden Age and of the ages that came after it, and the story of Prometheus, a culture hero who brought the benefits of agriculture and fire to his people.

*Boas, George and A. O. Lovejoy, *Primitive and Related Ideas in Antiquity* (Baltimore; Johns Hopkins Press, 1935).

Similar myths are found in almost every recorded culture, past and present, and thus since history began most men have divided themselves into two camps—the optimists and the pessimists. The optimists have always believed in a never-ending progress toward the day when man will have mastered "the arts of life" completely; the pessimists have always harked back to a "Golden Age" when life was better, when the streams ran clean and pure, the world was clothed in verdure, gardens yielded luxuriant crops, and herds waxed fat on the hillsides.

Today, the optimistic Prometheans hold center-stage, their faith and admiration turned to the new tribal-culture heroes—the big-business tycoon, the inventor, the scientist, the technologist, the manufacturer. The optimists accept the implicit promises of their new gods to provide not only magical new gadgets, but also limitless new substitutes for food and for diminishing resources. And they seem to imagine that all succeeding generations will enjoy still more glorious products of Promethean invention. The faith of these optimists, however, is a fantasy—a delusion perpetuated by seeing only the promise of science and refusing to recognize its warnings, among them the admonition that since men themselves are biological entities ultimately dependent on a biological environment for their own ultimate salvation, they must exist in harmony with it and live in equity with it.

What were the sources of these still-prevalent Promethean myths, in all their variations, and of the opposite, the myth of the "Golden Age?" It appears probable that neither is wholly mythical. Both represent the distillation of actual historical experiences in a past that was replete with alternating periods of hardship and comfort, of chaos and ordered stability. From such historical sources as the Bible and Egyptian records, plus observations of events well into the twentieth century, such as the Russian famine of the early 1930's and that of Bengal in 1943, we know that periods of famine have almost always followed times of abundance; and we can find no reason to believe that they will not continue to do so. The food and energy crises of 1973-74 illustrate the inevitability of these resource trends and rhythms.

It has always been man's fate to suffer from natural catastrophes—droughts, floods, and plagues of insects—in whose various wakes have come famine, uncontrollable epidemics, genocide, wars, and revolution. With each repetition of such disorder, storytellers, and later scholars and writers, tell of a bygone Golden Age that might never return. But the plagues pass, having reduced the size of populations. Soon thereafter, and in large measure as a result of reduced population density, food once more becomes abundant, a new Golden Age dawns, and optimistic myths of Prometheus are reborn.

In view of man's long experience with problems arising from the pressures of large population, why have people been so slow to recognize human numbers as a crucial aspect of man's dilemma? Perhaps because the inexorable forces of uncurbed reproduction—the forces propelled so irresistibly by our potential for "excess" procreation, our biokrene— move so slowly as to be almost imperceptible. Nonetheless, man is capable of ultimately reaching astronomical numbers so long as an increasing death rate does not sometimes intervene to control his biological potential. Indeed, even now, our options are being steadily reduced.

It is sheer folly to presume that without planned population controls we will not ultimately devastate the earth and all its wondrous resources. The earth cannot even accomodate the present numbers of the generation now in its infancy. During the past two hundred years, while merely growing to our present numbers, we have gutted the United States of most of its oil and metal resources. Further cutting of per capita consumption, a lowering of living standards, may enable our country to exist as a viable nation for a few more decades, but revolution could put an end to democracy as we know it. There is no need to wonder about the generations to follow. The depletion of non-renewable natural resources (fertile soils included) will render the inevitable verdict. Perhaps the most reasonable question today is not "When shall we commence a rigorous program of population and resource management?" but rather "When should we have begun?"

It has been said before, but it cannot be said too often: we must now take the first steps. We should at long last direct our conscious attention to the grim history of mankind's proclivity to outbreed its resource base, and cease our persistent ignoring of the vital relation between the irresistible potency of reproduction and the finiteness of the resources needed for civilization. We must look realistically at what is truly necessary for survival. Above all, we must understand the natural processes that maintain the balance of nature.

The basic requirements of all living things, including ourselves, do not comprise the mineral products required by organized industry and mechanized farming. The elementary essentials for living consist simply of food, water, air, and shelter. Countless generations of our remote forbears survived with nothing more. All of man's food consists of plants and of secondary supplemental protein products derived from the ingestion of plants by other animals. The entire natural system from which we have sprung requires only sunlight, the gaseous components of air, the essential chemical elements in the soil, and water. The regular alternation of sunlight and darkness and the seasonal fluctuations with their effects on winds, evaporation, and precipitation maintain an endless sequence of use and renewal. Together these sustain a system that does not require the depletion of the numerous finite resources that modern man has come to consider essential.

In this complex of sun, air, soil, and water, living things and their endless nutrition-providing, biokrenic recycling destroy nothing essential. The interaction between plants and animals constitutes a system that is in perfect equilibrium, the "balance of nature." That system has been refined throughout more than a billion years of trial and error and continuous mutual adjustment. These simple requisites for the sustenance of unnumbered generations comprise the substances known as renewable resources. Conservation of these marvelously generous materials seems obviously simple, requiring only the maintenance of a sustaining balance between the numbers and kinds of users that exist at any one time. In unmodified, freely operating nature, regulation of the harmony

between numbers and resources has long been established
and inexorably sustained through the extremely high death
rates that effectively recycle the elements of which all living
things are made. The biokrene continues to function unflag-
gingly, and the potential for excessive multiplication never
diminishes, but rather is counterbalanced by the limits of existing resources.

In this context of natural processes the human struggle can
be seen more objectively. Among all living things, death has
always been the prime requisite for continued and renewed
life—death for the many is the eternal price paid for survival
of the few. It is the very heart of evolution. In essence, it is
also the phenomenon that has precipitated mankind's ceaseless struggle for "progress" through technological inventions.
It is this phenomenon alone that mankind, by one device or
another, has blindly been trying to modify or defeat. But mankind will meet defeat unless it recognizes that there can be
no permanent preservation of even the renewable resources
until it once again submits to the rule of the limit of numbers
and thus re-establishes a balance among all living creatures,
including its own species. This is a universal law that no
amount of artificial manipulation can for long abrogate, and
whose operation and compulsion can be deferred, but never
evaded. The available supplies of water, minerals, soil, food,
or even space, cannot forever expand to meet the limitless
potential of untrammeled reproduction.

This sermon has been preached before. Paradoxically, however, there are still many wildlife conservationists who do
not recognize this threat of human population; they appear
to believe implicitly that the long-range objectives of conservation can be achieved without control of human numbers.
As a result, present methods of conservation consist essentially of laws that prohibit destruction of wildlife, killing of
songbirds and migratory birds, and uprooting and picking
of wildflowers; laws that establish "bag limits" on game, attempt to prevent pollution of rivers, lakes, and territorial
waters; and most importantly, establish "islands" of natural
conditions in the form of state and national parks, wilder-

ness areas, forest preserves, and recreation areas. But no
matter how immediately helpful and essential these laws may
be, they should, nevertheless, not be viewed as long-range
solutions to the problems of preservation.

As measured by the lifetime of a species (ours included),
these steps can suffice only as necessary short-term expedi-
ents. We should view them as immediately imperative steps.
If we ignore this larger threat of an exploding population,
how effective are the conservationists' pleas to preserve us-
able resources "for posterity" or "for perpetuity" likely to be
in the face of the consuming demands of the multitudes?

It is more frustrating that even some of those conservationists who do recognize the problem shy away from publicly asserting the connection between conservation and man's
numbers, and from predicting the irreparable effects of too
many people. Their reluctance, however, is perhaps understandable. Such predictions bring on unbelieving distress,
even anger, of merchants, industrialists, financiers, and speculators—all of whom see in multiplying numbers of customers only increasing financial returns—and those forecasts
alarm the ignorant and prejudiced, who become vindictive
when confronted with unpleasant facts. Thus often even public leaders who understand the situation are forced to be silent. Public statements on this subject have often incurred
bitter personal attacks, as though to state a fact were equivalent to creating or condoning it. For politicians publicly to
acknowledge the need for birth control is, in many countries,
still tantamount to professional suicide, and advocates of
population controls are accused of genocidal intentions by
those who would profit most.

But we must look at the cost of silence. We must see that
even short of suffering and famine, even in the midst of material prosperity, overpopulation has treacherous effects. Let
us try to grasp the life-defining values of forested hills and
flower-spangled valleys, the clear outlines of lavender-shaded
distant mountains and the color of their verdure close at hand.
Let us contrast clear and unpolluted air, enriched by the natural fragrance of the countryside, with the noisome aerial

garbage that rises from too many exhausts from too many cars, created and rendered noxious only by *too many people.* And think about the joys of glass-clear streams swarming with fish and free from industrial and human waste, clean lakes without a scum of oil from too many motorboats and with shores that do not reek with the odor of overflowing cesspools, undefiled beaches where the sound of the surf is not lost in the cacophony of radios or screaming humanity, and clear dawns on the marshes, silent but for the gentle cries of water birds or the singing of wind across the reeds.

On a hot summer day as long ago as 1960, the sun bathers of southern California between the Mexican border and Ventura County, some fifty miles north of Los Angeles, could claim an average of only 2.5 linear feet of beach per person. The supercities of our state spread insinuating fingers ever farther into the countryside; look-alike tract houses multiply insidiously, with only a tiny square of lawn fabricating the illusion of space between neighbors; freeways proliferate, choked at almost all working hours with cars pouring their exhaust into the already smog-filled sky; the price of land rises to astronomical heights. The West Coast paradise offers an excellent field laboratory preview of the future America. The Golden State is rapidly becoming tarnished, and its luster will continue to fade as long as too many people bury the very beauty they are seeking beneath their sheer numbers. Although California's annual gross income is greater than that of any but the largest Western nations, its overcrowded slums, clogged highways, and ever-rising taxes plague its residents and provide ample working evidence of the damage excessive numbers can wreak. Even its remote mountain trailways, its wilderness areas, its "untouchable" deserts are being seriously endangered by *too many people.*

The beauty that gives meaning to life, and value to our environment, is the diversity of face, form, and mind that can exist only in conjunction with an unencumbered landscape and continued freedom to move about from one landscape to another, to think and act with an exuberant spontaneity unchecked by the pressures and insecurities fostered by excess numbers. It is sheer madness to implement plans that will only increase the world's population and at the same time ignore the quality of life. We cannot, we must not, forget that it is inevitable that by unlimited multiplication we will ultimately thwart every effort to preserve the very things we need and love. The effort to care for our physical needs will become so great that the aesthetic side of living must, of necessity, become secondary and subordinated to the drive for material security and, at last, for bare survival. And even should we survive, even should we avert the final threats of famine, epidemic disease, and social chaos, we will survive in a world without natural aesthetic value. The struggle will have been lost.

Index

(Page numbers in italics refer to illustrations.)